THE MAHDIST WARS SOURCE BOOK

VOLUME I 1883-1885

Edited By
Patrick R. Wilson

Comprising Materials Originally Appearing In

SAVAGE AND SOLDIER

Magazine

Plus New Contributions By Douglas Johnson, Andrew Preziosi, Richard Brooks, Eric Cox, et al

Contents Copyright ©2007 By Patrick R. Wilson
Published by "The (Virtual) Armchair General"
10208 Haverhill Place, Oklahoma City, OK 73120-3922 U.S.A.

www.thevirtualarmchairgeneral.com
TVAG@att.net
First Printing, April, 2007
2nd Printing September, 2009
First Amazon Edition, February, 2015

Table of Contents

Article or Feature Title	Where Originally Published	Author/Artist	Page
Introduction		Editor	4
THE ARMIES			
The Egyptian Army: 1880-1900	Savage & Soldier Vol. VIII, #1	Douglas Johnson	7
Bashi-Bazouks In The Sudan	Savage & Soldier Vol. XVII No. 4	"	22
British, Egyptian, & Empire Units in Egypt/Sudan 1882-99	New Material	"	29
The Suakin Field Force		"	33
OPERATIONAL STUDIES			
Weep For Hicks	Savage & Soldier Vol. XIII No's 3 & 4	Lt. Dave Bullock	35
General Gordon And The Fall of Khartoum	Savage & Soldier Vol. VIII No. 4	Peter Clark	56
On Gordon's Death	Savage & Soldier Vol. VIII No. 4	Douglas Johnson	67
The Gordon Relief Expedition: The Desert Route & The Camel Corps, 1884-85		"	68
The Gordon Relief Expedition: The Nile Route, 1884-85	Savage & Soldier Vol. XVII No. 1	"	78
Wilson's Dash To Khartoum: The Last Heave to Save Gordon		Gerry Webb	91
The Wars In The Eastern Sudan Part 1: The Rise of Osman Digna	Savage & Soldier Vol. XVII No. 3	Douglas Johnson	104
Wars in Eastern Sudan Part 2: Baker & El Teb	Savage & Soldier Vol. XIX No. 2	"	116
Wars in Eastern Sudan Part 3: Graham's First Expedition of 1884	Savage & Soldier Vol. XX No. 1	"	132
Ginnis: A Battle of Lasts And Firsts	Soldiers of the Queen, #11	"	151
APPENDIX			
Orders Of Battle For The Sudan Campaigns And Actions 1883-1885		Andrew Preziosi	158

Introduction

Since the modern war games hobby began with the works of H.G. Wells early in the 20th Century, one of the most popular and enduring areas of interest has been that of the "Colonial Wars." That is, conflicts involving the 19th Century Era of Imperialism and Colonization throughout Africa and most of Asia. Practically speaking, this most commonly means the wars and campaigns waged by the British Empire against a wide variety of different peoples of equally varied geography and technology. Though by far the world's largest Empire, Britain's was not the only colonizing enterprise, and the imperial aspirations of France, Germany, Italy (among others), and ultimately the United States, are also popular grist for the Colonial War Gamer's' mill.

In 1965, hobbyist and budding historian, Douglas Johnson, produced a home published magazine dedicated to the enjoyment of Colonial Era history and games and called it *Savage And Soldier*. Not always well supported by commonly found sources in those days, much effort was put into finding what was available, not only in English language sources, but others as well. As the hobby itself grew, so did interest in more diverse wars and combatants, spurring ever wider study by many contributors over the years. In time, S&S grew in stature and erudition, ultimately becoming the nexus of Douglas' own—and others'—researches of interest to war gamers, especially miniaturists. Details of uniforms, weaponry, tactics, organization, flags, and more in campaigns as diverse as the Zulu War, Tai-P'ing Rebellion, Boer Wars, the wars of suppression in British and German East Africa, French interventions in Dahomey, Madagascar, Mexico, and beyond became regular fare for the readership.

After Douglas had moved on to Editor Emeritus status and was succeeded by Lynn Bodin as the active Publisher/Editor, S&S continued to grow to meet the ever rising standards of quality material demanded by the hobby.

Then, in the mid 1980's, Douglas and Lynn collaborated on a compilation of previously published articles dealing with the Sudan and the Mahdist Wars of 1883-1899. Modestly printed, though with four specially commissioned color uniform plates by regular contributor Greg Rose, the "Sudan Special" (as it has been known ever since) became a sort of legendary work that has been continuously in demand by those who have heard of it. Robert Burke, "Archivist" for the considerable number of back issues of Savage And Soldier, for years has kept the flame burning and is still the only source for all of the magazine's original back numbers, as well as the "Sudan Special."

In 1996, S&S seemed to have reached the end of its run. Then current Editor, Milton Soong (who succeeded to the post following the premature death of Lynn Bodin) had to devote his full time and energies to his job and family. Despite efforts to do so, no one could be found to take the helm and continue to keep the magazine at its regular quarterly publication schedule, and it's remarkably high standard of content.

Then, in 2006, Richard Brooks, Editor of another very long-lived Colonial War Games fan publication, *The Heliograph*, arranged with Milton Soong to bring *Savage And Soldier* back for one last year. It was not long after Richard began soliciting new material that I approached him with the idea of reprinting the "Sudan Special." At the time, it seemed an easy matter of simply reformatting the original articles and graphics in order to print a more sophisticated version.

However, the project quickly outgrew that simple design as we were able to re-establish contact with Douglas Johnson. His studies having continued over the years, and having had the good fortune to travel to the Sudan in the 1970's to visit the fields of Omdurman and Shaykan, he was able to offer much new information and some remarkable color photos.

Soon enough, it was decided to add related articles printed in S&S long after the "Sudan Special" had first been published, in addition to new and original material not seen elsewhere. The sheer volume of this material, covering as it does many obscure aspects of the Mahdist Wars, quickly grew to the point where an essentially new work resulted. Indeed, while many fine books, both scholarly and popular in nature, are available describing the course of the Mahdi's short rise to power, and the long fall of what he tried to establish, we are confident that no other source has the sheer amount of detail that war gamers and miniaturists seek.

Not only are there organizational, tactical, and uniform details, but with the participation of Andrew Preziosi, readers will find herein the most complete Orders of Battle for the Mahdist Wars available anywhere. By campaign and individual battle, the exact units, their leaders, and numbers are provided. Similar details for the Mahdist forces are also listed, though the sources for these are unfortunately not as complete as historians—and war gamers—might like!

Graphically, the original color uniform plates were retained, though whenever possible more illustrations have been provided as well. The seminal article describing the appearance and design of Mahdist Flags by Douglas Johnson has been amplified and the original sketches of examples have been replaced with high quality, full color renderings by graphic artist Eric Cox. Additional examples of Egyptian Army flags as well as the personal flags of the Mahdi and his Khalifa Abdullah have also been provided for the first time.

The limitations of this work are still in some ways those of the original. As stated in the Preface to the "Sudan Special," no attempt is made at a general history of events. Rather, this Source Book assumes some basic familiarity by the reader with the background to the Mahdist Wars and their general course. Articles have been included that spotlight some of the lesser known campaigns and battles not well represented elsewhere. Again, the thrust here is towards a single source of hard data which may be referred to on a "need to know" basis, particularly by newcomers to war games set in the Sudan.

Within these pages should be virtually everything needed to help war gamers and collectors alike to organize their miniatures, paint them in proper uniforms, and even to march under the proper flags. Players and designers of war game rules will find tactical and doctrinal information that will allow them to represent the behavior of the many different combatants in the harsh—if not bizarre—conditions of the Sudan.

More even than most anthologies, this work is a truly collaborative effort. As Editor I have been blessed with the whole hearted cooperation of Richard Brooks and *Savage And Soldier* "Archivist," Robert Burke, the tireless researches and contributions of Douglas Johnson, as well as the graphic talents of Eric Cox. A dip of the colors is also due to Messrs. Mike Embry and Ben Checota for their own contributions in our flag researches. Ultimately, they and the other individual authors are the true creators of the work, and without their enthusiasm for their subjects and curiosity to find otherwise obscure facts, none of this would have existed, either 25 years ago, or today.

Special thanks are due to the Indispensable Man, Editor Emeritus Douglas Johnson, for his encyclopedic knowledge of the Sudan and its grim history. He has dug deep into his personal collection of photographs (including those taken on the

Omdurman Battlefield in 1975), uniform sketches made *in situ* at displays in El Obeid and Khartoum, maps, arcane publications, and more. As a former Archivist for the Southern Sudanese Government, he is still engaged in personal efforts to help bring stability (dare we say "peace?") to that still troubled land.

As Editor of this work, I have tried to regularize the spellings of remote and distant places and people, and corrected errors when encountered, or updated original articles with new information as it has become available. All that is sound and useful is from the original authors, while all remaining faults are entirely my own.

Patrick R. Wilson
The (Virtual) Armchair General
April, 2007

Preface To The Original Edition

This book is not intended to be a comprehensive survey of the Sudan Wars. Instead, it is a collection of articles on various aspects of the *Mahdiyya* and the their wars which previously appeared in *Savage And Soldier* and *Soldiers Of The Queen* magazines over the 1970's and 80's. Most of the issues in which they appeared have long since been out of print and there have been numerous requests for reprints of individual articles. We thought it best to gather the best of the articles together in one booklet, rather than to reissue them piecemeal. We have taken this opportunity to offer better illustrative material than was available for the earlier articles, and to correct and update the text with information also not available when they first appeared. We hope this will provide a core of reliable information for all those interested in the military history of the *Mahdiyya*.

Special Acknowledgement

The Editors (past and present) of *Savage And Soldier* Magazine would like to take this opportunity to express our sincere thanks to Mr. Ian J. Knight, Esq., Editor of *Soldiers Of The Queen* (the Journal of the Victorian Military Society, London) for his kind permission to reprint articles which appeared in past issues of that magazine. Mr. Knight's cooperation and assistance has been greatly appreciated by all who have worked on this special issue. As both magazines are the publications which regularly address the military history of the Victorian Era, cooperation of this nature can only be beneficial to both journals. Thank you again, Ian.

Douglas H. Johnson	Lynn E. Bodin
Oxford, England	Redmond, Washington State, USA

Publisher's Note

All illustrations contained in this work are, as much as possible, contemporary with the history presented.

No claim is made by the Publisher to ownership of any such images.

The Egyptian Army, 1880-1900
By Douglas Johnson

Egyptian troops battling the Mahdiyya. Painting on display in the Military Museum of the Egyptian Army.

Colonial war gamers have a hard time assessing the Egyptian Army. The defeats of Tel el-Kebir, El-Obeid and El-Teb stand out in their minds as primary examples of Egyptian cowardice and ineptness. Much praise is given to the Sudanese battalions, and this is deserved. Contempt is reserved for the Egyptian battalions of 1881 and 1898, but this is inaccurate. The task of an accurate evaluation is not made easier by the patronizing remarks of British observers who had no real experience with the Egyptian Army. However readable the accounts of Steevens, Churchill, Burleigh, etc, only one was a military man, and not one knew Arabic or had ever commanded Egyptians in battle. Their knowledge was at best second-hand.

It is unfortunate then that war gamers (and others) have tended to adopt their prejudices, and this article hopes to reform them.

The Early Years

The Egyptian Army had a checkered career in the 19th Century. Capable of extensive conquests under Muhammad Ali, by the 1880's it was in a sad state, especially so since its defeat by the Ethiopians in the late 1870's. The best Egyptian battalions were kept in Egypt, and those Egyptians sent to the Sudan (especially officers) were often sent for punishment. The best troops seem to have been the Sudanese battalions raised from the Africans of the South. Still, some of the original Egyptian garrisons in the Sudan fought well in the early days of the *Mahdiyya*, as with Slatin or in the defenses of El-Obeid, Sennar, Sinkat and Kassala. The soldiers sent down with Baker and Hicks were certainly not up to the standard of the Egyptian garrisons already in the Sudan. In fact, they were men who were considered unfit to be enrolled in the new Egyptian Army of Sir Evelyn Wood.

Wingate relates an incident on the disarming of the Egyptian Army after Tel el-Kebir:

> "...Later on in the day came a regiment of veterans from the fort of Abukir, who had until now believed that their guns would destroy the English fleet.... These old soldiers marched in silence up the long line of railway trucks, halted in silence under the level ranks of the Shropshire and Sussex regiments, and were disarmed. They hurled their rifles into the wagons, tore off their accoutrements and flung them after them, then turned and marched sullenly away without a word. Sir Evelyn Wood was there, and perhaps he marked these men's demeanor. Whether so or not, he never had the slightest doubt as to what kind of soldiers he was going to make." (Wingate, pp 204-5)

In the early 1880's, the Egyptian Army battalion consisted of four *Buluks* (companies) of approximately 200 men each. The Sudanese garrisons followed this organization while the new army under Wood in Egypt underwent a complete reorganization.

The New Egyptian Army was formally raised in 1883. A total of 6,000 men was raised in eight battalions for four years' service in the army, and then four each in the police and the reserves. British officers seconded to the Egyptian any were given a commission of one or two ranks above their own. Egyptian ranks (as well as the drill) were in Turkish. They were: Sirdar (Commander-in-Chief), Farik (Lt.-general), and Lewa (Major-General), all of which were addressed as "Pasha;" Miralai (Colonel), Kaimakan (Lt.-Colonel), both addressed as "Bey;" Bimbashi (Major), Yuzbashi (Captain), Mulazim awal (1st Lieutenant) and Mulazim tani (2nd Lieutenant) all of which were addressed as "Effendi." Although the first eight battalions were formed into two regiments, the first commanded by British officers under Brigadier Grenfell and the second under native officers under El Lewa Shuhdi Pasha, in fact the practice soon came to be that there were no British officers below the rank of Bimbashi and few Egyptian officers above Yuzbashi.

Throughout the campaigns of 1884 and 1885 few units of the new army were sent to the front. Some served on the frontier, in garrison duty at Suakin, and hauling boats for the Nile Column. Forty men of the Camel corps (at this time consisting of only one company) were with the British at El-Teb and Tamai in 1884, and another detachment with one camel battery saw action at Kirbekan in 1885. But by and large the Egyptians were kept strictly out of the fight. Plans were even floated to raise a Turkish battalion for the war in the Sudan rather than use the Egyptians. When this fell through, it was decided to raise a battalion of Sudanese veterans from the old Dongola and Berber regiments. This was the IX Battalion and served on garrisons at Suakin and on the frontier. (It was conventional to distinguish the Sudanese battalions from the Egyptian by using Roman numerals).

Growth of the Army

By the end of 1885 the Egyptian Army totaled nine battalions of infantry (25 British officers, 181 native officers, 4,646 men), eight troops of cavalry (one British officer, 27 native officers, 540 men), four batteries of artillery (one British officer, 18 native officers, 403 men), and three companies of Camel Corps (two British officers, seven native officers, 203 men) (Colville, I, p. 277). Two battalions of infantry, two troops of cavalry, one battery of artillery and fifty men of the Camel Corps were stationed at Suakin while five battalions of infantry, five troops of cavalry, one camel battery of artillery and the rest of the Camel Corps were stationed between Wadi Halfa and the frontier. (Ibid.)

Both the infantry and the Camel Corps were armed with the Martini-Henry rifle and triangular socket bayonet, weapons they retained into the 20th Century. The cavalry were armed with the Martini-Henry carbine and saber. It was not until the 1890's that the front ranks of the cavalry were given lances. The artillery used both mules and camels in each battery, alternating the mounts depending on the type of terrain (mules being used for rocky or hilly country and camels for the desert). At this time the artillery was armed with seven-pounder mountain guns and small caliber Krupps. Despite the lightness of the guns, the batteries were designated Field Batteries, a term

Officer, Egyptian Camel Corps

used throughout the rest of the century.

In 1886 four new battalions were raised. Two, the Xth and XIIIth, were Sudanese. However, later on in the year the 11th and 12th Egyptian battalions were disbanded for reasons of economy. One Sudanese battalion of Valentine Baker's Gendarmerie was used on the frontier and in Suakin as regular infantry in 1886 and 1887, until it was finally incorporated into the army on May 1, 1888 as the XIth Sudanese. A XIIth Sudanese battalion was raised the same year, and the Camel Corps was increased to four companies.

Enlistment in the Egyptian battalions was changed in 1888 to six years in the army, five in the police, and four in the reserves. The Sudanese, on the other hand, were enlisted for life and kept until too old to fight. Their treatment when "retired" contrasted unfavorably with their Egyptian counterparts, for very little attention was paid to their fate, aside from occasional donations from individual British officers. It was not until after the re-conquest of the Sudan that the government took a more active role in setting up pensions and "retirement" villages.

In 1890 the Sudanese battalions were expanded from four companies of 170 men each to six companies of 150 each. The Egyptian battalions remained at four companies. By 1891 there were fourteen battalions of infantry (the last six were Sudanese), five squadrons of cavalry (of 100 men each), six batteries of artillery (113 men each, except the one horse battery which had 137 men), and six companies of Camel Corps (at 152 men each), totaling 12,633 men (Wingate, p. 225). The cavalry were recruited exclusively from the Egyptian peasantry (*fellahin*) primarily from the Fayoum oasis (Steevens, p. 15). The Camel Corps had originally been all Egyptian, but now included two companies of Sudanese. By 1898 the Egyptian infantry battalions also had six companies each (Pritchard, p. 206).

When the re-conquest of the Sudan began in 1896, the army had been increased by four squadrons of cavalry and the 15th and 16th Egyptian battalions had been raised from the reserves. In 1897 the Camel Corps was increased to eight companies (four Egyptian and four Sudanese), the cavalry to ten squadrons, and two more reserve battalions (the 17th and 18th Egyptians) were raised. In 1898 another battalion of infantry was included when the Askaris of the Italian garrison at Kassala were re-designated the "Kassala Irregulars" after the garrison was handed over to Egypt. The army now totaled 18,000 men.

The field artillery continued to use 6.5cm Krupps up through the Dongola campaign. These were carried on four mules (or camels) but also had a shaft that could be attached to the gun trail for draught (Headlam, p. 243). In 1897 they began to be replaced by Maxim-Nordenfelt 75mm quick-firers which fired a 12.5 pdr shell, or an 18.5 pdr double shell. This was a compact gun that also could be carried on four mules. At Atbara only the 1st and 2nd Field Batteries had Maxim-Nordenfelts, but at Omdurman all four Field Batteries were armed with them, though No.3 battery retained two of its Krupps (Headlam, p. 245). The Horse Battery was armed with antiquated 7.75cm Krupps (sometimes referred to as a 7pdr), which lacked brakes, had a slow rate of fire, and often had poor quality shells. Each gun was drawn by a team of eight Syrian horses, and had ammunition wagons accompanying them into battle. Multi-barreled Gardner and Nordenfelt machine guns were used through 1896. The first Maxim guns manned by Egyptians appeared in 1897; until 1898 all Egyptian machine guns were Maxims, including the famous "Galloping Maxim" of the cavalry, which were drawn by teams of six horses. While artillery batteries had six guns each, the machine gun batteries had only two.

Attack Formations of The Sudanese Battalions

Both Egyptian and Sudanese Battalions marched in columns of double companies, but the Sudanese, having six (as opposed to the Egyptian's four), advanced to attack in a line of four companies with two more in reserve behind the center at a distance of one company. In this way, the two flank companies could swing around to form a square if necessary. Bayonet charges were launched in this formation, which was adopted by the Egyptian Battalions at Omdurman as well.

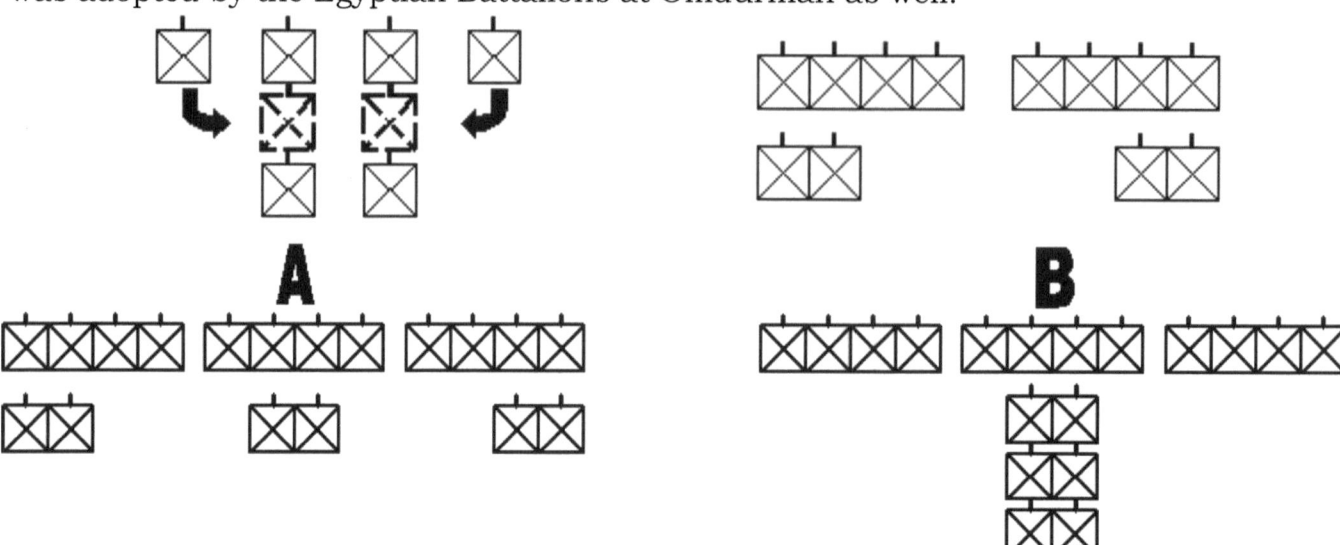

When advancing in brigades, the same formation was adopted, with two battalions on the fighting line, each with two companies out of their six behind in support (Knight, p. 117).

A brigade of four battalions had three battalions in front [Figure A] with one in column (sometime in double companies [Figure B) in support to the rear.

The Frontier 1885-96 and Re-conquest

Numerous frontier skirmishes took place at the end of 1885 as the British retreated and the Mahdists advanced. The new Egyptian Army got its first test in December, 1885, in the battles around Kosheh and Ginnis. Unlike later actions with the British army, the Egyptians were not brigaded separately. The 3rd Egyptians, one company of the Camel Corps and one Field Battery were with the 1st

Five-barreled Nordenfelt machine-gun used by both British and Egyptians throughout the Mahdist Wars, though three and two barreled models were more common. Fired by rapid hand crank, it was the first machine-gun adopted by the British Army.

Egyptian Army Cavalry Scouts at the time of the Re-conquest. Note arrangement and style of saddles and tack.

Brigade; and the 1st Egyptians, IXth Sudanese, one company of Camel Corps and one squadron of cavalry were with the 2nd Brigade.

Kosheh and Ginnis were a revelation to the British on the ability of the Egyptians. Together the Cameron Highlanders and the IXth Sudanese cleared a Mahdist village near Kosheh, the IXth alone capturing two cannon. The Egyptians, too, cleared part of the village of Ginnis in stiff hand-to-hand fighting and captured four Mahdist guns.

After Ginnis the British force at the Frontier was progressively reduced until only one company remained at Assouan by 3 January 1888, and this was withdrawn to Cairo in June. The defense of the Frontier and of Suakin was, for all practical purposes, left entirely to the Egyptian Army from 1886 on. British troops were either entirely absent, or played only a supporting role. The defeat of Wad al-Nujumi at Toski was done entirely by Egyptians and Sudanese, the 20th Hussars being the only British troops involved.

Most of the fights that took place were skirmishes and small actions, with both the Egyptians and the Mahdists advancing and retreating around the villages of Serras, Gemai, Suarda, Argin, and others. Usually the Mahdists remained in Serras and Gemai while the advanced posts of Egypt were at Argin and the Khor Musa Fort. After Toski the Egyptians advanced up to Serras, though they generally remained on the defensive up to 1891.

Many of these skirmishes ended in Egyptian defeats, but they were defeats of a type that proved the steadiness of the new army. Only a few examples need be cited.

In a skirmish near Khor Musa Fort in October, 1887, the Camel Corps and cavalry were caught in a melee by a superior Mahdist force while withdrawing. Yet they were able to continue their retreat in good order, while fighting, until the rifles of the IXth Sudanese could come to their aid (Royle, p. 470). The disastrous Handub expedition three months later, which nearly cost Kitchener his life, could have ended in a massacre but for the valor of one company of the Xth Sudanese that was with the force. This company was caught unsupported when 300 "friendlies" routed in the face of Uthman Digna's troops. A force of 150 men faced 1,000, of which 600 were entrenched with rifles. The Xth held out until Kitchener could bring up his reserves of cavalry and Camel Corps. Despite losses of 40 percent the remnants of this company covered the retreat of the entire force. One British officer later wrote "...Had it not been for the gallantry and steadiness of the Xth, we must have all been scuppered" (Hunter, pp. 6-9).

A similar incident happened at the Khor Musa fort the night of August 29, 1888. The Mahdists managed to enter the fort at night and occupy half of it while part of the Egyptian battalion there, under the command of an Egyptian major, was able to hold the other half until relief came in the morning in the form of cavalry, infantry, an armored train and a gunboat (Royle 1900, p. 472).

Various British writers date the "transformation" of the Egyptian Army from Toski in 1889, or Tokar in 1891, and some even as late as Omdurman itself. But it is clear that the transformation was earlier than that for one cannot think of a greater contrast between El-Obeid and El-Teb than the above incidents where the Egyptians remained steady when outnumbered and outgunned, surprised or actually overtaken by the enemy. Toski and Tokar were the largest tests, but they only showed the British public what the British officers in the Egyptian Army already knew.

In late June, 1889, reports came that Wad al-Nujumi was advancing into Egypt with a force of about 4,000 fighting men. Immediately a Flying Column of about 1,940 men and four steamers under Colonel Wodehouse was formed to make contact with the enemy. This they did at the village of Argin where, by fortifying the village, setting the guns across the river overlooking the village, and skillfully using the steamers filled with men to rush reinforcements from one sector to the next, the Flying Column repelled the Mahdist attack. The force then spent the rest of July trailing Wad al-Nujumi and preventing him from reaching the river while the Sirdar, Sir Francis Grenfell, gathered a larger force of Egyptians and called in British reinforcements.

The Egyptian force was concentrated at Toski and reformed into two brigades. Grenfell hoped to delay action until the British arrived, but it turned out he needn't have worried. On August 3rd, two days after the Sirdar's arrival at Toski, a battle was unexpectedly precipitated.

At first the Mahdist rifle fire was so heavy that the Camel Corps and cavalry were forced out of two defensive positions. But in a series of rushes the Sudanese and Egyptian battalions were able to storm and seize the Mahdist hill-tops. The last hill was taken by a united charge of the IXth, Xth and XIIIth battalions. The ensuing Mahdist retreat was harassed by the Egyptian cavalry aided by the 20th Hussars, the only incident where British troops came into action in the nearly two month long expedition. (See Hunter, pp. 17-18; Royle 1900, pp. 480-484; Wingate, pp. 406-432).

With their defeat at Toski the Mahdists retreated south to Suarda. Minor raiding continued until 1893, but the frontier was quiet after that. Only Suakin needed security. In 1891 Colonel Holled-Smith, commander of the Suakin garrison, was sent to secure Tokar.

Taking Handub first on January 27, 1891, he arrived at the old government buildings of Tokar on February 19th. The battle there was not the dramatic event some writers later made it to be. A force of three battalions of veterans (two had been at Toski) was attacked by a smaller force of some 2,000. There was no question of whether the Egyptians would hold, or whether the square would break. The main attack came against the XIIth but firing was general all along the perimeter. Once the Mahdist charge was checked, the XIth launched a counter charge which cleared the field. Uthman Digna was forced to fall back on Kassala and for the next five years made only occasional raids against Suakin and Tokar.

Egypt, through the army, had now established secure frontiers which could also serve as bases for its own invasion of the Sudan.

The Re-conquest

It is natural that British authors give more attention to the few British troops involved in the conquest of the Sudan, but this gives a distorted view. In one sense the conquest of the Sudan was a British victory, for the designers of the military and political strategy were British. The Egyptian Army was remodeled by British officers and British infantry and artillery did play a considerable part at Atbara and Omdurman. Yet it is as untrue to claim the re-conquest a British victory as it would be to claim that the Normandy landings were an American victory. Even in substituting "Anglo-Egyptian" for "British" the emphasis should be on Egyptian, for it was the Egyptian Army that won the battles.

When the decision was made to advance on Dongola in April, 1896, the Egyptian Army was momentarily caught off-guard, only in that no campaign was expected that year. Two new battalions were raised from the reserves, an Indian contingent was sent to replace the garrison at Suakin, and the North Staffordshire Regiment moved south to occupy frontier posts for the Egyptian Army. The force that crossed the frontier was on its own. The first engagement at Firka on June 7th was carried out entirely by the three Egyptian brigades and mounted support. While the North Staffordshire Regiment was at Hafir, that battle was primarily an artillery duel between the Mahdist guns and the Egyptian flotilla. It fell to the Egyptian artillery and two companies of the Xth Sudanese to cross over the neighboring island of Artaghasi and silence the Mahdist redoubt at close range. Dongola fell to the gunboats.

The consolidation of 1897 again was done solely by the Egyptian Army. Abu Hamid was captured by four battalions and the artillery on August 7, Berber was taken by Ja'alin "friendlies" on September 6th. Kassala was handed over by the Italians to the 16th Egyptians on December 25th.

It was not until February, 1898, that one brigade of British infantry began to arrive at the frontier. This brigade was a great help at Atbara, and all are agreed that the bulk of the fighting done was by the two Highland and six Sudanese battalions. Yet it was the Sudanese who, having the longest distance to travel and coming under the heaviest fire, breached the *zariba* first. It was the Xth that captured the Mahdist Commander, Mahmud.

The 21st Lancers did not come out from Cairo until August, nearly six months after Atbara. They seem to have been a totally superfluous regiment as most reconnaissance was conducted by the Egyptian cavalry either in small groups, or as at Atbara, in force. Together with the Camel Corps, the horse battery and the "Galloping Maxims," the Egyptian Cavalry could form the advance force for the entire army, engaging the enemy with rifles, artillery and machine-guns. The "Galloping Maxims" even allowed the cavalry to fire while withdrawing, though the effect at full tilt must have been erratic. This potent formation was used effectively at Omdurman in "soaking off" the forces of Sheik al-Din and Ali wad Hilu. But, as so often before, the slow moving Camel Corps nearly got overwhelmed by the enemy's fleeter movement, and the entire force might have come to grief without the intervention of the gunboats. By the end of the battle the Egyptian cavalry and the Camel Corps were still able to attempt the pursuit of the Khalifa. This pursuit, or rather the prevention of the Khalifa's escape, was supposed to be the job of the 21st Lancers who had wasted their opportunity by being tricked into their charge. They were in no condition afterwards to pursue anything but their own glory.

Another brigade of British infantry, plus two batteries of artillery were sent to reinforce the Egyptians after Atbara, though one wonders if they were needed. The artillery support at Omdurman was effective. The first Mahdist charge was directed mainly at the British brigades but finished in front of Maxwell's. This was scarcely the whole battle. The main attack, first by the Black Flag, then by the two Green Flags, was directed at the Egyptians, and particularly against Macdonald's Sudanese. The credit for meeting both of these threats, delivered almost simultaneously, should go equally to Macdonald and his men, for he gave the orders, but they carried them out perfectly. The eventual support of the 10th Lincolnshire Regiment hastened, but did not dictate the end of the Mahdist charge. That was already decided by the 2nd Egyptians and the IXth, Xth and XIth Sudanese. One English officer with the 2nd Egyptians wrote home after the battle, "I also saw (from newspaper clippings) that 2 cos. of the Lincolns came up and saved us!! Certainly 2 English Regiments came up to our support but after we had finished our job, they never formed up into alignment, much less fired a shot" (Ready Ms, NAM).

The actual capture of Omdurman was carried out by the Egyptian Army, with the XIIIth Sudanese entering and taking the citadel just too late to capture the Khalifa.

With Omdurman captured the British troops left the Sudan. The Guards and the 21st Lancers returned home to cheering crowds while the Egyptian Army continued the year-long hunt for the Khalifa and his remaining Emirs. Gedaref, the last major

Mahdist stronghold was taken by the 16th Egyptians and the "Kassala Irregulars." The largest battle after Omdurman was at Rosaires on December 26, 1898, when a few companies of the IXth and Xth attacked Ahmad Fadil in a well-entrenched position. The Mahdists had two tiers of riflemen concealed in sand hills and scrub and subjected the Sudanese to a fire that many compared to the fire the Mahdists received at Omdurman. The Xth alone lost nearly a quarter of its strength. Yet when they halted and were rushed by the Mahdists, they returned an equally devastating fire at close range which completely repulsed the Mahdists (Hunter, p. 52).

The Khalifa was finally met and killed at El Gedid (Umm Diwaykarat) on November 23, 1899, by the IXth and XIIIth Sudanese. Among the trophies carried off by the IXth were the Khalifa's own leather and silver encased *dombeya* (elephant tusk horn) and the Mahdi's original modest green flag.

The Sudanese Battalions

In making a critical assessment of the Egyptian Army it has to be admitted that the Sudanese battalions were universally regarded as the pride of the army. In numerous battles they were placed in the firing line first, with the Egyptians in support. Though there may be something in the attitudes toward war in the Sudanese culture to account for their reputation, it would be a mistake to explain it solely by the "martial race" theory.

A better reason for their reliability is found in the set-up of the Egyptian Army itself. The Sudanese battalions were recruited from the Blacks of the Southern Sudan and the Nuba Mountains. Many were veterans of the old Egyptian Army who had fought in Mexico and Turkey. Some later served with the Mahdists in the *Jihadiyya*. Many of these had-been commanded by Hamdan Abu Anja, the greatest tactician and general of the Mahdist army. The first Sudanese battalion, the IXth, was raised from ex-soldiers still in Egypt. The next two, the Xth and XIIIth, were drawn mostly from the survivors of three Sudanese battalions in the Eastern Sudan who had escaped, *en masse*, from the Mahdists In 1885. After every major battle, a few recruits from the *Jihadiyya* prisoners were sent off for additional training to replace losses. Thus, in the beginning and throughout the long war against the *Mahdiyya* the Sudanese battalions were able to recruit almost exclusively from veterans with many years experience fighting under a variety of conditions in the Sudan. Unlike the Egyptian battalions, the Sudanese were recruited for life, so these veterans were retained from campaign to campaign.

This experience told in the soldiers' relations with their British officers. One subaltern who served with the IXth on the frontier reports several instances of being corrected by his men. Prior to Toski he was assigned to fortify a house and walled courtyard with part of one company:

"I had two 3 barreled Nordenfelts and on my making a position for them at one corner, which had a good field of fire, I was checked by an old Shilluk (one of the tribes of the Southern Sudan) for doing so, as he said that the Dervish would be sure to make for the corner of the fort, and then our machine-guns would jam; whereas three or four men would be ever so much safer, and then there were their bayonets. There was a lot in what he said." (Mitford, part 2, p. 226).

Bandsmen of the XIth Sudanese pose proudly for the photographer.

At another point during the battle of Toski he was ordered

to fire on a body of Mahdists same 900 yards away to prevent their advance north:

> *"I noticed some of the volleys seemed very weak, so watched the muzzles and spotted that no smoke appeared an the word of "Atesh", so, seizing one man by the ear, asked him why he had not fired. He said, 'No, Bimbashi, not yet, it is far; let us wait until we see the whites of their eyes; the day will be long, and we shall want all our cartridges before it is finished.' I had to quickly explain that we must prevent the foe going north."* (Mitford, part 3, p, 66).

Thus there seems to have been a continuous rapport between the Sudanese and their officers: sharing combat experience, explaining, relying on initiative, and a general keeping everyone on his toes. This did much to maintain their standard of fighting.

There has been much criticism about Sudanese fire-discipline. The authority most often quoted on this is Churchill, whose greatest criticism is voiced regarding incidents he did not witness. He claims that Sudanese firing at Atbara "was of the wildest and most reckless description," though he himself had not been at Atbara (Churchill, I, p. 934). His criticism compelled his editor, who had served with the Egyptian Army throughout the re-conquest, to comment "The shooting was generally very free, and no unit can be either entirely exonerated or severely blamed." (Ibid.) Churchill then gives a very long and vivid description of the wild nature in which the Sudanese of Macdonald's brigade wasted ammunition. Yet at this time he was nowhere near the scene of the action and his seemingly eye-witness account appears more and more like the imaginative reporting for which he was known. A more reliable authority reported that when Macdonald's brigade was drawn up to face the Mahdists the artillery and maxims opened fire prematurely, and this set the Sudanese off at independent firing. Macdonald brought this to a halt, company volleys were opened up at four hundred yards, and "from that time on they worked like a machine" (Pritchard p. 206). The real problem the Sudanese faced was a shortage of ammunition, which is not surprising considering they bore the brunt of the battle (Zulfo, p.227). The official report records that Macdonald's brigade repulsed the attack by their own firepower (SIR, p.7). This was only one of three attacks the Sudanese repulsed with firepower during the battle. There were other battles, Firka, Hafir and Rosaires, for instance, where the effectiveness of Sudanese firepower drew special comment (Knight, p. 123, Atteridge, p. 212, Hunter, p. 52).

The Egyptian Battalions

If the praise for the Sudanese Battalions is sometimes as wild and free as Sudanese firing was reputed to be, the praise for the Egyptians is more restrained, almost defensive. "Though the Sudanese might be considered the flower of the army," wrote one British officer, "the *fellaheen* cavalry, artillery and infantry were absolutely trustworthy troops. (Maxse, p. 132). "Excellent soldiers, but not heroes," is the type of remark one is apt to hear about them. It is a general feeling, rarely substantiated by specific instances. Some of the examples can be questioned in their interpretation, and others do not merit being turned into blanket generalizations.

The Times Correspondent was impressed with Egyptian performance at Firka:

> *"I had already noted in the course of the action, that the Egyptians were perfectly steady under fire, and they have always had the reputation for being so, but few gave them the credit for possessing the dash they displayed on this occasion"* (Knight, p. 123).

A new reputation should have begun with Ginnis when the 3rd Egyptians cleared several houses at the bayonet and captured four guns, or with the early string of "gallant actions" of the Camel Corps. Yet the memory of El Obeid and El Teb, as un-indicative of the new army as they were, lingered.

I have already noted the veteran status of the Sudanese as one reason for their reliability. Egyptian soldiers were recruited for only six years, so that only officers and NCO's were likely to be veterans of the widely separated campaigns. Seven years had elapsed between Toski and Firka, with only one Egyptian battalion having served in the 1891 Tokar Expedition. It is not likely that any battalion had the accumulated experience of the Sudanese. It is not surprising, then, that some of the reservist battalions distinguished themselves quite well, though generally kept out of the battle. The 15th Battalion, unsupported, took Shendi before Atbara. The 16th Battalion did so well at Gedaref and other actions along the Blue Nile that even Churchill was moved to say that it "won greater distinction than any *fellahin* troops during the war" (Churchill, II, p. 266).

The Officers

The common explanation for the fighting ability of the new Egyptian Army is that it was now "properly led by British Officers." Though nothing should be detracted from the real achievements of the British Officers and NCO's that trained and led the Egyptian Army, it is time that this emphasis on the officer be dropped. When properly lead and trained, by anybody, any army can fight well. It is not true than an army is only as good as its officers—the British Army has proved that over and over again in the 19th Century, and especially WW I. An army is only as good as its soldiers, and again the British Army has proved that.

There were certainly some very good officers seconded to the Egyptian Army. Those who came early and were in command of a company or two, who had a close contact with their men, seem in many ways better than those who straight away commanded a battalion or larger force. They had a better understanding of their own men, knew their capabilities and how to reach them. It also seems that those who came out in the 80's or early 90's and stayed on became the best officers in the army. Certainly there was a difference between them and those who came much later, for the last phase of the Re-conquest. There were some brand new officers who came out in 1898 just in time for Atbara and who could not converse fluently in Arabic on military matters until after Omdurman! One might also suggest that those in the Sudanese Battalions seemed to advance further than those in the Egyptian. It is more than a coincidence that during the Re-conquest the commander of the Egyptian Division, General Hunter, and three out of four brigade commanders—Lewis, MacDonald and Collinson—all had served in Sudanese Battalions.

Native officers were often belittled. It was often said that the 7th Egyptians at Omdurman, the only battalion with no British Officers, wavered in the face of the enemy. The fact that it was commanded by native officers was seen as sufficient explanation. Unfortunately, no one has yet gone into the matter more thoroughly.

There were many instances on the frontier and the Dongola Campaign where troops under their own officers fought quite gallantly. The case of the Egyptian major defending Khor Musa Fort has already been cited.

There was a difference between Egyptian and Sudanese officers. Almost all Egyptian Officers (many of whom served in Sudanese Battalions) were trained at the military academy in Cairo. All Sudanese Officers came from the ranks. These officers won high praise from the *Times* Correspondent in 1896, and he could by no stretch of the imagination be described as a negrophile.

Relations With The British

Churchill attributed the transformation of the Egyptian Army to the regimental pride adopted and instilled by the British Officers. "The officer's military honor is the honor of his men... whatever they are, or wherever they are, the officer who leads them believes in them and swears by them" (Churchill, I, p.412). This may not be a major reason for the change, but it certainly was an element. Officers in the Egyptian Battalions despised the Sudanese. Officers with the Sudanese knew that their men were best. Both resented the officers of the British Regiments. At Ginnis, a British Officer in the Egyptian Army was the first to enter the Mahdist camp. He went rushing about grabbing Mahdist banners yelling, "Don't let the English get the flags! Don't let the English get the flags!" It was only after intervention by Grenfell that he reluctantly gave up a few of the trophies he had gathered for the Egyptians (Haggard, p. 376).

The same rivalry was sometimes displayed by the men. One Sudanese Battalion fired warning shots over the heads of the Grenadiers as the latter tried to pull in front in the rush to be the first to enter Omdurman after the battle. When one officer nervously inquired about the shots, another answered, trying to sound cheerful, "Oh, it's the Gyppies behind... they always do that if you get in front of them" (Ziegler, p. 191). Nor did the "Gyppies" let the Guards remain in front for long. Smith-Dorrien led his XIIIth Sudanese through the back alleys and outskirts of the town, re-entering the main road in front of the Guards, and then spread his companies out across the width of the street so that no else could pass (Ziegler, p. 196). As it was, the Sirdar chose the XIIIth over the Guards to be the first to storm the citadel.

There were friendlier relations between individual battalions. In commemoration for their joint defense of Kosheh, the Cameron Highlanders presented the IXth Sudanese with their own Color. Friendly interest continued between the two regiments until 1930 when the IXth was disbanded. The IXth insisted on returning their Color to the Camerons for safekeeping, and also gave them their two most prized trophies: the Khalifa's war horn and the Mahdi's original green flag. The Xth Sudanese had a similar relationship with the 10th Lincolnshire Regiment while the latter was stationed in Egypt, but this friendship was based on the fact that both shared the number "ten." On the march into Omdurman, both battalions cheered as they passed and re-passed each other on the way. The band of the Xth played the "Lincolnshire Poacher," and finally gave the 10th a Mahdist flag to carry in front as a trophy. In reciprocation, the 10th presented the Xth with a color of their own after the campaign. The Grenadier Guards also presented the Xth with a Drum Major's staff.

Conclusion

The conquest of Africa was carried out by European Governments, but primarily through African Troops. The old Askaris do not figure as prominently in modern history as their enemies who resisted European domination. "Mercenaries" they are sometimes called, and mercenaries they often were, but not in the image that word now evokes. Thus dismissed by Africanists, they fare no better with modern British writers who, with extraordinary ingratitude, ignore the soldiers who won for them the empire they remember so fondly.

The Egyptian Army was raised with the conquest of the Sudan as its main—and almost sole—purpose. The defense of the Suez Canal and British interests were left to the Royal Navy and British Troops in Egypt. This purpose the Egyptians achieved through a long frontier war, in battles on their own, and finally in battles aided by the British Army. The officers who served in the Egyptian Army have long since died. The battalions who bore Ginnis, or Toski, or Firka on their flags have been disbanded. They have no regimental historians or museums to maintain the credit due them. Many recent books by British authors on the Colonial period have emphasized such notable British traits as a sense of "fair play," yet there has been little that is fair in the treatment of the memory of the Egyptian Army. There is still the need for fairer and more analytical accounts. They may come in the near future, but they are long overdue.

Uniforms, Flags, and Numerals

The army retained its white uniform of the earlier period up through 1885. Sometime in 1885 the new Khaki uniform was introduced. The cavalry and camel corps at Suakin were still in white by the end of the campaign (Haggard), but the Desert Column met Egyptians in khaki and puttees when they returned to Egypt in June and July (see Gleichen, Camel Corps).

While the Egyptian battalions had khaki drill early the Sudanese were less uniform. The IXth did not get full khaki drill until 1887, and did not even have a full issue of boots before 1886 (Mitford, p. 181). At first they wore a dark blue jersey and puttees, fez, and white pants. They had no regulation equipment, each man being issued a bit of leather out of which he improvised his own bandolier, same of very ornate design (Mitford, p. 175). When they finally did get their khaki drill and regulation equipment, they retained the blue jersey, and most men also kept their own bandoliers in preference to the new ammunition pouches which were stiff and often did not close properly (Mitford, p. 181). The XIth Sudanese began as a Gendarmerie battalion, and as such wore a Zouave style uniform of dark blue cloth, red cummerbund, white spats and yellow piping (Mitford, p. 177).

They retained this uniform for some time after they were incorporated into the regular army, though one photo of the battalion at Suakin in 1891 shows them in the regular khaki drill (Scrapbook, Gordon Highlanders). This same Zouave uniform was issued to all Sudanese battalions as a winter uniform in 1890, though the other battalions wore light blue piping. At this time the uniform was dark blue cloth, though a later photograph (1898) shows a uniform that is either medium or light blue (Khalifa's House, Omdurman).

The color of the khaki drill used by the Egyptian Army has been described as yellow and brown, the brown referring to the jersey the Egyptians wore. Churchill describes it as darker and not as yellow as British khaki (Churchill II, p. 427). All branches wore the jersey for marching order: the Egyptians wore brown and the Sudanese (including the Sudanese companies of the Camel Corps) wore dark blue.

Chevrons were red and were worn on the right arm of either the jersey or the khaki jacket. Officers, both native and British, never wore jerseys. One photo of an Egyptian officer shows him in a coat considerably darker than his trousers. Officers generally wore gaiters, though some wore puttees. British officers occasionally wore the fez, but this was mainly for ceremonial occasions. Most of the time they wore the Egyptian pattern sun helmet, which had a wider brim than the India pattern then in use by British regiments.

The fez (sometimes called *tarbush*) was tall, though shorter fezzes of earlier times seem to have been wore through the 80's and into the early 90's. It was sometimes worn plain, but there were four styles of *immas* (turbans) worn around it. The plain khaki *immas* with neck cloth was worn most often by all troops. It covered the top, and sometimes the neck cloth was tucked up under the fez leaving the back of the neck bare. So sketches in Churchill, however, show Egyptian cavalry with the neck cloth worn in front, part of it tucked under the fez to stiffen it like a hat brim to shade the eyes. The Sudanese battalions also had a plaited straw *imma*, stitched in back, with neck cloth, but leaving the top of the fez bare and tassel free. A plain white cloth was also sometimes worn by all leaving the top of the fez bare. Another variation of this was a bulky white cloth wrapped around the entire fez, covering the top as well. Regimental flashes and stripes were worn on the khaki and straw *immas* only.

Drums of the XIth Sudanese Battalion

Bandsmen wore the same uniform as the regular soldier. However, at times Sudanese wore their red sash over their blue jerseys. Each battalion had a drum and bugle band, while the brigades had full brass band. About 1886 the first bagpipe band was raised for the IXth Sudanese by a pipe-major from the Cameron Highlanders. By the end of the century almost all infantry battalions, Egyptian and Sudanese, had pipe bands. Bag covers and drums were dark green. The drums were trimmed in red along the top and bottom, had white tension ropes, and bore the regimental number and battle honors.

Flags

Each infantry battalion was issued a plain green silk flag, about 40"x 32", with white Arabic (Hindu) battalion numbers on the center and were carried into battle.

The one battalion at this time that did have a distinctive regimental color was the IXth Sudanese. This was presented to the battalion by the Cameron Highlanders on May 27, 1886, and returned to the Camerons when the IXth was disbanded in 1930. When first presented it had only Kosheh and Ginnis as honors, others being added later. It was of red (maroon) silk. The fringe was red and gold, the scrolls were buff edged in gold with black lettering, the central wreath was gold with green leaves, and the staff had a gold crown and crescent star on top. One side of the flag was in English, the other in Arabic.

In addition to the battalion flags, each company had a small rectangle of colored cloth with a white numeral in the center giving the company's number. The color of each flag varied with the company and were: 1-blue, 2-black, 3-white, 4-amber, 5-green, 6-vermilion (Steevens, p. 90). These flags were attached to spear shafts and carried in front of each company as they marched.

The national flag of Egypt at this time was in fact the Turkish flag: red with a large white star and crescent in the middle. The Khedive's standard was red with three small stars and crescents on the half of the flag nearest the staff.

Numerals

Those used in the Egyptian Army might cause some confusion. In English documents it was customary to use Arabic numerals when referring to the Egyptian battalions, and Roman numerals for the Sudanese. here are some documents that use either for both. The real confusion begins in the regimental flags and flashes of the regiments. For Arabic does not use what we call "Arabic" numerals, but a series of numbers based on a Hindu model. Unlike the language itself, the numbers are read from left to right, with the tens first and the units last. Here is the Arabic numeral system, in the most common orthography, as they would be used on the *imma* flashes of all regiments.

Egyptian Soldier's Summer Uniform under the reign of Khedives Ismail and Tewfik (1863-1882) and the first years of the Mahdist Revolt.

9th Egyptian Battalion Flag

Khedive's Color

National Color (Turkish)

Officer's uniform in the reign of Khedive Ismail. (1863 — 1879 A.D.).

Company Flags Within Each Battalion

No. 1	No. 2	No. 3	No. 4	No. 5	No. 6

Egyptian Army Standard, most likely for a Cavalry Regiment, bearing Honors including Omdurman. Cavalry did not carry Standards into action during the Mahdist Wars.

Reconstruction of the flag of the IXth Sudanese as it appeared at the end of the Mahdist Wars. Note the flag is in English on one side and Arabic on the other, with Roman and Arabic Numerals.

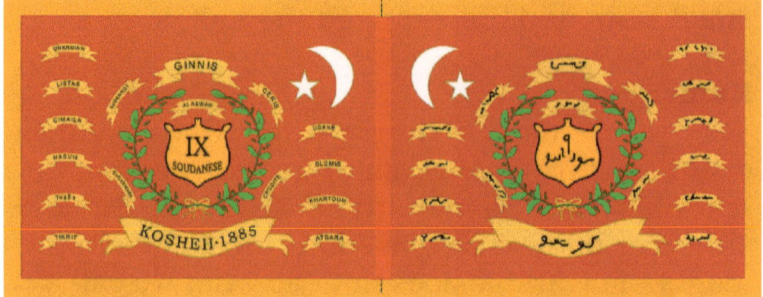

Note: Egyptian units were identified by the flashes worn on the front of their fezzes. These flashes were as follows:

- 1st Battalion: Green diamond
- 2nd Battalion: Black triangle
- 3rd Battalion: White diamond
- 4th Battalion: Red and Green rectangle
- 5th Battalion: Bright Blue Diamond
- 6th Battalion: Violet Rectangle
- 7th Battalion: Red and Green diamond
- 8th Battalion: Yellow triangle

The Sudanese Battalions did not have specific shapes of flashes as the did the Egyptians, rather they just had flashes of colored cloth worn on the sides of their fezzes. The Sudanese wore the flash outside the straw *imma* as well.

IXth Battalion: Green
Xth Battalion: Black
XIth Battalion: Scarlet
XIIth Battalion: Yellow
XIIIth Battalion: Blue
XIVth Battalion: White

Figure A
Sudanese Infantry in Zouave Style dress. Red fez with white turban, light blue uniform w/yellow trim, red sash. Brown belt, black boots, white gaiters.

Figure C
Corporal Piper in khaki kit. Regulation khaki uniform. Green pipe bag and possibly ribbons. Martini sword bayonet.

Figure B
Egyptian Infantry in winter Parade uniform. Red fez, black tassel, medium blue uniform, off-white collar, shoulder straps, trim and trouser stripe.

10th Sudanese infantry in uniform of post 1889

Figure D
Sudanese Infantryman in campaign (blue) kit showing the method of wearing the straw *imma* around the fez with the Battalion flash color in place.

Sudanese Infantry at bayonet work with Ansar near Suakin. Note the Egyptian Officer at left.

Bashi-Bazouks in the Sudan
by Douglas H. Johnson

Brigands always seem to be colorful characters in the popular imagination, and the Bashi-Bazouks (brigands almost to a man) were certainly some of the most colorful of all the colonial troops employed in the 19th Century Sudan. They were a mixed group with a mixed reputation. Their individual fighting ability and collective ferocity were rarely questioned, but so was their love of plunder

"North African" Bashi's posing to match their reputation.

and lack of military discipline. They were unreliable as a force after the first rush of conquest, yet they survived in the Turco-Egyptian Sudan up through the fall of Khartoum. Students of the early years of the Mahdist Wars are interested in the origin, career and dress of these somewhat mysterious soldiers.

"Bashi-Bazouk" (or, more correctly "Bashi-Buzuq") means "His head is irregular." It has been translated as "cracked-brain" or "madman" (Hill 1967: ix), but the Dutch traveler Schuver, who visited Turkey as well as the Sudan, claimed that the term did not refer to the soldier's lack of discipline but to his status in the army. His "head" being his commander, who was not regularly employed by the Sultan but raised his soldiers on his own initiative (Schuver: 4). Thus they were irregular troops, as opposed to regular soldiers. This explanation is consistent with the way in which these soldiers came first to Egypt and then to the Sudan. With Napoleon's defeat of the Mamlukes, and his subsequent retreat from Egypt, the Ottoman Sultan reasserted his authority in the country by sending soldiers from Turkey to curb the remaining authority of the Mamlukes. A number were Arnaut, a name given to soldiers from Macedonia, the Morea, Albania and Rumelia: all parts of the Ottoman Empire which are now contained in the modern nations of Greece, Albania and Yugoslavia (Rumelia bordered on Bulgaria). Thus while all were Turkish speaking, as Turkish subjects, many also spoke Greek.

Muhammad Ali was one of these Arnaut, and he used them first to crush the Mamlukes and then to gain ascendancy in Egypt and virtual autonomy from the Sultan. His army up until the 1820's contained the same mixture of Ottoman subjects as had been sent to Egypt. They dressed in their national costumes, rather than in uniforms, used weapons of their own preference, and were organized around and fought under their own leaders. There was no real organization in the army; it was a collection of different bands in Muhammad Ali's service (Weygand: 152). It was this army which invaded and conquered a large portion of the northern Sudan in 1820. It included Turks, Albanians, Syrians, Circassians, Kurds and North Africans.

After the initial conquest of the Sudan, a new army was formed, the Nizam al-Jadid, a regular army modeled on Napoleonic lines. It was originally composed of Sudanese slave soldiers, but as the manpower of the Sudan was not sufficient for Muhammad Ali's needs, Napoleonic-style conscription was introduced into Egypt itself.

The Nizam al-Jadid was gradually expanded throughout the 1820's until it embraced all arms of the service, but irregulars continued to be used in various parts of the Egyptian Empire. The number of irregulars grew even as the Nizam al-Jadid grew: there were 41,000 regulars and 12,000 irregulars in 1828, and 150,000 and 22,000 (respectively) in 1839 (Weygand: 222).

The irregulars in the army of occupation in the Sudan were originally drawn from the old war bands in Muhammad Ali's service prior to the conquest. These were mainly Albanians, Circassians, Kurds and Slavs. Eventually they included a number of other local levies. The first Arnauts sent to Egypt had been cavalry, and most Bashi-Bazouks in the Sudan were also cavalry, though as late as 1838 there were also some Turkish and Arnaut artillerists (Deherain: 153). Since the main function of the Bashi-Bazouks was to collect taxes and raid for slaves (two almost indistinguishable tasks), they remained mounted for many years.

There was no central Bashi-Bazouk command. The commanders of local detachments usually raised their own units from their own people, paid them and outfitted them with horses and muskets themselves. Each such chief was under the orders of the provincial governor. Each troops or company (*Buluk*) varied in size, and the company commander (*Buluk Bashi*) were called *Sanjaqs*. By the late 1860's some *Sanjaqs* were given the rank of *Yuzbashi* (Captain) in the regular army (Hill 1959: 27, 47, 114).

The term Bashi-Bazouk first applied to Albanians, Kurds and Slavs in the Egyptian army, but it was later applied to many other types of irregulars in the Sudan. Some Maghrabis (North Africans) were also called Bashi-Bazouks, as were the Sha'iqiya Arab horsemen who accompanied many Egyptian slave raiding expeditions into the Ethiopian foothills or into the northern most fringes of the Southern Sudan. In the Eastern Sudan during the 1883-4 campaigns there were a number of non-Turkish Bashi-Bazouks as well. The Sinkat Bashi-Bazouks were mostly Egyptians or men of Turkish descent recruited locally around Suakin, an old Turkish port; the Tokar Bashi-Bazouks were old soldiers and Egyptian convicts; the Massawa Bashi-Bazouks were none of these, but local Abyssinian (or Eritrean) frontiersmen and hill men, armed with firearms, skilled in their own type of mountain warfare, and dressed exactly like the Beja of the Red Sea (Wylde 1:109, 128-9).

The Bashi-Bazouks in the siege of Khartoum were a mixture of Sha'iqiya Arabs, townsmen, African slaves and ex-slaves. In general, though, the term was usually applied to any type of Turkish soldier recruited in Egypt or the Sudan, and in accounts of both Hicks' and Baker's armies the terms Turks and Bashi-Bazouks are usually interchangeable, though some of Baker's regular *gendarmerie* included Egyptian Turks.

Reliability and Performance

One of the first descriptions of the Arnauts sent to Egypt notes that they imitated the fierceness and endurance of the ancient Spartans, and that they were hardy, undisciplined, but excellent marksmen (MacLean: plate XXVII). The German traveler Frederick Werne was not impressed by their sobriety and discipline on the campaign in Taka in 1840, but he was amazed by their hardiness. The night before one march was spent in a drunken orgy, with correspondingly severe hang-overs the next morning. But when the order to begin the march was given, the Turks, the greater number of whom were Circassians, Kurds, Arnauts, or Albanians, who an hour before could hardly put one leg before another, were now changed men; the instant they were in their saddles they were galloping like madmen round the Pascha, and thrashing their horses with as little compassion as if they had been intoxicated with opium. (Werne: 28)

When Britain occupied Egypt there was some misguided anticipation, based on the racial prejudices then current in both England and Egypt, that Turkish soldiers would form the elite of the new Egyptian Army. The Turks soon disappointed the English and Egyptians, and Sudanese were used instead. Some Turks were sent to the Sudan with Hicks and Baker. Hicks was escorted from Suakin to Khartoum by 350 Bashi-Bazouks purged from Baker's gendarmerie. He, too, put great store in the Turks and Albanians to be included in his army, but his first look at his Bashi-Bazouk bodyguard on his way to Khartoum gave his some doubts. "They look like fighting," he wrote, "but also like thieving and murdering" (Daly: 22).

He liked the look of the Albanian Bashi-Bazouks already camped at Khartoum better, but all these, unlike those of the earlier years in the Sudan, were infantry, and he had been hoping for cavalry. Eventually he scrounged some horses and mounted some of the Bashi-Bazouks but was not pleased with the result: "...Found horses and saddles pretty good, but the men! Such a set of ruffians—unable to ride and each carrying in his hands a gigantic rifle" (Daly: 72). He may have rearmed them before setting off for El Obeid, for throughout the rest of his letters the Bashi-Bazouks are described as having carbines. His final disillusionment came with the beginning of the march into Kordofan.

Frank Power (the *Times* Correspondent) described the force as containing "1,000 cavalry (Bashi-Bazouks) that have never learned to ride..." (Power: 20), and Hicks found that they used their horses more to loot than to scout. When Hicks disarmed the local tribes, the Bashi-Bazouks sold them back their guns. Hicks decided they were so untrustworthy that he could not put them in line with the regular troops (Daly: 92-4).

There were Bashi-Bazouks defending El Obeid before the Hicks expedition. They manned the outer entrenchments of the town, armed with long "Abu Lafata" percussion rifles (anonymous account of al-Ubbayyad, SAD 40,41,10). We know how stubbornly El Obeid was defended. The "Turks" and Bashi-Bazouks of Baker's column put on a more varied performance. There were at least 400 "Turkish" and Albanian infantry, extracted mainly from the *gendarmerie*, and some 150 Bashi-Bazouk cavalry. The cavalry started the panic at El Teb by riding straight into and through the square, but the Turkish infantry held until overwhelmed.

Costumes and Uniforms

Since there was no single style of clothing for the Arnauts and Bashi-Bazouks, the flavor of their appearance is best conveyed by citing several descriptions.

There is a plate of an Arnaut soldier in T. MacLean's *The Military Costume of Turkey* (1818). The Arnauts are described as being armed with a pair of pistols stuck in their waist sash, a long *handjar* knife or dagger, and a long barreled musket. The figure in the plate is dressed in a long white shirt extending to his knees, short white trousers, a red hat, red vest and red sandals which lace up almost to the knee. His hair appears to be dressed in a long plait hanging down his back.

The Asiatic (i.e. "Turkish") troops sent to the Sudan in 1820 are described by a contemporary observer as dressing as they liked, in green, blue, red, brown and white. Some soldiers wore turbans around their heads, but the Albanians wore no turbans, only large red caps covering their ears and foreheads (the forerunner of the *tarbush*?). Most soldiers wore three or four long shawls wrapped around their waists, capable of stopping a pistol ball from 15-20 meters. They armed themselves with a long musket, a pair of pistols, a sword and a *yatagan*, or knife (Douin: 110).

One of the most colorful descriptions of the Arnauts comes from Werne, who described them in Cairo and in the campaign in Taka, the Eastern Sudan in 1840. One group of Rumelian and Albanian Arnauts he saw in Cairo wore:

> *"...Dirty ragged tarbushes dragged down low over the eyes or carelessly hanging on one side of the head, the bull-like neck and brown breast ever bared, a jacket, always at first of a yellow color, but now from age, holes and dirt, colorless, and under it a gay vest of many hues; the once white Albanian or Grecian shirt (Fustanella) with large wide sleeves, but now black or brown, as washing it never knew. The shirt falls like a tunic over their short breeches; their leggings generally fastened with innumerable buttons, are of a different color from the jacket, usually bright red or green, and the naked foot is thrust into old slippers. Over an old torn scarf or shawl is worn a leather girdle, in which are carried their ornaments, all valuables, and deadly weapons of every kind; at the back hang two small leathern pouches for powder and ball, along with a small flask holding oil for their arms; during war they carry a long musket, and with it, in spite of its short and awkward stock, they take sure and deadly aim"*
>
> (Werne: 116-7).

During the campaign in Taka, Werne observed "The Turkish cavalry, in their national dress of every hue and color, with yellow or green standards and small kettle-drums..." (Werne: 27). A number of contemporary prints from the 1830's-50's in the author's collection show a variety of Albanian costumes. The shirt is always white, with long and wide sleeves, and the shirt itself comes down to the knees, and sometimes below, in many pleated folds. The soldiers wear sleeveless waistcoats over the shirts and sometimes long-sleeved jackets over this. Many are draped in sheepskins or drab-colored blanket-like cloaks. The caps vary in size and a turban is only occasionally worn. The waistcoats and jackets are usually brown, buff, red (the most frequent color), green or blue. The caps are red and the tassels blue or black, but other colors may also have been worn.

The variety of costume continued into the 1880's. The *Graphic's* illustration of Hick's troops shows Albanian, Bosnian, Syrian and Greek Bashi-Bazouks, along with Kurdish cavalry, all retaining their national costumes, and looking identical to Turkish and Balkan irregulars in the Turkish army during the Russo-Turkish war of 1877.

We have another vivid description from one of Hicks' officers:

> *"...Some with their many-colored spear-tassels (large tarbush tassels) dropping to their shoulders; others again with their white turbans bound round the tarbush, and others with the linen folds thrown negligently from the "burnoose" over their head. Some had neatly embroidered jackets, as worn in their Albanian and Rumelian homes; others Anatolian dandies, vied with the former in their rain-bow colored scarves girt to the loins by crimson and buff stamped leather belts, containing cartridges, silver-mounted pistols, murderous knives, and pockets carrying their worldly wealth. Many wore long 'caftans' of silk, and many the Albanian knickerbocker trousers, leaving the knees uncovered, and wearing around the calf and skin a richly embroidered gaiter laced tightly around the ankle—the bare foot being sandaled. Planted defiantly before the marquee of their commander flowed their green standard...."*
>
> (Colborne: 46-7).

The Bashi-Bazouks of the Eastern Sudan were not all of this Anatolian and Balkan flavor. The "Old Soldiers" of the Suakin and other garrisons wore a plain white *jallabiyya* and white trousers, but these were not "Turkish" Bashi-Bazouks. The commander of Baker's 400 Turkish infantry, Yusef Bey, dressed himself in greater style, wearing an embroidered *Zouave* waistcoat and jacket, loose dark cloth trousers, embroidered leggings and Turkish shoes. He had a red silk sash twisted in several folds around his waist, with a scimitar tucked into the right side and two silver mounted flintlock pistols tucked in front. He had buckled over the sash a belt with three or four silver filigree boxes for powder, shot, etc (Sartorius: 186).

In fact, Bashi-Bazouk commanders frequently "dressed like stage villains" (Hill 1959: 26), no matter what their men wore. Our last description of Bashi-Bazouk style dress comes from the Egyptian frontier as late as 1887 when Ali Bey, a Cairene Turk, patrolled the frontier with a contingent of Sha'iqiya, whose sheik he had become. He carried a scimitar and wore

"...A big soft tarbush, with a large tassel, coming down over his ears, tied tightly around with an imma (turban); a Zouave coat, waistcoat, and baggy trousers of some dull color, not khaki, a large red sash around his waist, red leather socks in shoes with very turned-up toes. He was about five feet seven inches in height, with small hands and feet, and very large sweeping moustache."

(Mitford: 202).

If we can generalize then, the "average" Bashi-Bazouk in the Sudan from 1820-1884 wore a large red hat, often with a large tassel. In the early years no turban was worn, but later Bashi-Bazouks wore a number of coverings over the hat, some being turbans, some being the flowing burnoose. The white shirt had wide sleeves and came down in pleated folds almost to the knees, giving an *Evzone* appearance. Over this a Balkan or Turkish *Zouave*-style jacket or sleeveless waistcoat was worn. The jackets were many colors: buff, brown, red, green and blue, with embroidery of many colors. Trousers were usually short, coming to the knees, and often baggy, but white or drab in color.

Sashes around the waist were voluminous, often bright red, sometimes multi-colored. The lower legs were usually covered by leather gaiters, the feet were usually sandaled in Turkish-style shoes (often red) which covered the toes and were laced all the way up the calf. The weapons were flintlock pistols, scimitars, large daggers, and long-barreled muskets.

The accompanying illustrations give a further idea of the variety of Bashi-Bazouk dress in the Sudan. Bashi-Bazouk proved to be extremely versatile: they were used in many campaigns in the Sudan from the conquest in 1820 to the fall of Khartoum in 1885. Miniatures of Bashi-Bazouks can also be used as Turkish irregulars in war games throughout the same period, such as the Crimea, for instance.

The "Abu Lafata"

This is described by one author as a short percussion cavalry weapon, made between 1820-30 (Salmon: 89). It seems more likely to have referred to any muzzle-loading percussion firearm, whether musket or rifle, being the colloquial name for a type of weapon, not a specific manufacture. There were a number of Abu Lafata infantry rifles and single-barreled pistols and their percussion caps listed in the Omdurman arsenal in 1898 (Sudan Intelligence Report no. 60, appendices 25b & 26).

An ornate "rat Tail Flinter" such as a Bashi might thrust into his cummerbund and carry with typical panache.

References

Colborne, J., WITH HICKS PASHA IN THE SOUDAN, London, 1885.

Daly, M. W. (ed.), THE ROAD TO SHAYKAN: LETTERS OF GENERAL WILLIAM HICKS PASHA WRITTEN DURING THE SENNAR AND KORDOFAN CAMPAIGNS, 1883, Durham, 1983.

Deherain, H., LE SOUDAN EBYPTIEN SOUS MEHEMET ALI, Paris, 1898.

Douin, G., HISTOIRE DU SOUDAN EBYPTIEN, TOME 1ER: LA PENETRATION 1820-1822, Cairo, 1944.

Hill, R., EGYPT IN THE SUDAN, London, 1959.

Hill, R., A GEOGRAPHICAL DICTIONARY OF THE SUDAN (2nd ed.), London, 1967.

MacLean, T., THE MILITARY COSTUME OF TURKEY, London, 1818.

Mitford, B. R., "Extracts From the Diary of a Subaltern on the Nile in the Eighties and Nineties," SUDAN NOTES & RECORDS, 19/2, 1936.

Power, E., LETTERS FROM KHARTOUM WRITTEN DURING THE SIEGE, London, 1885.

Salmon, R., "The Story of Sheikh Ahmed Abu 6elaha, a Sudanese Vicar of Bray," SUDAN NOTES & RECORDS, 21/1, 1938.

Sartorius, E., THREE MONTHS IN THE SUDAN, London, 1885.

Schuver, J.M., REISEN IN OBEREN NILGEBIET, Gotha, 1883.

Werne, F., AFRICAN WANDERINGS, London, 1852.

Weygand, General, HISTOIRE MILITAIRE DE MOHAMMED ALI ET DE SES FILS, Paris, 1936.

Wylde, A.,'83 TO '87 IN THE SUDAN, Vol 1, London, 1888.

An uncharacteristically sedate group of Albanian Bashi-Bazouks whose dress is clearly influenced by almost every Balkan/Turkish fashion.

Costume of a Kurdish Bashi-Bazouk

Examples of Albanian Soldiers and their dress shared by Bashi-Bazouks.

Unspecified study from 1855

Yatagan with sheath

Egyptian And Sudan Campaign Tables
Compiled by Douglas Johnson

The following list covers the period 1882-99, including the campaigns and battles that took place between the withdrawal from the Sudan in 1885 and the commencement of the Reconquest in 1896, and the post-Omdurman campaigns against the remnants of the Mahdist army. This list does not necessarily correspond to official battle honors or medal clasps.

British, Indian and Colonial Units in Egypt and Sudan, 1882-1898
- 1882: Egypt
- 1884: Suakin (El Teb, Tamai)
- 1884-5: Nile & Desert Columns, Ginnis
- 1885: Suakin (Tofrek)
- 1889: Toski
- 1891: Tokar
- 1896: Dongola
- 1898: Atbara/Omdurman

Egyptian Army Campaigns, 1884-99
- 1884-5: Suakin, Nile Column, Kosheh, Ginnis
- 1888: Handub, Gemeiza
- 1889: Argin/Toski
- 1891: Tokar
- 1896-7: Dongola, Abu Hamid
- 1898: Nile Expedition (Atbara/Omdurman), Gedaref, Rosaires
- 1899: Gedid (Um Diwaykarat)

ROYAL NAVY UNITS	1882	1884	1884-5	1885	1896	1898
R. Naval Brigade	X	X	X	X	X	X
Royal Marine Light Infantry (RMLI)	X	X	X	X		
R. Marine Artillery	X					

BRITISH CAVALRY REGIMENTS	1882	1884	1884-5	1885	1889	1898
1st Life Guards	X					
2nd Life Guards	X					
Royal Horse Guards	X					
4th Dragoon Guards	X					
7th Dragoon Guards	X					
5th Lancers				X		
10th Hussars	X	X				
19th Hussars	X	X	X			
20th Hussars					X	X
21st Lancers						X

BRITISH INFANTRY BATTALIONS	1882	1884	1884-5	1885	1896	1898
1st Grenadier Guards						X
2nd Grenadier Guards	X					
3rd Grenadier Guards				X		
1st Coldstream Guards				X		
2nd Coldstream Guards	X					
1st Scots Guards	X					
2nd Scots Guards				X		
1st (5th) Northumberland Fusiliers						X
1st (6th) R. Warwickshire						X
1st (10th) Lincolnshire						X
2nd (18th) Royal Irish	X			X		
2nd (20th) Lancashire						X
1st (35th) Royal Sussex	X			X		
1st (38th) S. Staffordshire	X			X		
1st (42nd) R. Highlanders	X	X		X		
2nd (46th) DCLI	X			X		
1st (49th) Berkshire	X			X	X	
1st (50th) West Kent	X			X		
1st (53rd) Shropshire LI	X				X	
2nd (56th) Essex				X		
3rd (60th) K.R.R.C.	X	X				
1st (63rd) Manchester	X					
1st (64th) N. Staffordshire					X	
1st (65th) York & Lancs		X				
1st (72nd) Seaforth High.	X					X
2nd (73rd) East Surrey				X		
2nd (74th) Highland LI	X					
1st (75th) Gordon High.	X	X	X			
1st (79th) Cameron High.	X			X	X	X
2nd (84th) York & Lancs	X					
1st (87th) R. Irish Fusiliers	X					†
2nd (89th) R. Irish Fusiliers		X				
Connaught Rangers					†	
2nd (95th) Derbyshire	X					
2nd (96th) Manchester	X					
2nd (106th) Durham LI				X		
2nd Rifle Brigade						X

† Machine gun section only

ROYAL ARTILLERY BATTERIES	1882	1884	1884-5	1885	1898
A, D, H, F/1, R.A.	X				
1/1, Southern Division, R.A.			X		
4/1, London Division, R.A.	X				
5/1, London Division, R.A.	X				
5/1, Scottish Division, R.A.	X			X	
6/1, Scottish Division, R.A.	X	X		X	
M/1, Scottish Division, R.A. †		X			
7/1, Northern Division, R.A.	X				
I, N/2, R.A.	X				
C, T/3, R.A.	X				
32nd Field Battery, R.A.					X
37th Field Battery, R.A.					X
16/E, R.A.					X
N/A, R.H.A.	X				
G/B, R.H.A.	X			X	

† *Ad hoc* unit

ROYAL ENGINEER COMPANIES	1882	1884	1884-5	1885	1896	1898
2nd (Fortress)					X	X
8th (Railway)	X					
10th (Railway)				X		
11th (Field)	X			†		
17th (Field)	X			X		
18th (Field)	X					
21st (Field)	X					
24th (Field)	X			X		
26th (Field)	X	X	X			
Telegraph Section	X		X	X		

† Mounted detachment of 1 officer and 27 men

COMMISSARIAT & TRANSPORT COMPANIES	1882	1884-5	1885
3rd			X
5th			X
8th (+ signalers)	X		
9th	X	X	
10th	X		
11th	X	X	
12th	X		X
15th	X		
17th	X		

EGYPTIAN ARMY UNITS	1884-5	1888	1889	1891	1896-7	1898	1899
1st Egyptian Battalion	X		X	X	X	X	
2nd Egyptian Battalion			X		X	X	
3rd Egyptian Battalion	X				X	X	
4th Egyptian Battalion		X		X	X	X	
5th Egyptian Battalion					X	X	
6th Egyptian Battalion					X	X	
7th Egyptian Battalion					X	X	
8th Egyptian Battalion					X	X	
9th Sudanese Battalion	X	X	X		X	X	X
10th Sudanese Battalion		X	X		X	X	
11th Sudanese Battalion		X	X	X	X	X	
12th Sudanese Battalion		X	X	X	X	X	
13th Sudanese Battalion			X		X	X	X
14th Sudanese Battalion					X	X	
15th Egyptian Battalion					X	X	
16th Egyptian Battalion						X	
17th Egyptian Battalion						X	
18th Egyptian Battalion						X	
Kassala Irregular Battalion							X
Camel Corps	X	X	X		X	X	
Cavalry	X	X	X	X	X	X	X
Artillery	X		X	X	X	X	

INDIAN & COLONIAL UNITS	1882	1884-5	1885	1896
28th Bombay Native Infantry			X	
7th Bengal Native Infantry	X			
17th Bengal Native Infantry			X	
20th Bengal Native Infantry	X			
26th Bengal Native Infantry				†
29th Bengal Native Infantry	X			
15th Sikhs			X	
35th Sikhs				†
Madras Sappers & Miners	X		X	
1st Bombay Lancers				†
2nd Bengal Cavalry	X			
6th Bengal Cavalry	X			
9th Bengal Lancers			X	
13th Bengal Lancers	X			
5th Bombay MT Artillery				†
Canadian Voyageurs		X		
New South Wales Regiment			X	
New South Wales Artillery			X	

† Sent to garrison Suakin; took no active part in the campaign

Suakin Field Force
Compiled by Douglas Johnson

UNIT	TOTAL	EL TEB	TAMAI
1st Brigade (Buller)			
1st Btn (75th) Gordon High.	747	720	712
3rd Btn (60th) K.R.R.C.	630	338 (1)	565
2nd Btn (89th) Royal Irish Fusiliers	350	329	343
26th Co. Royal Engineers	98	79	62
6/1 Scottish Division, R.A. (2)	125	111 (+107 E.A.)	107
2nd Brigade (Davis)			
1st Btn (42nd) Royal Highlanders	766	740	623
1st Btn (65th) York & Lancs	500	474	435
R.M.L.I. & R.M.A.	-	383	478
Naval Brigade (3)	-	125	163
M/1 R.A. (4)	-	-	69
Cavalry Brigade (Stewart)			
10th Hussars	280	256	251
19th Hussars	477	373	362
Mounted Infantry	150	120	124

Notes:

Most sources disagree on the total number of troops sent to Suakin and the numbers actually an the battlefield at El Teb. Where figures are not given in regimental histories, I have relied on Royle (p. 138) and Jackson (pp. 206-7), who used official reports as their sources. Even here it is not clear whether the figures given are for those who disembarked at Trinkitat or for those who marched to El Teb. There is, fortunately, almost universal agreement on the numbers engaged at Tamai.

1) Only 4 companies were at El Teb; the rest were at Fort Baker.
2) Formed into 2 camel batteries (A & B). Originally given 84mm bronze rifled guns of the Egyptian Artillery, but being unused to these, borrowed eight 7-pdrs from the Royal Navy at Trinkitat. These were mounted on Egyptian camel battery carriages with leather collars around the trunnions to make them fit. There were also 66 camels, carrying 90 rounds per gun, and 107 Egyptian artillerymen as camel leaders. During the march to Tokar the guns were dragged, so as that camels would not disturb the square formation.
3) Armed with 3 Gatlings and 3 Gardner guns.
4) An *ad hoc* unit formed at Suakin, using two 6-cwt and two 8-cwt guns (both called 9-pdrs), complete with field carriages and limbers, borrowed from the Royal Navy. These were carried by 52 mules, who also carried 86 rounds per gun.

Principal Rifles Of The Mahdist Wars

Egyptian Army issue Remington Breech Loading Rifle in 11mm. This single shot weapon was bought by Egypt in quantity in the 1870's and thousands fell into the hands of the Mahdi in the early years of the war.

The British Army's first purpose built breech loading rifle, the Martini-Henry in .45 Caliber. Used from the first engagements against the Ansar until the last by British Troops, then Egyptian, and finally Indian, numbers were captured and used by Mahdists as well.

The Belgian Albini breech loading rifle issued to their troops in the Congo also fell in limited numbers to the Ansar in remote areas like Equatoria.

The Lee-Metford was the first bolt action, magazine fed rifle issued to the British Army beginning in 1888, though taking years to complete. By Omdurman, this is the weapon—alongside the Maxim Gun—which shattered the Mahdist dream once and for all.

Converted to the first breech loading rifle used by the British Army, the Snider was standard issue to East Indian troops who fought in the Sudan. As the Lee-Metford began to replace the Martini-Henry, the latter was passed down to the Indian troops, finally retiring the Snider.

A Krupp Gun lies abandoned on the field at Omdurman with two of its crew dead beneath the carriage. Note the characteristic Krupp square breech block. Prior to its last battle, there is no telling how many actions this gun had seen since likely being captured from Hicks or even Khartoum itself some 15 years earlier when the Mahdi's Ansar seemed unstoppable.

Weep For Hicks
By Lt. Dave Bullock

Col. William Hicks ("The Hicks Pasha," or "Huksi")

I. *"Today, this day of days, we are all gathered together in one place, strong young warriors and maidens; soak the men in blood, drive away the backs of the enemy."* (1)

The Sudan lay festering, an immense land of varying waste graciously watered by the Nile and her tributaries. From 1819—when Ismail Ali marched from Egypt to subdue the Sudanese tribes—until 1883, Egypt held unchallenged dominion over her larger southern neighbor. "Her rule was not kindly, wise, or profitable" (2).

Egyptian garrisons pinned the country into an increasingly unhappy submission, harnessing the populace with a corrupt and painful system of taxation. Adding little of their theoretically superior culture, the Egyptians fed off the slaves, gum, ivory, and ostrich feathers of the Sudan. By 1879, (the then Colonel) Charles Gordon was to write, "The government of the Egyptians in these far-off countries is nothing else but one of brigandage of the very worst description" (3).

Forty-thousand of the Egyptian Army were scattered amongst their host country in eight major garrisons and many lesser posts. In a vast, road-less, train-less area, the army was seldom paid, poorly trained, and the officers were "distinguished for nothing but their public incapacity and private misbehavior." A posting to the Sudan for commissioned and private soldiery alike was usually the result of disgrace or disfavor (4). More unpromising army material could rarely have existed.

By 1881, two fateful events began gestation. The first was the rise of Mohammed Ahmed, the second was the rise of Arabi Pasha. Arabi's coup was the quicker and the lesser lasting. Stemming out of army grievances and problems caused by foreign influences, the Arabi revolt overturned Khedive Tewfik in 1882 and threatened Britain's lately acquired Suez rights. Arabi brought down the wrath of Her Majesty's Empire who promptly dispatched a naval force to bombard him at Alexandria, and a land expedition to quash him at Tel-El-Kebir. Tewfik was reinstated as a British marionette and the Empire became embroiled in a worsening situation she first sought to avoid and was later forced to combat. This came from the Sudan.

Mohammed Ahmed, the self-proclaimed "Expected One" of Hadith prophecy, began brushing with Egyptian officials in 1881. Few took his "rebellion" seriously, this poor man of an obscure family who had pretensions of tracing ancestry to the Prophet. This Mahdi, with the gap between his front teeth—a Sudanese symbol of good luck—gained an early series of escalating victories. Amusingly, the strategy behind these was concocted from his avid studies of Mohammed's victories in the Koran.

His first battle was at Abba Island where he had 313 men—the same number as the Prophet in his first encounter over 1200 years earlier. The Governor General of the Sudan, Rauf Pasha, dispatched Abu Su'ud upriver to Abba. Dividing his forces in twain, Abu promised promotion to the first officer to take the "Mahdi." They disembarked from steamers and converged on the village simultaneously. Thinking the Mahdist standards were those customarily placed on graves, the Egyptians allowed the Dervishes to come close and then panicked, opening up a cross-fire into the other Egyptian group. Although outnumbered, the Mahdi's five standards exploited the confusion and cut the Egyptians to pieces.

Now the Mahdi's earlier wanderings to gain promises of local support bore fruit as Sheikhs sent in congratulations and submissions. Cleverly, the Mahdi retreated to Kordofan with his new following. Yet another enterprising Egyptian, based at Fashoda, sought to destroy him.

In October, 1881, Rashid Bey marched to Khor Maraj with 1200 men. His secrecy betrayed by a spy, Rashid was met in December by a Mahdist force of 8,000, drawn up in classical Islamic fashion—rows of infantry lined as in prayer, and cavalry on the flanks. Rashid was annihilated and the Mahdi took up quarters for training.

In March, 1882, al Shallali organized another government expedition at Kawa. Abetted by spies, the Mahdi lured them into the interior to Jebel Jarrada. On 28 May, the Egyptians went into *zariba* for the night. It was their last. At dawn, the Mahdi's Army, swollen to 15,000, divided into four blocks, each assaulting one side of the square, and pierced them all. The Khalifa Abdullahi sagely bore off the captured rifles and guns (5).

Mohammed Ahmed, "El Mahdi" (The Former "Hermit of Abba Island")

An early Mahdist attack scenario often assumed the following characteristics: Waiting until the Egyptians were occupied—drawing water, unloading camels— or were lethargic. Then the simple charge in a dense mass, exploiting enemy confusion with speed and surprise. Women and children commonly followed, beating small drums and shouting war cries. The men came on with large flat-headed lances which they used to protect their faces. Oddly, eyes were often shut in the advance.

Conversely, Egyptian faults were simple and notable. After unpacking, a *zariba* would be formed, normally with no outposts, scouts, or vedettes. Also, encumbering most expeditions were the many wives and followers to which they were so inexorably attached (6).

The Mahdi's next objective was El Obeid, the rich capital of Kordofan. It was a logical prize and deep enough into his new "territory" to subdue. With El Obeid gone, the approach to Khartoum would be paved. One-by-one, throughout the rainy-season, government posts fell—Abu Haraz, Birka, Azhaf, Tayyaara and Dilling. Bara was besieged—the second most important town in Kordofan.

El Obeid was defended by 6,000 Egyptian troops. Its defenses were not so awesome. The walls were of 20-foot-thick earth, but only nine feet in height. A scattering of numerous straw huts, a ditch enclosed only a few of the government buildings. On September 1, 1882, the Governor, Mohamed Sayyid, was offered surrender. He hanged the emissaries.

The next week, the Mahdist Army, now bloated to an estimated 5,000 horse and 50,000 foot, assaulted the city head-on, and for the first time Mohammed Ahmed reeled with a bloodied nose. After losing thousands, a lesson in firepower was taught, and the Khalifa Abdulahi's firearms were sent for from Qadir. Abu Anja was given a new command, that of black rifle troops which were proclaimed the *Jihadiyya*.

As the siege tightened that autumn, malnutrition and dysentery hit the defenders. Peter Clark's excellent *The Hicks Pasha Expedition*, illustrates the conditions of horror as skins, gum and dogs were consumed. Carrion birds ate dead bodies, and the soldiers shot and ate the birds, thus renewing the human cycle.

In January, Bara capitulated and its former defenders joined the Mahdists and "verbally tormented those in El Obeid." On January 17, El Obeid—a thoroughly doomed city—fell and its Governor and leaders were executed. Kordofan was sacked by the rebels and Darfur Province was isolated beyond hope.

Jihadiyya Rifleman

II. *"The most important thing is submission to the Emir who organizes the battle. As the Prophet Mohammed said, 'Whoever obeys my Emir obeys me, and whoever disobeys my Emir disobeys me.' I have warned time and again of the need for the Brethren to submit to their Emirs, and to their Khalifas, and all to the Khalifa 'Abdullahi.'"* (8)

The Mahdi's Army was becoming more sophisticated as he divided it into Standards (*Rayya*), each under the direction of a Khalifa. His army was composed of three tactical elements:

1. Reconnaissance Forces—These horse would cut supply lines, maintain speedy communications, carry out long-range skirmishes, spread propaganda, and ruin wells. Headed by Abu Qarja, there were about 3,000.

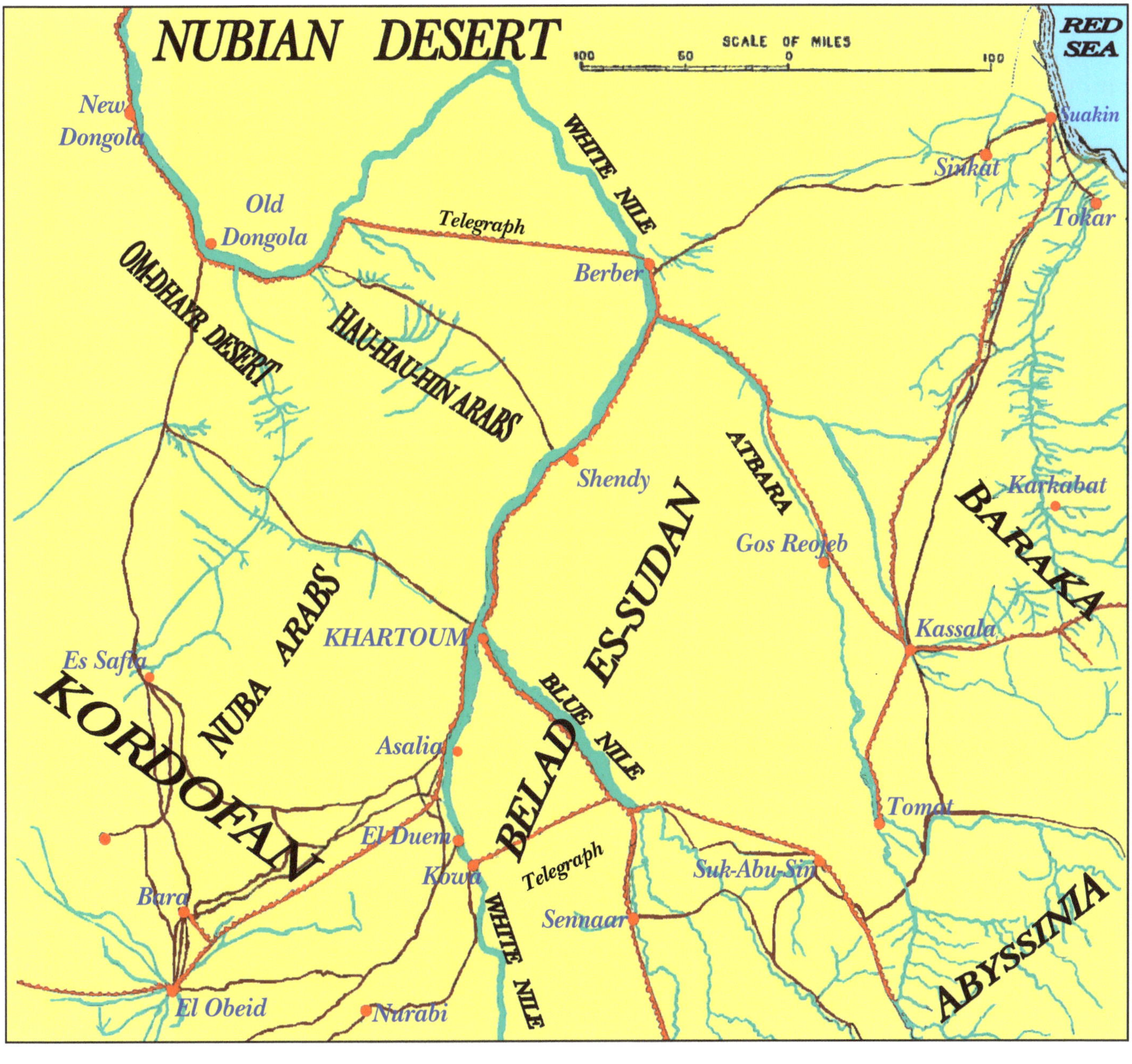

2. Attacking Forces—Mainly sword and spear, augmented by some horse under Wad al Nejumi. Several main leaders commanded these 50, 000 to 60,000.

3. *Jihadiyya*—Mostly black soldiers developed and commanded by Abu Anja. Armed with Remington rifles, there were about 7,000 troops and these were regularly paid.

> III. "Rainless storms dance tirelessly over the hot, crisp surface of the ground... The earth burns with the quenchless thirst of ages, and in the steel blue sky scarcely a cloud obstructs the unrelenting triumph of the sun." (10)

The topography into which the Hicks Expedition was to plunge was bleak. An American ex-Confederate Officer (Stone Pasha) perhaps knew it best of anyone, but he would not be available. The Egyptians themselves possessed maps of no special detail, and the water sources were ambiguous.

Against this mysterious backdrop resided an unending, rolling dry steppe that was Kordofan. Nowhere over 2,000 feet in altitude, there existed no streams, no rivers, and only a few wells offering scanty enough sustenance, and most of these at great depths. Naturally enough, areas with water at all, or at best luck shallow wells, rapidly became population centers (e.g., El Obeid, Bara, and Melbeis). Besides wells, Kordofan was watered during *kherif* from early June to late September. Three lakes existed, varying in depth and purity at different times of the year. Shirkeleh, with a six square mile area, was normally dry before *kherif*. Kordofan was overall a sparsely populated, largely unproductive land whose main exports were salt, iron, gum and ostrich feathers imported from Darfur (11).

> IV. "I promise you this in His Highness' name, with the weapons in your hands, if you only use them properly, you can not fail to be victorious over the enemy, who are for the most part only armed with rude weapons. All that is required of you is firmness and steadiness, and you must always win the day." (12)

Early in January, 1883, the Sudanese Governor, General Abd el Kader (who had earlier replaced Rauf Pasha), appointed a series of European Officers to high posts in the Sudan as a last ditch gamble at turning the rebel juggernaut. Colonel William Hicks was named Chief of Staff of the Army of the Sudan, a post "nominally" under the Governor-General with the unwritten understanding that Hicks was supreme in military matters. It was thought this arrangement would offset the Mahdi's propaganda and that the Sudanese Army was commanded by a Christian.

Hicks Pasha had begun service in 1849 in the Indian Army and had seen action in the '57 Mutiny, and in Abyssinia under Napier. In 1880 he was appointed an honorary Colonel in the Reserve and was retired. In December, 1882, with Sir Evelyn Wood reorganizing the Egyptian Army, Baker Pasha—commanding the gendarmerie—wired the invitation to the 52 year old Hicks. Described as handsome, courageous, and energetic, Hicks, with little real command experience, gladly took up the reins (13).

Hicks' intermediary in Cairo was the British Consul General Sir E. Malet. He protested to the Egyptian Govern-

Hicks in Egyptian Service

Bashi-Bazouks (Albanians, Kurds, Bosnians, Syrians, & Greeks), Sudanese and Egyptian infantry, cavalry, and camelry who constituted Hicks' army.

ment that the British had no responsibility toward the Sudan. Gladstone's recently formed government, based as it was on retrenchment and anti-colonial adventurist policies, was embarrassed by the 1882 intervention forced on them, and still more embarrassed by recent events in the Sudan to which her new child, Egypt, had an umbilical attachment. When both Hicks and Egypt tendered papers presenting the necessity of increased financial underwriting, Gladstone, the Cabinet, and the Chancellor of the Exchequer determined to clarify proceedings. The Sudan was Egypt's baby. They refused responsibility and support (14).

Hicks and staff traveled from Cairo on February 7th by train to Suez, steamer to Suakin, and from there took to the desert via camels. Bound for Berber, which they reached on 1 March, they were protected en route by 100 Egyptian regulars and 350 Bashi-Bazouks.

Bashi-Bazouks—those colorful mercenaries in white turbans, gay colored coats, and bellies thoroughly accoutered in knives, pistols, and swords—were almost universally hated in the Sudan. Gordon had small use for them. These hashish smoking individuals from the Balkans, Turkey, and the Levant were often described as disorderly brutes. However, Col. Colborne praised their fighting ability and they were nearly always seen with Hicks—Arab Huscarls, as suggested by David Johnson's *Bugles in Kordofan*.

News of El Obeid's demise reached Hicks at Berber. Khartoum officials exhorted him to hurry south. Arriving on 4 March, the welcoming ceremony held nothing of the gathering gloom that lurked in the narrow streets of Khartoum, nor of the overt fear attending the western provinces. Addressing the citizens through his Arabic interpreter, Captain Evans, Hicks sought to instill Khartoum with hope for the upcoming expedition and to banish the rumor he was to lead the Army of the Sudan into the desert to die.

Hicks put his soldiers to work on target practice and within three weeks Captain Forrestier-Walker arrived from Cairo with some Nordenfelts to supplement the artillery. Colborne's diary recounted Forrestier-Walker's training show:

> *"When the guns were attempted to be brought into action, dire confusion reigned. Men ran against each other; the ground was strewn with cartridges; hoppers were placed anywhere but where they ought to have been. No one appeared to have the slightest knowledge of how to feed, aim, or discharge the pieces."*

Hicks swore "He had never seen such a disgraceful thing in his life." Colborne further commented on the bad Gippy rifle practice—how they leaned backwards to fire instead of forwards, the jerking of triggers, the loose-holding of the rifles, and the tendency to fire into the air. In disgust, Forrestier-Walker trained a hard three days more, then fell victim to sunstroke and was invalided back to Egypt (16). (He would later be killed at El Teb when Baker's square was broken). It was an un-fortuitous start.

In the next weeks, efforts at training continued unabated. Most of the European Officers lived in Khartoum, that Eastern palm-treed city of 60,000 surrounded by mud walls on three sides and the Blue Nile on the fourth. The usual ritual was to rise at 0500 taking bath and coffee, hopping a steamer to Omdurman, training the men until 1000, then breakfast. At 1700, Hicks took his staff for a gallop before evening retreat and conversation (17). It was a lull of mellowed kindness before the storm.

During this time, traveler's news reported a questionable 100,000 Mahdists dispersed throughout outlying areas. Closer and more certain were 7,000 assembled at Marabiyeh and Abu Djuma, and these included 1,800 Cavalry. Another group was reported at Jebel Ain. In spite of the good work he had done, Abd el Kader was replaced for criticizing superiors and events. In his stead as Governor-General was placed Ala al Din—a man of inferior status, and on paper, still Hicks' superior.

Hicks was eager to strike the Mahdists before the *kherif* rains. This expedition to drive them from Sennar province was to come in two waves and was to relieve the Egyptian positions at Kawa 150 miles up the White Nile. Col. Colborne's group started first up the Nile—the Colonel in the lead steamer—and eight troop-loaded *merkebs* (25 ton sailing boats) following.

Colborne contacted Kawa, which was commanded by Hussain Pasha. Five battalions, or 3,000 men, were encamped there—three battalions inside the fort. Sentries were posted at a wasteful "every two yards" and Hussain refused Colborne's suggestion of outlying pickets on the grounds that it would be dangerous for the men involved.

Hicks landed at Kawa on 6 April with the second Khartoum force, this one of 5,000 "officially" under the command of Suleiman Pasha. Four days later, Hicks and a small party on the steamer *Bordein* pushed ahead to *reconnoitre* as far as Abu Zed. The enemy had collected in force (estimated 20,000) at Jebel Ain and due to supply shortages, it was mandatory that they be quickly dislodged. Hicks raced up and down the Nile by steamer with his omnipresent Nordenfelts and Bashi-Bazouks, egging the expedition on.

One of Hicks victories As portrayed by The Illustrated London News

Suleiman Pasha, leaving 1,000 men at Kawa, marched south with his field force as Hicks and 200 Bashi's made a steamer dash to capture the strategic and well-defended ford at Abu Zed near Jebel Ain. Hicks accomplished this on 23 April with *élan*.

Suleiman was to complete his 45 mile task in 3 days. But instead of marching in open column ready to form square, he ordered his men into square immediately and thus cut his speed to six useless miles a day. Colborne's efforts to change Suleiman's tactics failed. The four-and-a-half battalions, four Nordenfelts, and the mounted Sudanese and Bashi's slogged at this torpid pace under heat and through scrub brush.

Meanwhile, Hicks had learned the Mahdists were advancing to the attack and he set off by steamer, reaching Suleiman's column on the 25th. Captain Massey galloped to the main body with the news that now an estimated 30,000 were coming on (18).

The next day an alarm sounded with the advent of 1,000 rebel horse. O'Donovan of the *Daily News* recalled that the Egyptian square formed rapidly as rockets and guns blazed at the circling cavalry 1,000 yards away. The Mahdist horse broke off and for the next two days the Bashi's rode ahead as a mounted screen (19).

On the 29th, the column was attacked. Of all the Dervish options of attack, they had picked the worst. Hicks' force deployed into square, hurling out the "crow's feet" spikes (caltrops) that Egyptian soldiers carried to discourage a charge. Eight hundred yards of open ground surrounded the square. The charge developed into a surging mass without plan, a rushing, plunging crescent shape, the cavalry in the front ranks.

Hicks had deployed his guns in the usual fashion outside the square itself, as he feared the natural gaps they made when formed into the line. Colborne admired the way the Mahdists rode fearlessly up to the muzzles of the guns before being swept away like chaff (20). The rocket tubes and howitzers were positioned in the faces of the square. Hicks at first had difficulty in getting them to fire, and when they did, some rockets exploded above his own men. Spears were actually penetrating the square. Incredibly, when the firing stopped, there were only seven casualties. The Dervishes lost over 500 men and 12 Emirs, including the leading Chief, Amr el Mararshef, and most of these had died within 400 yards (21).

The famous colonial tactician Col. C. E. Callwell remonstrates that if Hicks had possessed real cavalry, his success would have been more complete instead of having allowed a successful Mahdist retirement. Equally of note was the general lack of reconnaissance which allowed potential ambushes to surface. But for the jubilant Egyptians, this was not time for ominous recrimination and self-examination—the Province of Sennar had been saved.

> V. *"The force we have is not sufficient to undertake the Kordofan campaign. Every ounce of food must be taken from here. We march through a hostile country, inhabited by powerful tribes. The lines of communication must be kept open, and depots must be formed which must be sufficiently garrisoned. Each convoy will require escort. Our available strength will be under 6,000: Of these many will likely be sick after the fever season."* (22)

The Egyptian Government decided to embark on the re-conquest of Kordofan to regain prestige. There were those who considered the decision at best injudicious. Among these were Hicks. Pondering the cataclysm a further failure would now demand, Hicks concluded, "Taking into consideration the whole state of affairs in this country, I am convinced that it would be best to keep the two rivers and Province of Sennar, and wait for Kordofan to settle itself."

The renowned Sudanese adventurer, Colonel Stewart, was in concordance. Gordon, who would be maneuvered onto a limb from ensuing events, later commented in his *Journals At Khartoum* that Hicks would have stayed in Khartoum with better success and could have "worn out the Mahdi."

Hicks' organizational problems were immense. In May he urged his formal acceptance (under pain of resignation) as official commander-in-chief, a request not granted until August. This news came with the qualifying rider that Governor-General Ala al Din, with whom Hicks had constantly been at odds in the Sennar Campaign, was to accompany the expedition. This was an extra monkey to shoulder.

Hicks had no transport and little or no money. The troops' pay was months in arrears. He needed an extra force of at least 10,000 able bodied men with a further 2,000 to guard the lines of communication. As Cairo was under going the reorganization of the Egyptian Army, they sent him a denigrating 3,000. And 1,800 of these were the unwanted scum of Arabi's former mutineers, men rejected for defects from the Egyptian New Model Army. This force was to recapture El Obeid in the heart of rebel held Kordofan.

That summer, Hicks' petitions for more troops were rejected, especially his requested levies from the New Model Army. He even offered to trade 5,000 for which he had already pleaded for four battalions of the New Model, and then to return them in six months. Instead, men were shipped to him in chains (in spite of which, 31 men of his Krupp battery still managed to desert). Two soldiers in Egypt blinded themselves with lime to avoid service in the Sudan.

By August, the expedition was consolidated. Ala al Din had managed 4,000 camels, albeit inefficiently, and the "cavalry" had arrived—although none of the men were trained to ride! On 9 September, the Hicks Pasha Expedition marched from their base at Omdurman toward Duem, 110 miles distant (25). The force totaled:

7,000 regulars
500 untrained cavalry
400 mounted Bashi-Bazouks
100 chain-mailed Cuirassiers, mounted
4 Krupp field guns
10 mountain guns
6 Nordenfelts
2,000 camp-followers
5,500 camels
500 horses (24)

"Morituri te Salutant"
Standing (from left to right): Captain Massey, Colonel Arthur Farquhar (Q.M.G.), Major Warner, Sergeant Brady (Hicks orderly), Captain Edward Baldwin Evans (intelligence officer, interpreter), Captain Forestier Walker. Seated (from left to right): Colonel John Colborne, Major Martin, General William Hicks Pasha, Colonel Henry de Coëtlogon Pasha.

Personae Vitae

Major General Billy Hicks Pasha— Commander-in-Chief

Ala-al-Din— Governor-General of the Sudan, former Turkish cavalry officer and appointed second in command by Cairo.

Colonel Arthur Farquhar— Formerly Coldstream Guards, "dashing" but inflexible, Chief of Staff to Hicks.

Major Baron Gotz von Seckendorf— Cavalry leader, "fit," "quick-tempered," bearded, blond.

Major Edward Evans— Intelligence Officer and the only Arabic speaking European, a veteran of the Sudan.

Major Warner— Cavalry leader.

Captain Massy— Dashing Cavalry leader.

Captain Hearlth— Austrian cavalry leader of the Bashi Bazouks.

Captain Matygna— Austrian cavalry leader of the Bashi's. Colborne disliked him as being prone to dis orderly behavior.

Kordofan—With Hick's Projected & Actual Routes of March

Hicks' general formation along his line of march.

Lieutenant Brody— "Cuirassier" leader, former Royal Horse Artillery Sergeant-Major.
Surgeon-General George Bey— A Greek, chief physician.
Sergeant-Major Rosenberg— Leader of the camp followers
Hussain Pasha Mazhar— Overall Egyptian C.O. of the Regular Infantry.
Miralai Rajab Bey— C.O. 4th Battalion.
Miralai Salim Bey— C.O. 1st Battalion.
Edmund O'Donovan— *Irish Daily News* reporter, extensive traveler.
Frank Vizetelly— Reporter, *Illustrated London News*

Notably absent, and a blow to Hicks' stability, were Colonel Colborne (invalided to Cairo from sunstroke), and Lt. Colonel de Coetlogon, Garrison Commander at Khartoum. Rashid Pasha, appointed to command a Brigade, artfully declined (safely from Kassala), because of "urgent local matters." (25)

Hicks Pasha and staff leaving Suakin for Khartoum, February 18, 1883.

Hicks' army on the march—-the reality was even worse than the artist could imagine.

VI. *"You must know that here we are 1300 miles away south of Cairo, in the midst of a wild, almost unexplored country. The Egyptian Army, with which I am here camped on the banks of the Nile, will have but one chance given them—one tremendous pitched battle."* (26)

The original plan of march to El Obeid was via the northern route, about 136 miles from Duem, last post on the Nile before striking into the desert. Bara was to be captured first, then used as a depot springboard into El Obeid. This would be the beginning of the end for the Mahdi. But the plan changed.

The march to Duem, south down the Nile, was accomplished by the following line of march: Two camel scouts, the armored Cuirassiers, the General Staff, an Infantry Battalion in line, then the artillery flanked by eight Battalions in column—and in the rear—a Battalion in line, the cavalry, the transport animals, the Bashi's, and the Irregular Horse.

An hour before each dawn the men stood to in the *zariba* while the cavalry went out to *reconnoitre* and camp was struck. The army kept near the Nile for protection and made only slow progress in the 115-degree-plus heat through brush and sand. The telegraph had already been cut by forward elements of the Mahdi's minions. In the foreboding future, probably with an eye to all security being left farther behind with every slogging step, Hicks confessed in a letter "At times all this weight of anxiety and responsibility (are) too much for me." And later at Duem he felt like "Jesus Christ in the midst of the Jews" (27).

At least one benefit from the march was the perfection of "going into square," the whole procedure, including rockets and guns, being honed to 2.5 minutes (28). Hicks was at least showing that even troops of such low calibre could be improved. One military criticism of the march would have to be the employment of the Bashi's and Irregular Horse behind the baggage animals instead of thrusting them forward of the line of march.

At Duem, Hicks caught up with the main force after having taken care of lingering administrative details in Khartoum. Ala al Din had not been asleep. He immediately coaxed Hicks to take the southern route to El Obeid. His returning scouts had solemnly assured him of the abundance of water from Duem to Nurabi, a ninety-mile jaunt hitherto believed to be waterless. From Nurabi, Khor Abu Hable was sandy and along this 100 mile route was a torrent flowing from Jebel Kulfan, itself fifty miles south of El Obeid (29).

There was more. The northern route was hostile and even Hicks was puzzled as to how he was to establish the necessary posts to anchor his lines of communication. It so happened King Adam of Takalle promised Ala al Din succor if only the expedition would pass through his lands—and these were on the southern route. Hicks demurred and Ala al Din had his way. The journey had just increased 114 miles in distance, or nearly doubled. Thus, the plan of a week overruled the plan of a summer.

Hicks Pasha's column moved out of Duem after a four day rest on 27 September 1883, headed for Shatt, sixteen miles to the south. There they would link with their advanced party of 2,400 infantry, two Krupps, four mountain guns, and Bashi's who had taken the village wells (30).

VII. *"It was in Ramadan when first we heard that an army was being prepared against us and that the name of its leader was Huksi."* (31)

The Mahdi had taken up comfortable headquarters in El Obeid. From there his power base swelled. Gordon, who consistently underestimated the Mahdi, put his strength at 4,000—this being as ludicrous as the estimation of 300,000 by a Copt. The truth lay between with most spies and travelers postulating 60-70,000. At that stage of the rebellion, those figures are likely still high, although Major Ismat Zulfo, the modern Sudanese scholar, also calculated 60,000.

The Mahdi now called for his organization to work for him. Moving east of El Obeid his warriors trained in camp and his horses had guns fired near them for battle acclimatization. Abu Qarja and 3,000 were sent out to dog Hicks after leaving Duem—to close his route behind him, and to destroy the wells (32). Qarja was to skirmish as soon as Hicks had penetrated westward, to cause him loss of sleep and to fray his nerves. The tribes en route were instructed to abandon their lands, leaving nothing in their wake.

The Mahdi had the luxury of intelligence with which to foster his plans. He could select from two options: to await Hicks' arrival at El Obeid and deal with a weary enemy, or to march out to a battleground of his own choosing and timing. The Mahdi sent Abd al Oadir with 1,000 horse to the pools of al Birka. This move would force Hicks' advance toward al Melbeis through the dense forests of Shaykan (33).

> VIII. *"All the expeditions which preceded us during the past two years have been defeated with disaster. Let us hope ours won't share the same fate."* (34)

Facing a powerful external threat, the expedition members were quick to provide an internal one—that of quarreling among themselves. The main force entered Shatt in such confused formation that Hicks and Hussain Pasha crossed heated public words and had to be taken aside in Ala al Din's tent where Abbas Bey (the Governor-General's secretary) interpreted and calmed them down. Hicks had strongly urged that either he or Hussain Pasha should be sent packing. Hussain Pasha and Rajab Bey had already jealously quarreled the week prior. Most unfortunate of all was the compromise. After Shatt, Ala al Din and his staff had to be consulted before orders would be carried out. A corporal deserted that afternoon to bring the Mahdi these glad tidings.

On October 1st, Hussain Pasha disobeyed decampment orders issued by Colonel Farquhar by marching out of the *zariba* in square, a more time consuming process. But he considered it safer. He was supposed to quickly march out in succession and form on the outside.

Then came the outpost crisis: Whether or not to leave behind posts to guard the supplies and the retreat. Hicks thought it advisable as did Hussain Pasha. The Battalion commanders thought it would be a further critical dissipation of strength even though it was a good idea. Hicks and Hussain Pasha now quarreled as to where the outpost manning could come from. Ala al Din was very placatory to all, but said that they were too weak already for this scheme. None of the tribes offered submission so that any post left behind would be isolated and massacred. They must keep together. Hicks asked for everyone's opinion in writing and left to think. The outpost scheme was dropped and Hicks' last communication to the outside world carried the details of this decision. And so behind them, Abu Qarja closed their communications and their wells.

On 4 October the Expedition gained Um Sadena where a false alarm was sounded. Then to Rahad el Abid, then to Serakna where they made their *zariba's* in a thick woods. Colonel Farquhar pointed out the chancy aspects of this to Hicks and Ala al Din and they moved on at the morn's light.

On the 7th, the column proceeded for Khor es Sagh and learned the Mahdists

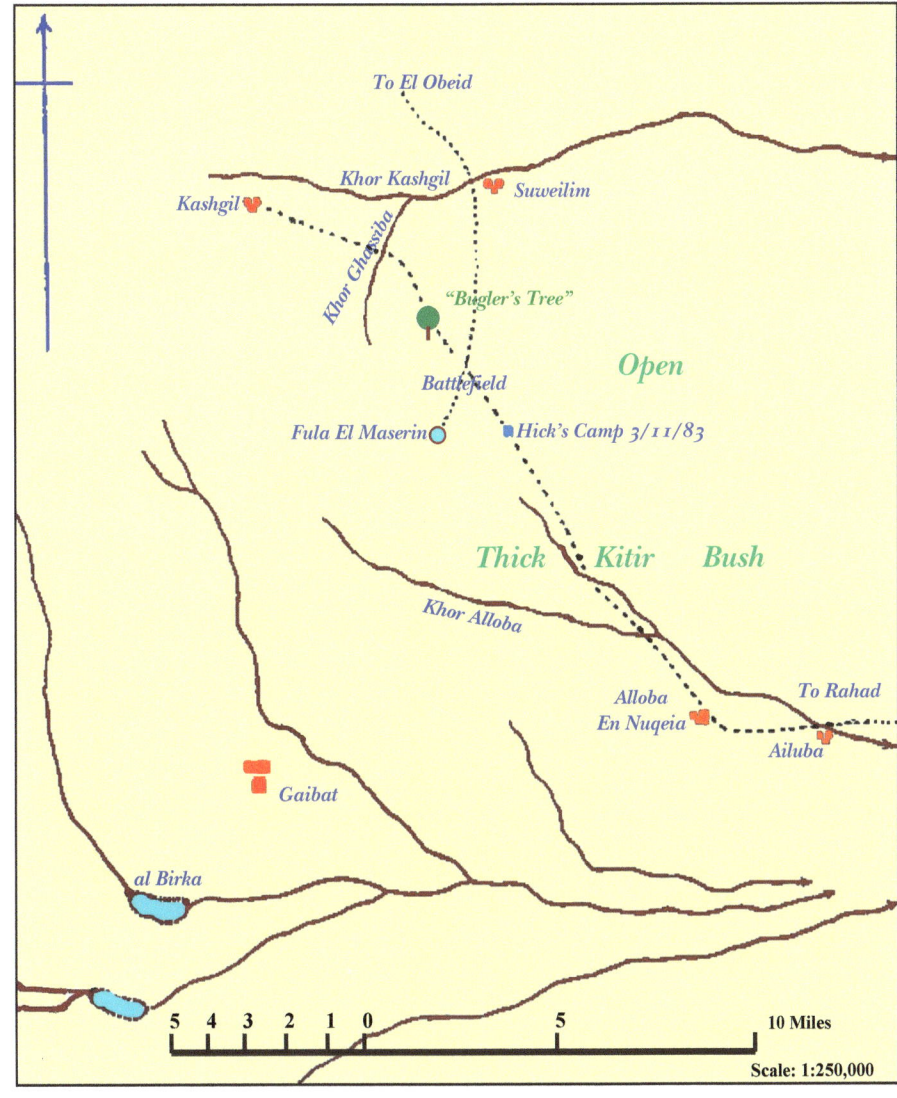

Hicks' Approach to Kashgil ("Kazgeil") from a map by E.F. Aglen on location in 1936.

were gathering at Nurabi. The next day some guides were ambushed. A heated public argument ensued between Hicks and Farquhar over the authorization of an order. From Abbas Bey's diary it would seem Hicks was either slightly at fault or had put Farquhar in a difficult situation.

Next day's water was at a brook about four hours east of Aigella. On the 10th, the guides lost the route to water-precious Aigella and after a waterless march became strung-out over 2,000 disorganized meters. Tempers flared and stragglers dropped out to perish horribly at Dervish hands. When Captain Hearlth's cavalry spotted ducks and traced them to water, the expedition scarcely had pitched camp and had not gone into *zariba* when the infection of desperate thirst spread and the army literally charged the brook. When Hicks ordered Hussain Pasha to collect the force he answered: "There is their Commander, let him keep order if he can because I am not able to do so." Hicks then commented to Abbas Bey, "Hussain Pasha quite forgets all this disorder is entirely due to his own mismanagement. I shall refuse to keep him as my Second-in-command." Hicks organized whomever he could to build the *zariba* (35).

From 10 October, no man left camp unarmed. The animals could no longer roam at any well and only eat what they found inside the square. In desperation, the hungry camels ate the straw pallets cushioning their wooden saddles—which caused them painful lacerations as the wood now chaffed their unprotected skins. The men had been eating too much *ful Sudani* (local beans) and as a result, aggravated their thirst. This complication was partially offset by the occasional finding of watermelons (36).

Hicks has been frequently criticized for his moving square formation. Certainly over open ground it seems an excessive precaution, especially as the cavalry could have been used as a screen. By marching in square the movement of the whole is restricted to the rate of the slowest animal. It is a double-edged sword. With unreliable troops, or in an area of difficult terrain, (i.e. rolling hills and scrub or forest) a marching square is often mandatory. Hicks had to countenance both of these criteria.

The value of the square in the Sudan was proved by the successful 1852 exploits of Giegler Pasha, a Bavarian in the Khedive's employ. Hicks had again proved it at Marabiah using indifferent troops. Colonial tactician Colonel Callwell attaches two riders to the square's success: that fire discipline can be maintained as long as the terrain is reasonably open, and that the attack is not a surprise. The Mahdi was seeking to exploit both of these tactical considerations (37).

On the 11th, there was a brief skirmish before Aigella and Ala al Din thanked his men "for their gallantry." Morale improved for a while and through the feast of Bairam on the 12th. Sohan was reached on the 13th.

The march continued to Balashik, then to Albi where a skirmish revealed that the Krupps had been neglected, and they failed to operate. The transport animals were tired and officers had failed in supervising their men's water conservation. At Um Debakar, two muddy brooks offered some relief.

On the 20th of November, Colonel Farquhar twice led the column through almost impenetrable bush in response to the dictates of his compass. The troops and transport intermingled hopelessly, and Hicks and Ala al Dish were separated as all formation was lost. Abbas Bey wrote, "Is this what they call the skill of the English to lead us blindly against the advice of our guides into a dense bush?" An uneasy pall of disaster crept through the ranks. "I thank God the enemy had not fired the grass or the result would have been terrible."

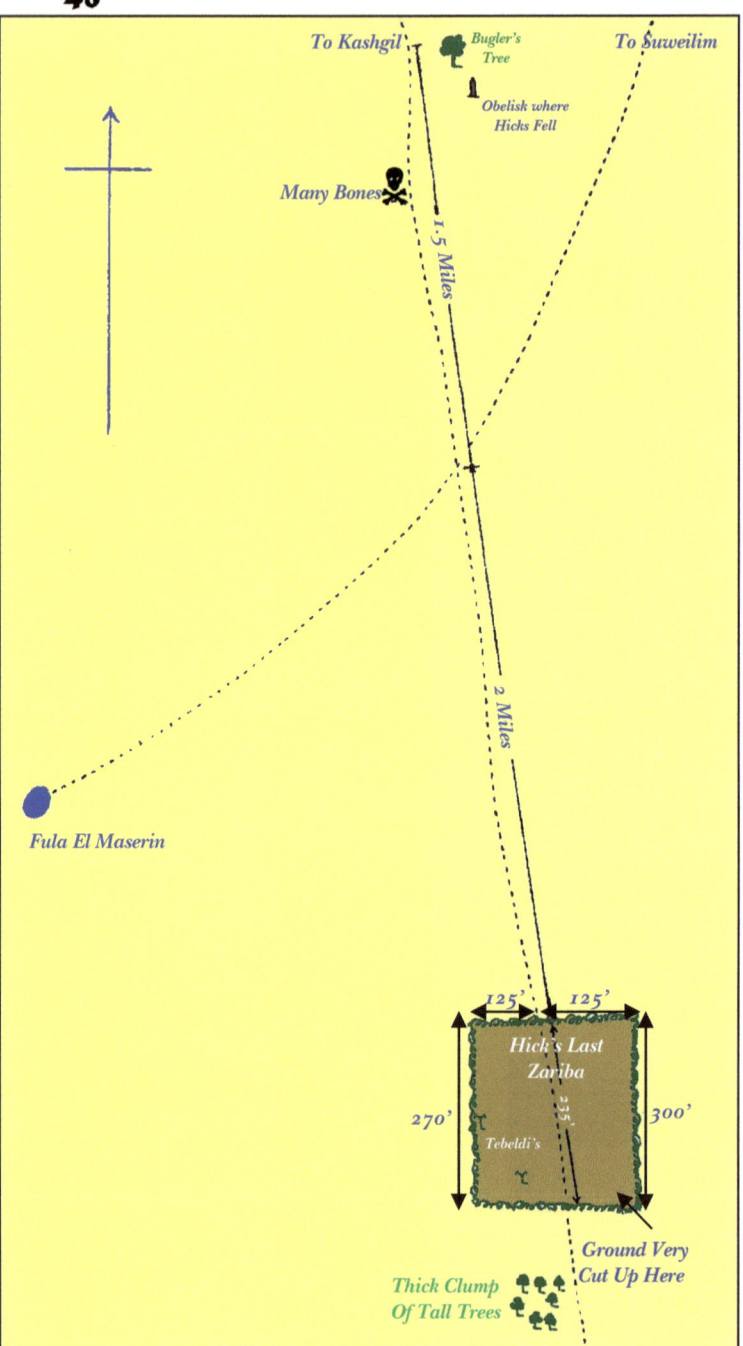

E.F. Aglen's reconstruction of the Shaykan Battlefield based on his 1936 inspection of the site.

Next day at Baliab, the Mahdists sniped with effect. Hicks directed artillery at them and ordered a Battalion across the *khor* to make a *zariba* on the opposite bank. Then Hicks and Ala al Din held a heavy conference about suspected treachery among their guides. Hicks was advised not to interfere with the Governor-General's selections.

Sniping again on the 22nd. Marching for the pools at Rahad, the column was attacked before Audia on the 23rd. Hicks maneuvered onto a hilltop and dispersed the Dervishes with guns, but later while on the march, the column was raked by three-sided fire. At Audia batches of the Mahdi's propaganda leaflets to surrender littered the ground. While Hicks burned many of these religious tracts (38), the rank and file found them handy as toilet paper (39).

The 25th—sniping. The 26th—the outposts were attacked just after dawn. Hicks broke up the bodies of enemy troops with guns at 2,000 yards. At Rahad's pools they lingered from the 24th to the 30th, resting. They would march to Alwayah, to Kashgil, then to Melbeis to reorganize before El Obeid.

On the 27th an abortive attempt to gain prisoners miscarried. On the 28th some Rahad villagers laid a trap while pretending to submit. More skirmishing. The artillery officers complained to Colonel Farquhar that the Staff Officers were "interfering" with them.

On the 30th, the march resumed en route to Aloba. More sniping. The 31st ditto. November 1st—they made Aloba.(40). Abbas Bey's diary, meticulously maintained, ends here as does all written word concerning the column. Mystery had descended like a cloak of doom over the Hicks Pasha Expedition.

> IX. "With the flashing sword in his hand, the Mahdi remained standing in the middle of the clearing. His Ansar all saw him there as they rushed howling against the enemy." (41)

The events of the final four days must remain as sketchy as were the numerous collections of eyewitness accounts. However, enough stories trace a similar vein so that the major events can be reconstructed.

With Abd al Qadir ensconced at the pool of al Birka, Hicks was forced to take the Melbeis track from Aloba through the forests of Shaykan with its thorn trees and o *tebeldi's* from whence he hoped to reach Kashgil. The Mahdi himself had moved to al Birka. As soon as Mohammed Ahmed was convinced Hicks had ignored al Birka and was heading north, he dispatched cavalry to make Hicks believe he was surrounded by the entire Dervish Army. This distraction purchased time for Abu Qarja to mount two or three *Jihadiyya* upon each horse and to disperse them on both sides of the track through which Hicks must pass. Wad al Nujumi moved with cavalry and assault infantry to block the north. Abu Qarja then sealed off the south (42).

As late as at Rahad, Hicks had boldly hurled back the Mahdist challenge to surrender: "I refuse," he answered the Mahdi's emissaries, "Even if the sky falls, I have enough bayonets to hold it up, and if the earth tries to rise I have a big enough army to keep it down" (43).

On Saturday the 3rd, Hicks headed for Fula al Musarin, a seasonal pool ominously named "Pool of the Entrails" from a past military disaster. The Mahdi himself shifted his power base there.

On the 4th, the column left its probable last well-built *zariba* for the insecurity of the march. Suddenly, Abu Anja's *Jihadiyya* caved in the rear of the tight square. The front battalion, wheeling, succeeded in driving off the Mahdists, but not before several guns and many water-laden camels were lost. That night Hicks held his last officer council amidst withering fire. They were trapped. Few must have believed El Obeid a reasonable goal. Hicks asked for suggestions and got none. (This information came from Captain Hearlth's diary which Father Ohrwalder saw before it was destroyed).

It must be to Egyptian credit that after dawn the morning of the 5th they tried to advance, and indeed, had managed to form-up in square. The testimonies of several Sheikhs bore out the deadly fire exchange which stripped the bark from the surrounding trees. Densely packed as the column had been the night before, the ratio of bullets fired to bullets struck home must have been very favorable.

The hopeless plight as the Expedition set out that morning must have hung like a death sentence. The ensuing pitched battle was more intricate than many accounts have suggested. The European deserter, Gustav Klootz, enumerated seven eyewitness phases to Father Ohrwalder:

1. First Attack
2. Resistance
3. Orderly Retreat
4. Renewed Dervish charge against the last disciplined square.
5. This square marches into second trap.
6. It is broken.
7. Europeans make a stand under trees toward Kashgil village.

    E.F. Aglen visited Shaykan battlefield in 1936 and was able to form his own conclusion while tramping the lie of the land. Signs of Hicks' *zariba* on the 3rd were visible, 3.5 miles south of the *tebeldi* or "Bugler's Tree." One-half mile south of the tree, or three miles north of the *zariba*, was the "killing ground" with hordes of bone fragments attesting to the wholesale slaughter. This would be where the squares perished.
    The "Bugler's Tree" is where the last stand took place by Hicks and staff and those who broke free from the carnage long enough to fight back to back. The tree itself is so named because as legend has it Hicks ordered his bugler up the tree to assess the situation. The report was so disheartening that the bugler was quickly shot so as to avoid spreading panic. The skeleton hung in the branches for years (44).
    The final attack took place at about 0600. Faraj Sadik, a bugler, claimed he and survivors of two companies fled out of the *zariba* and escaped toward Kadara (45). Some accounts put the final onslaught at mid-day, and according to one account, after a successful cavalry action the day before.
    The final formation Hicks assumed is also questionable. Both excellent articles of David Johnson and Peter Clark portray the last advance as being in three equidistant squares with 300 yards separation and cavalry on the flanks and rear.
    Klootz' testimony would lend evidence to this: "There they lay, in three huge mounds of dead bodies, spread over a distance of two miles." But why? Hicks had marched in his single square since leaving Omdurman. This was the natural formation to continue as his men understood it, and it was easier to form, taking less time and dangerous confusion. Further, human psychological insecurity at this stage of tactical degeneration would naturally serve to keep the men as close together as possible. The only factors gained by three squares would be in forcing the enemy to break three smaller squares rather than one: In rough terrain, three smaller squares would be more maneuverable. Note that some frontage of firepower is masked, however, and even more so if the enemy got into the gaps between the squares. The Egyptians would

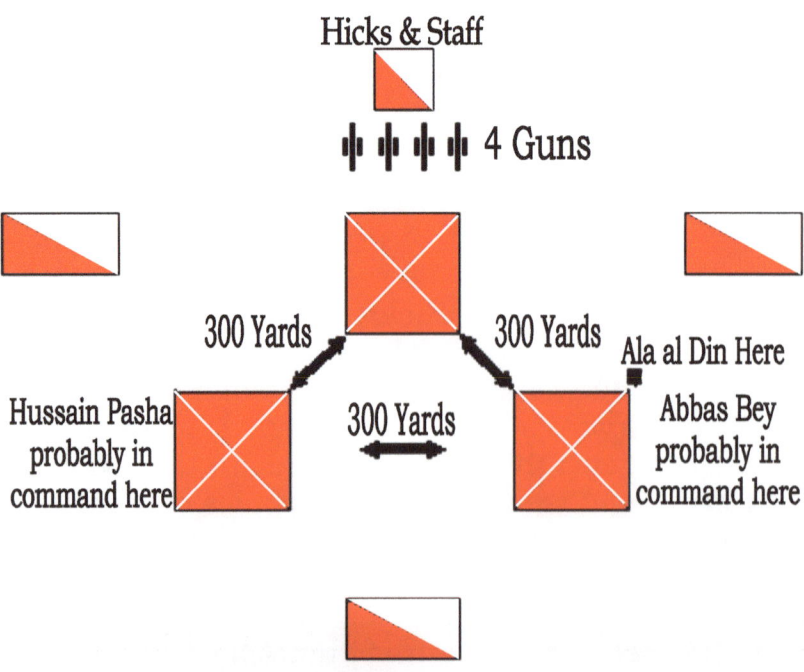

The "Three Squares" Theory of Hicks' Deployment

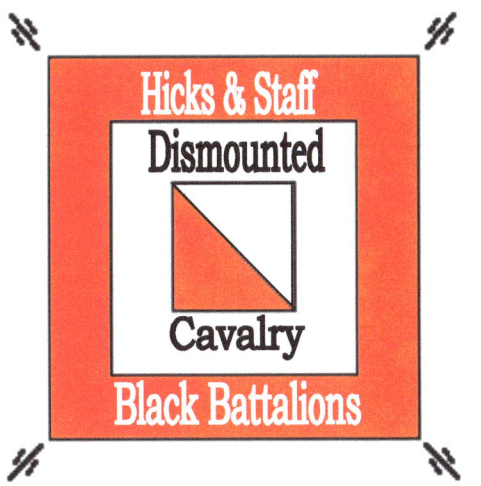

*The "Single Square" Theory
(Based on Eyewitness Accounts)*

have to fire on each other to drive them out.

The majority of eyewitness reports indicate a single large square and the breaking of the front face. This would be Aglen's "heap of bones" where the square was massacred. One account had the cavalry fighting on foot inside the square. This seems logical as cavalry out flung in that forest were vulnerable. It is also logical from the standpoint of Hicks' past actions. And if the cavalry retired they could only mask the fire of the square while dragging a rampant enemy behind them, and only disorder a face of the formation during their interpenetration phase. At that stage they could have done little by themselves away from the main body—not even to affect their own escape.

Hicks' death assumed "a thousand stories and a thousand faces," all of them brave. There are three scenarios. All versions have him initially on horseback (one conveniently a white one). In the first scenario, Hicks and staff cut free of the carnage and reorganize under the *tebeldi*. Ala al Din is killed trying to reach them. Hicks loses his horse and fights to the last, sword in hand, teaching some everlasting saber lessons with his staff at his back. He is either speared or his wrist is slashed and he drops his sword first.

In the second scenario, Hicks and staff, all mounted, shoot their way free in a charge. Hicks attacks and wounds a mailed Emir, whom he believes to be the Mahdi, with his saber. Clubbed in the head, Hicks is unhorsed and his staff's horses are speared. Fighting together, he is the last to die.

In the final version he charges the survivors into the Dervish mass, emptying his revolver three times and using his sword so well that the Mahdists are in awe until he is lanced. As Mek el Tahir el Dud witnessed: "Hicks Pasha himself died fighting bravely by the *tebeldi* tree and I myself was there to see it" (46).

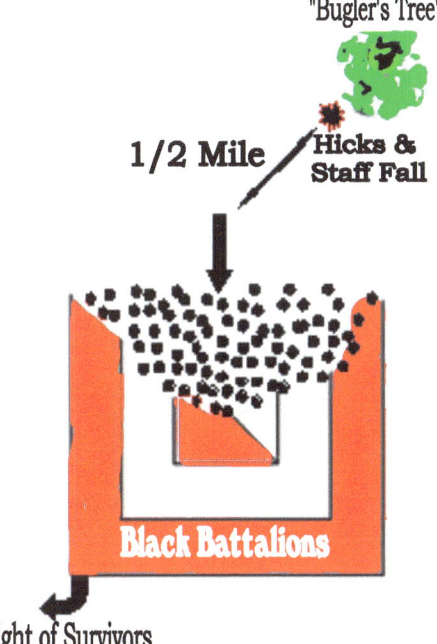

*The "Last Stand"
(Based on Eyewitness Accounts)*

CAPTAIN MASSEY, LATE OF THE DUKE OF CAMBRIDGE'S OWN (MIDDLESEX REGIMENT)
On Hicks Pasha's Staff

MAJOR WARNER, LATE OF THE 12TH FOOT (SUFFOLK REGIMENT)
On Hicks Pasha's Staff

COLONEL FARQUHAR, LATE CAPTAIN IN THE GRENADIER GUARDS
Chief of the Staff

HICKS PASHA, LATE COLONEL IN THE INDIAN ARMY
Commander-in-Chief of the Soudan Field Force

MR. EDMOND O'DONOVAN
Correspondent of the *Daily News*, and Author of "The Merv Oasis"

CONSUL MONCRIEFF
Killed at Tokar, near Suakim, Red Sea, Nov. 6

MR. EDWARD BALDWIN EVANS
Interpreter During the Trial of Arabi at Cairo, and Head of the Intelligence Department under Hicks Pasha

MR. FRANK VIZETELLY
The Artist who has Supplied *The Graphic* with Some of the Sketches of the Soudan Expedition

THE DISASTER IN THE SOUDAN—PORTRAITS OF SOME OF THE BRITISH OFFICERS AND OTHERS WHO ARE SAID TO HAVE FALLEN DURING THE RECENT FIGHTING, NOVEMBER 3—5

No Country for old men… or young ones, either.

X. *"... Isolated as it was in the desert with no line of retreat secure, it is most improbable that even if the termination of the fight had been less disastrous, the hapless army could have gotten back to the Nile."* (47)

The Hicks Pasha Expedition was worse than a failure. The immediate as well as long-range consequences were far greater than the annihilation of an Egyptian Army—bad enough as that was. Politically, the Mahdi received delegations and submissions from Islamic nations reaching from North Africa to Central Asia. Effectively, most of the Sudan was his. Those Sheikhs wavering before the slaughter now bowed to the Mahdi's will.

The Governor of Darfur, Rudolf Slatin, now had no hope of relief, and panic spread at Khartoum. A quarter of those inside the capital were thought to be rebels, and there were not enough garrison troops left to man the walls.

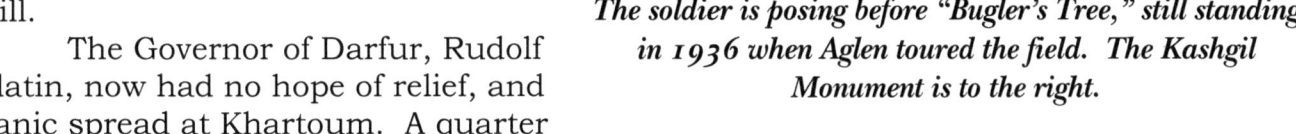

The soldier is posing before "Bugler's Tree," still standing in 1936 when Aglen toured the field. The Kashgil Monument is to the right.

The Dervish haul in booty was rich—thousands of Remington Rifles, the Nordenfelts, the mountain guns, surviving horses and camels, and an undetermined number of cartridges and shells which some have claimed to total a million rounds. Thus the army's destruction was a material Godsend delivered directly into rebel hands and at their power base, no less. Famous Colonial disasters often form one of two patterns. Either the adventure is based on fully erroneous conceptions from the start and should never be sent out, or a series of personalities and events combine in a string of snowballing consequences. The Hicks Pasha Expedition qualifies on both counts. With most of condition two's mistakes arising out of strong condition one.

That is to say, the Khedive's Government misread the strength of the Mahdist Rebellion. This would appear incredible after the line-up of failures preceding and necessitating the appointment of an Englishman to do an Egyptian's job. Hicks pleaded for additional troops and money for months, gaining little. He knew he was too weak, Colonel Stewart knew it—and said it. The gallant American ex-Confederate, Stone Pasha, also a Sudanese expert, had wanted three times what Hicks was given and had had wisely turned down the appointment.

The monument subsequently erected by the British to commemorate Kashgil, the greatest defeat of a "modern army" ever inflicted by native peoples. Of some 10,000 troops, less than 300 ever returned alive to Egypt.

On these grounds, the Expedition would have been better served policing Khartoum, Sennar Province, the Nile areas, and the North and East Sudan, buying time for the reconstruction of the New Model Army and concentrating on outmaneuvering the Mahdi with methods other than direct military confrontation. The expedition was directed to bite off more than it could chew.

Before leaving Khartoum, records research reveals

the overriding presentiment of the European officers as evidenced by letters, diaries, and official correspondence. In the face of this external threat, members broke down in the heat and fear with jealousy and squabbling. Negligence put the Krupps out of action at a critical juncture. European officers had to patrol at night to keep guards awake. Formations were bungled from misinterpreted orders, and even out of spite. The Expedition assumed the characteristics of a doomed drifting body—in front of it a triumphant, watchful, mysterious host, and behind it a hostile mobile force... no wells... no communications ... no retreat.

Hicks Pasha, a valiant man as proven in his steamer adventures and in his death, sometimes lacked the ability for high command. He marched with a force he knew inadequate for the task. Then, having carefully planned the northern route, he allowed Ala al Din to divert him south.

The paucity of troops caused the abandonment of the vital posts. To strip needed men from his main force and leave it too weak to fight or to abandon communications and gamble all on a quick battle—that was the question.

The answer was loaded against him either way. Staff misunderstandings, and his compromising to consult the Governor-General before issuing orders hurt his power of command. And where was he in Farquhar's compass charge into dense brush? By Alluba, the Expedition was a blind mass stumbling through the enemy's front yard devoid of real strategy. And before the final battle, Hicks had to ask his staff for ideas.

The Hicks Pasha Expedition ended on November 5th, 1883 as most had feared and as the rules of war demanded—the disastrous interment of the bleached bones of 10,000 men under the wastes of Kordofan. Today, only the hot, slumbering, thorny forest of Shaykan remembers the desperate struggle of the squares and of that last heroic stand under the spreading branches of the Bugler's Tree.

Footnotes
1. "Sudanese Soldiers Songs," *Journal of the African Society*, p. 315
2. Churchill, p. 13.
3. Ibid., p. 15, 1879, "Colonel Gordon in Central Africa."
4. Ibid., p. 16.
5. Zulfo, pp. 11-13.
6. Pimblett, pp. 20-21.
7. Clark, pp. 6-8.
8. Zulfo, p. 12.
9. Ibid., pp. 13-14.
10. Churchill, p. 6.
11. Gleichen, pp 38, 48-50, 59.
12. Colborne, p. 90.
13. Johnson, p. 11.
14. Clark, p. 50.
15. Royle, p. 53.
16. Colborne, pp. 78-81.
17. Johnson, p. 28.
18. Ibid., pp. 12-14.
19. Pimblett, p. 29.
20. Colborne, pp. 159-63.
21. Johnson, p. 14.
22. Clark, p. 11. Hicks' statement to Cairo.
23. Royle, pp. 60-64.

24. Abbas, p. 18124. Abbas, p. 181
25. Abbas, p. 181; Clark, pp. 12, 13; Johnson Pt. 3, p. 9
26. Pimblett, p. 42. (Seckendorf in a letter)
27. Johnson, Pt. 3, pp. 10, 15.
28. Royle, p. 64-65.
29. Johnson, Pt. 3, p. 15.
30. Royle, p. 66.
31. Johnson, Pt. 3, p. 19.
    (Statement of Shaykh Ali Gulla from *Sudan Notes and Records*).
32. Ibid.
33. Zulfo, p. 15.
34. Royle, p. 66, (O'Donovan's statement)
35. Abbas Bey, pp. 182-190.
36. Clark, p. 15.
37. Callwell, pp. 272, 299.
38. Abbas Bey, pp. 189-194.
39. Slatin, p. 132.
40. Abbas Bey, pp. 194-96.
41. Bermann, p. 182.
42. Zulfo, p. 16.
43. Faraj Sadik, *Sudan Notes And Records*, p. 155.
44. Aglen, pp. 142-43.
45. Sadik, p. 156.
46. Aglen, p. 145.
47. Caswell, p. 122.
48. Gordon, p. 241.

BIBLIOGRAPHY
Primary Sources
Aglen, E.F., "Sheikan Battlefield," *Sudan Notes And Records*, Vol. XX, Khartoum, 1937.
Colborne, J., *With Hicks Pasha To The Sudan*, Smith, Elder and Co., London, 1884.
Gleichen, Captain Count, *Handbook Of The Sudan, Pt. 1*, Harrison and Sons, London, 1898.
Gordon, C. G., *The Journals of Gordon at Khartoum*, Kegan Paul, Trench and Co., London, 1885.
Slatin, R., *Fire And Sword In The Sudan*, Edward Arnold and Co., 1930. (1st Edition 1898).
"The Adventurous Life or Faraj Sadik," *Sudan Notes And Records*, Vol. XXXII, Khartoum, 1951.
"The Diary of Abbas Bey," *Sudan Notes And Records*, Vol. XXXII, Khartoum, 1951.

Secondary Sources
Bermann, R., *The Mahdi Of Allah*, Putnam, London, 1931.
Churchill, W., *The River War*, N.E.I. Edition, London, 1973. (Originally, 1899.)
Clark, Peter, "The Hicks Pasha Expedition." No publication details. Text entrusted to
Mr. Douglas Johnson and delivered to this author in Oxford, England.
Callwell, C.E., *Small Wars*, General Staff, War Office, 1906. Republished by Greenhill Books, 1990.
Johnson, David, "Bugles To Kordofan, or 'Whatever Happened to Billy Hicks?'" *Tradition*, Issues 48, 49, 51-53.
Pimblett, W., *Story Of The Sudan War, 1881-1885*, Remington and Co., London, 1885.
Royle, C., *The Egyptian Campaigns, 1882-1885*, Revised to 1899, Hurst and Blackett, Ltd, London, 1900
Zulfo, I., *Karari*, Frederick Warne, London, 1980.

General Gordon And The Fall of Khartoum
By Peter Clark

General Charles George Gordon as Governor General of the Sudan

(Editor's Note: Peter Clark was Deputy Representative of the British Council in Khartoum. He was the editor and translator of Ismat Zulfo's book Karari, published by Leo Cooper. The following lecture was delivered at the Anglican Church's bi-weekly supper club on Sunday, January 25, 1976. We are grateful for Dr. Clark's permission to reprint it here.)

Ninety ore years* ago this evening was the last spent on earth by General Charles George Gordon, Governor General of the Sudan. He was killed at about 5 a.m. on the morning of Monday 26 January 1885 at the Palace about 100 yards from this spot. The dramatic circumstances of his death after a long siege are well known. Gordon's personality—quixotic, pietistic, utterly selfless—was much admired in British and European circles. He was idealized as a Christian hero and his death was seen in intensely melodramatic terms. His political mission and its failure were interpreted in terms of a polarization between Christianity and Islam, between the forces of darkness and of light. Parallels between Gordon and Christ were hinted at and a flood of devotional literature was unleashed dwelling on his martyrdom.

In the next few minutes I wish to concentrate on the political circumstances of Gordon's mission here. What were his practical problems? What alternatives was he faced with? What was the local context? Who were the besiegers? Who the Besieged?

In preparing this talk I must acknowledge my debts to three writers in particular. The first is Dr. Muhammad Ibrahim Abu Salim, Director of the Central Records Office, who has written a fascinating history of Khartoum, **Tarikhal Khartum**, unfortunately available only in Arabic. The second is Dr. Roland Stevenson, of the Church Missionary Society, whose article, "Old Khartoum 1821-1885" in *Sudan Notes And Records,* 1966, tells us much that can be known of Gordon's Khartoum. The third is a most competent book, recently published, written by Miss Ma'muna Mirghani Hamza. It is called **Hisar wa Suqut al Khartum** ("The Siege and Fall of Khartoum"). I have drawn from it liberally.

Khartoum in the early 1880's was the capital of the Sudanese dependencies of the Khedive, the ruler of Egyptian Sudan had been an Egyptian colony since the 1820's. The rule had been established to exploit the alleged miners wealth—especially gold—of the country. In fact it supplied slaves and soldiers for the Khedive's army. Khartoum and el Obeid became important commercial centers dealing with slaves, ivory, gum and ostrich feathers. The Egyptian rule was based on a series of garrison towns and penetrated the rural areas only to extract taxes. Certain aspects of industrial Europe were introduced to the Sudan for the first time, such as steamers, postal services, the telegraph, railways and 19th century governmental practices, hospitals and schools. We must not exaggerate the sophistication of these innovations. On the other hand in 1890 a letter from Khartoum to el Rasher took 11 days and from Khartoum to el Obeid 41 days.

Khartoum had a mixed population of about 50,000 in the early 1880's, of whom

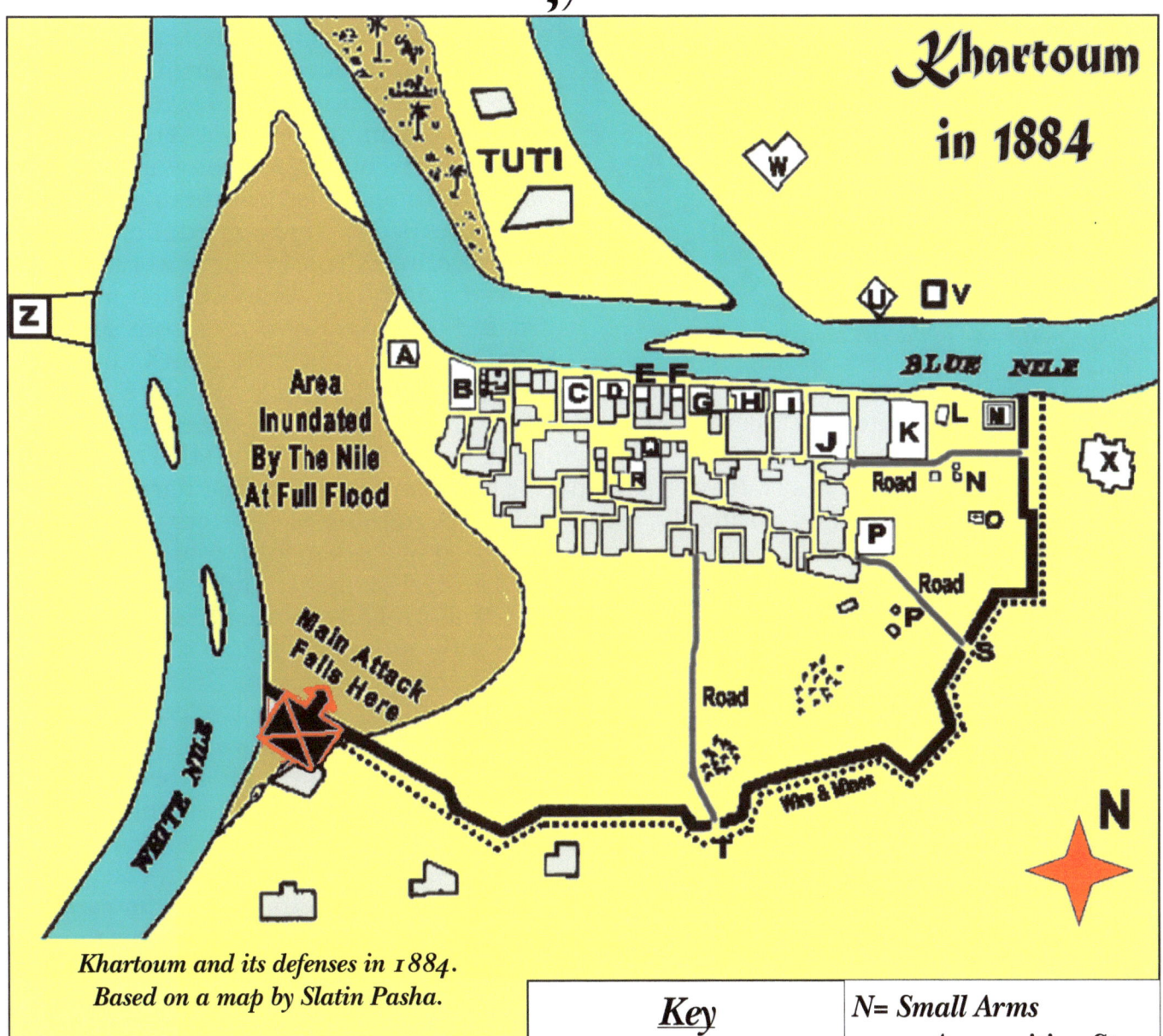

Khartoum and its defenses in 1884. Based on a map by Slatin Pasha.

Key

A= Fort Mukran
B= Gardens
C= Church
D= Sanitary Department
E= Post & Finance Offices
F= Austrian Consulate
G= Government House
H= Governor's Palace
I= Grain Stores
J= Arsenal
K= Barracks
L= Hospital
M= Fort Burri
N= Small Arms Ammunition Store
O= Artillery Ammunition Store
P= Cartridge Factories
Q= French Consulate
R= Italian Consulate
S= Bab el Messalmiah
T= Fort Kalakla
U= Eastern Palace
V= North Fort
W= Khojali Village
X= Burri Village
Y= Kalakla Village
Z= Omdurman Fort

perhaps 30,000—35,000 were, according to Colonel Stewart, Gordon's deputy, slaves. There was a wealthy class of Egyptian merchants and officials including Copts who were clerks, accountants and traders. Many northern Sudanese from Dongola and the Shaiqi and Ja'li tribes were small traders and sailors. Slaves tended to be Southerners, Nilotics and Bari, from the Nuba Mountains, Darfur and the Funj areas. The Europeans were a mixed bunch, a lot of Greeks, Austrians, and Italians, some British subjects, including Maltese and the odd Indian. There were also Jews, Syrians,

The north side of the city alongside the Blue Nile.

Algerians and Ethiopians.

In 19th Century Khartoum the river was far more important as a channel of communication. The best houses overlooked the river which was dotted with small jetties where grain and other provisions were landed, brought in from riverine villages. There were, of course, no bridges, but a regular ferry crossed to North Khartoum from some point near the present Roman Catholic cathedral. The Palace, built in the 1870's, had two stories. The present palace occupies the same site and it is interesting to observe that, like its predecessor, it is designed for approach from the river, from which it can be seen at its best. The town was mostly to the south and west of the palace. There were lots of rough narrow streets that got very muddy during the rainy season. A number of quarters were called *Hilla*, "village," and Khartoum was a compact collection of settlements. Hardly any buildings remain from that time—only the tombs in Shari' Baladiya and a wall in the buildings of the Commissioner of Khartoum which may go back to the 1850's.

Hillat Musa Bey was immediately west and south of the palace and was an area of offices and middle level residences. Along the river near the present Grand Hotel was Hillat Manjara where there were workshops for the river craft. To the back, south west of the town was built a sandbank about three feet high. Called the *Teras*, it was designed to protect the town from White Nile floods. It marked the end of the town in that direction, and just inside were a series of small houses and mud huts, the homes of tinkers and prostitutes. Coming to the east, on the site of the present central taxi station and the Sudan Airways headquarters, was the *suq* and mosque area. The main Khartoum mosque was built in the 1830's and the *suq* must have been like the *suq al 'Arabi* today: Some constructed markets and many small stores and displays, dealing with local produce and cheap imported luxury goods. Finally, the area now bounded by Palace Avenue, Hospital Street and Shari' Jumhuriya was the area called Salamat al Pasha. This was the residential area of the poorer Sudanese. It also contained then, as now, Khartoum's red light district.

Khartoum was a foreign town and represented the colonial power. The reaction to the foreigner and his ways was bitterest in matters of religion. The Egyptians introduced mosques and a government controlled hierarchy of religious officials that seemed to interfere with the popular piety of rural Sudan. Considering the innovations the regime introduced—and one of the words for innovation in Arabic, *bid'a*, has

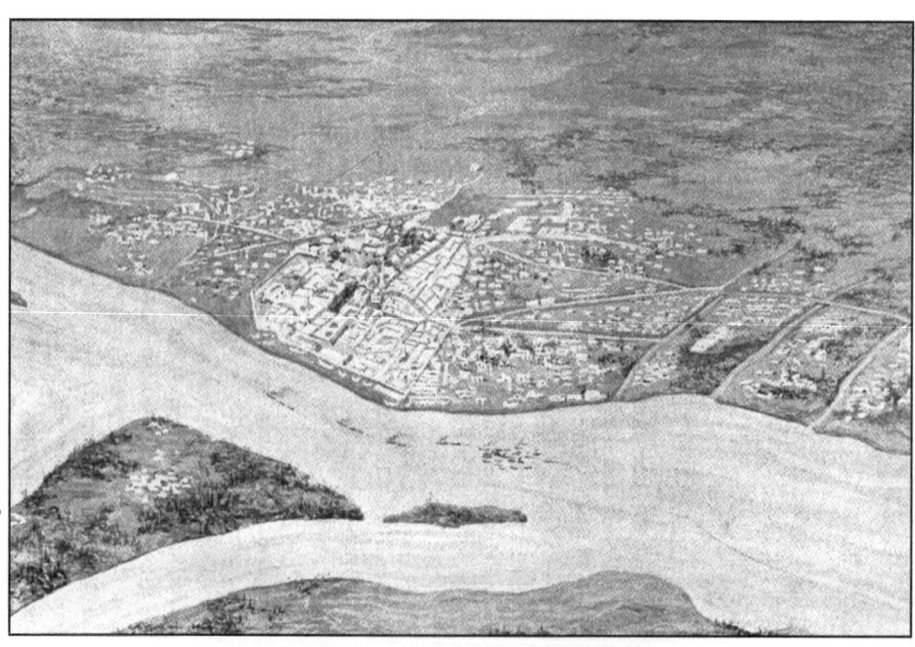

A bird's eye view of Khartoum

overtones of heresy—it is not surprising that opposition took a religious form. It became concentrated on the teachings of a holy man from Dongola called Muhammad Ahmad, who declared himself the Mahdi al Muntazar, the expected rightly guided one. In the years from 1881 to 1883 he built up a widespread popular movement based on the White Nile and Kordofan areas. Repeated military expeditions sent from Khartoum were defeated by the Mahdi and his followers. The movement had features in common with other Islamic fundamentalist movements that have emphasized the purity of the early years of Islam in contrast to the decadence of modern times. The extraordinary military successes of the Mahdi against organized and well-armed soldiers seemed to vindicate his claims. In January 1883 the second city of the Sudan—el Obeid—fell to him after a six month siege.

Coincidentally with the rise of the Mahdi, Egypt fell under European and particularly British control. In 1882 Egypt was occupied by British troops and the country was indirectly ruled by the British for the next two generations. Control was through advisers, and the principal British authority was the Consul General. In the summer of 1883, Evelyn Baring was appointed Consul General and was to stay until 1907. During these years of what has been called "The veiled protectorate," Baring, later Lord Cromer, was the effective ruler of Egypt, although the Khedive and Egyptian ministers remained nominally in charge.

In 1883, an Egyptian army officered by Britishers, led by Hicks Pasha, came to the Sudan to sort out the Mahdi. Hicks had innumerable problems before he set out from Khartoum for Kordofan. But the Mahdi's forces tracked him, harried him and dragged him further and further west. Finally his army was massacred at Shaykan, some 20 miles south of El Obeid on 5 November, 1883.

The news caused panic in Khartoum, consternation in Cairo and dismay in London. In Khartoum the wealthy foreign communities saw a threat to their property and welfare. In Cairo official circles feared a spread of revolutionary Mahdism in the towns and villages of Upper Egypt. In London Mr. Gladstone's Liberal government, already tottering from a series of domestic difficulties, was reluctantly forced to do something about this crisis in a far away country about which little was known and less understood.

In carrying out a decision in the Sudan there were now three centers of political decision making—London, Cairo and Khartoum. There were three areas of divided sovereignty and indirect authority. The seeds of Gordon's destruction were sown in this politically muddled situation.

The Cairo government at once agreed on the need to evacuate the Egyptian garrisons from the Sudan. In Britain a lively popular opinion somehow saw Major General Gordon as the answer to the difficulty. A weak and divided government gave in to the demands of public opinion and tried to urge Baring to accept Gordon as an emissary in Khartoum. An untried and doubting Baring gave in to the demands of the British government and tried to urge the Egyptian government to accept Gordon as an emissary in Khartoum. The Egyptian government, hamstrung by foreign advisers, accepted with alacrity, assuming that the responsibility for any unforeseen consequences would rest with the British government. The British government, led by an ailing old man and caught between a demanding public opinion and a vigorous needling opposition, breathed a sigh of relief assuming that the responsibility for any unforeseen consequences would rest with the Egyptian government. The Gordon mission was under way.

Meanwhile why Gordon? Gordon already had considerable experience of the Sudan. From 1874 to 1876 he served the Khedive as Governor of Equatoria. From

When Governor General, Gordon was widely admired and respected. It was said by the Sudanese that if he were only a Muslim, "He would be the perfect man."

1877 to 1880 he had been Governor General of the Sudan. In these roles he was a vigorous opponent of the slave trade. He was a strong Bible reading Evangelical Christian and his unorthodox character and methods gave his an enormous reputation among the newly literate non-Conformist lower middle classes of Britain. Gordon was now in his early 50's and most of his life had been spent as a soldier in distant parts of the globe. He was regarded as an authority in what was called savage warfare. In England Gordon had always shunned publicity but had spent a great amount of his time, energy and income on the welfare of destitute youths. All who worked with him were inspired by great devotion. Although his judgment was at times faulty, and his behavior impetuous, he was un-dogmatic, highly resourceful and never one to bear grudges. This was the man sent to Khartoum by two governments.

The British government charged him with going to Khartoum to report on the best methods of evacuation—an advisory role—and to accept any task given him by the Egyptian Government. The latter made him Governor General, an executive role. He was to carry out the withdrawal of Egyptian troops, to employ "The best means and arrangements which may be necessary for the safety of those troops and employees, and inhabitants and merchants, both native and foreign," who may wish to leave and to arrange for a successor government in the Sudan.

It is not clear who was to provide support and backing for this open-ended undertaking. Nor was it clear what was to happen if his advisory role conflicted with his executive. Again, who was to be evacuated? All garrisons? Including those in Equatoria and Bahr al Ghazal? And how binding would his advice be?

Gordon accepted his commissions, left England in January and reached Khartoum on 18 February, 1883. He immediately sought to weaken the appeal of the Mahdi by issuing some reforms. Taxation was halved. Some arrears were cancelled. Many prisoners were released. The Khedival ordinance banning slavery from 1887 was declared inoperative. By removing some of the more unpopular aspects of the government it was hoped to still opposition. Secondly, Gordon set about plans for the government of the Sudan after the withdrawal. He wanted a Sudanese of authority who would be an alternative focus of support. Zubair Pasha would be such a man.

Now Zubair was a vigorous old slaver living in exile in Cairo at the time. A Jaili from al Jaili, he and his family had been the main antagonists of Gordon in his previous tours of duty in the Sudan. Zubair had been Governor of Bahr al Ghazal, was a man of wealth, influence, of military and administrative ability. Gordon's suggestion was sound. Baring supported it, but the British government, submitting to pressure from the Anti-Slavery lobby, rejected the idea. Gordon's alternative was to build up a Council in Khartoum formed of tribal leaders, officials and merchants. He

Zubair (or "Zobeir") Pasha, Slaver Extraordinaire.

appointed the Mahdi Governor of Kordofan, requested that he stay there and expressed a hope for cordial relations. He attempted to isolate the Mahdi further by arranging for the *ulema,* the religious leaders of Khartoum, to write a letter refuting the exclusive claims of the Mahdi.

So much for Gordon's peace offensives. At the same time he looked at his military resources. He had a garrison of about 5,000 regular soldiers reinforced by probably the same number of irregulars. There was a fleet of steamers which maintained his communications with the outside world. Indeed, Gordon's dependence on his steamers was a characteristic of his conduct of the siege. It reflects the importance of the river to 19th century Khartoum—the river that linked the Sudan and Cairo. As one historian has observed, "The Egyptians depended on the Nile while the Mahdists feared it; the Mahdists built fortifications on the Nile banks (at Omdurman) but none on the desert side, while the Egyptians did the reverse."

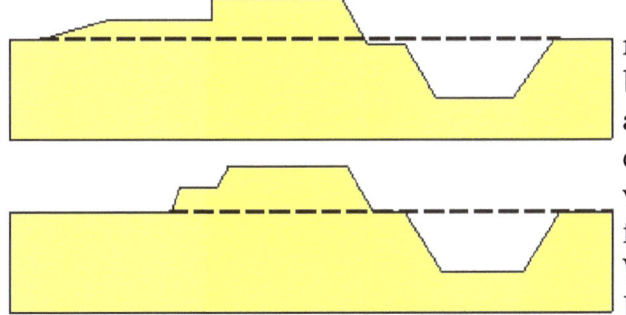

Cross Sections of Gordon's Parapet and Ditch.

The fortifications of Khartoum were a mile or two from the town. They were first built by a previous Governor General and Gordon set about repairing them. A ditch, three meters deep and four meters wide, was constructed with a parapet on the town side. The line of fortifications went from the Blue Nile to the White Nile. It started near the present Blue Nile Bridge and a gate, the Burri Gate, was the exit for the villages of the Blue Nile. There was also a Burri Fort, the site of which is in the University grounds. The parapet followed the railway line roughly (one or two small capstans still exist marking the site of the line of Gordon's ramparts) and after 3,000 meters, a little to the east of the present railway station, was another gate, the Masallamiya gate. (Masallamiya is an old town near Wad Medani.) By it was a second fort. Following the railway again, 1,500 meters further on was the third gate, Kalakla gate. (Kalakla is a village on the road to Jabal Aulia.) The site of this gate is the Hurriya Bridge over the railway on the road to Shajara. There was another fort a little to the west and then 4,000 meters of ramparts as far as the White Nile. Gordon had three other forts at his disposal—Mugran, roughly on the site of the present Mugran Gardens—near the White Nile Bridge, Omdurman; North Fort, opposite the Palace, originally a private residence; and Omdurman Fort, a little inland from the river to the south of the White Nile bridge.

Meanwhile, what was the Mahdi doing? Until August 1884 the Mahdi remained at al Rahad, sixty miles south east of el Obeid, organizing his forces. He issued his arrangements through a series of decrees—*manshurat*—in which he specified the chain of command in his army.

In the Sudan, religion calls upon powers of discipline and organization rarely found elsewhere. When we see Sudanese Muslims praying, men form themselves spontaneously into neat rows behind a leader in prayer, an *imam*. It is a most moving experience to attend an Islamic festival. A space with hundreds of men milling around will, within one or two minutes, form itself into a score of rows. The actions of praying—kneeling, bowing, standing—are performed in as regular and disciplined a way as well drilled soldiers on a parade ground. Such groups of worshippers behind the *imam* formed the basic fighting unit in the Mahdi's forces. Such organization and discipline bore fruit in the early military successes of the *Mahdiyya*. Like groups of worshippers, the number of these basic units could vary enormously in size.

The Mahdi rejected Gordon's offers of a Sultanate of Kordofan with scorn. He remained in Kordofan for several months, directing the siege from al Rahad. It was not until October that he arrived to take part personally. His basic policy in the early months was to impose a close siege on Khartoum. He issued *manshurat* to tribal and religious leaders calling on them either to join him in Kordofan or to take part in the siege. The call was answered, and within one month of Gordon's arrival his telegraphic communications were cut. Gordon was faced with the problem of a blockade. The Mahdi appointed his father in law, Muhammad al Tayyib al Basir, a holy man from the Halawiyin tribe in the Jazira, to the command of operations in Central Sudan. One of these earliest letters after the battle of Shaykan had been to the people of Salasat al Pasha, the Sudanese quarter of Khartoum.

The world press followed the siege with rapt attention. Punch printed this cartoon of a wistful Gordon wondering if relief had come or he was only seeing a "mirage."

By early May it was clear to Gordon that the chances of a political solution to evacuation were fast diminishing. In that month news came of the fall of Berber in the north. He had passed through Berber three months earlier on his way to Khartoum and had set up a local administration to take over after evacuation. The appeals of the Mahdi dissolved Berber's loyalty, and Gordon's careful administration collapsed like a pack of cards. Only a military solution seemed possible. Either Gordon must defeat the Mahdi and then confront the consequent political problems, or he must receive reinforcements from Egypt or Britain. His original instructions, vague and contradictory, now became irrelevant to the situation. This was abundantly clear to Gordon, but not to Cairo or London. Hence the slowness in appreciating the danger of his situation and the delay in sending out a relief expedition.

The following eight months of the siege can be seen as being in four phases: from May to July the Mahdi's grip tightened on the city; in August Gordon took the initiative but overreached himself; from September to December disaster followed disaster; by January the situation was utterly desperate, and the final fall came almost as a relief to the tension.

In the first phase the Mahdists took up their positions. Muhammad Uthman Abu Qirja, a Dongolawi from al Qitayna, arrived to take up command in April. He based himself at al Jirayf. The qadi of Kalakla who had been among Gordon's first Council had now joined the Mahdists and faced the city from the south. Another army settled at al Fitayhab, west of the White Nile. To the north two men, al Tahir Muhammad Badr al Ubaid, son of a very holy man of Umm Dubban, and Mudawi Abd al Rahman, completed the blockade north of the, city. (Both, incidentally, were to support Kitchener in his re-conquest campaign 1896-98). Abu Qirja, after capturing a steamer and some weapons at al Mak, 20 miles south of Khartoum, built a series of forts outside the fortifications, and his Krupp guns started to fire projectiles into the city.

August saw the high Nile. The rains and a high Nile were to the advantage of the besieged. Within their more permanent residences the heavy rains were less demoralizing than for those in tents or sleeping in the open. The high river assisted Gordon's steamers, facilitated transport and awakened hope. In late August-one of Gordon's

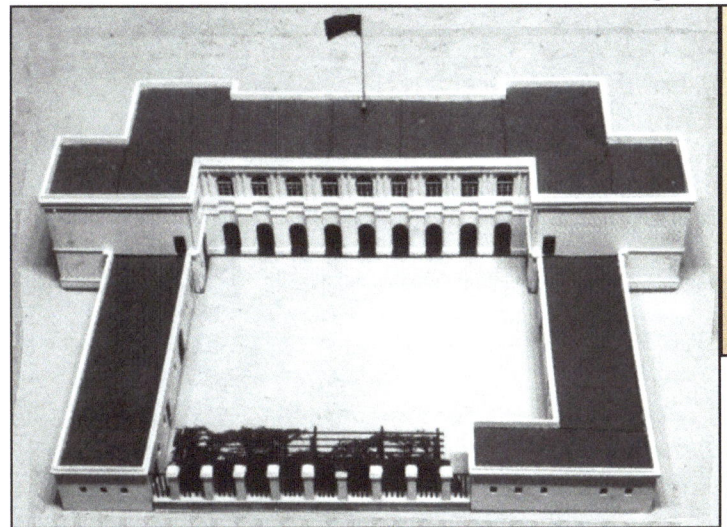

A model of the Governor's Palace dating from 1900. The original building was in ruins when the British finally arrived thirteen years after its fall.

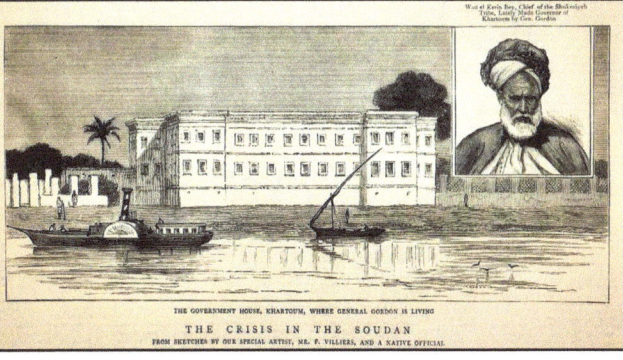

The Governor's Palace as seen from the Blue Nile.

most capable soldiers, Muhammad Ali Pasha Husayn, an Egyptian born at Manjara, known as the "Fighting Pasha," led a series of successful sorties out of the city. At al Jirayf he seized 1,600 rifles from the Mahdists. The Jirayf-Kalakla triangle was cleared, opening up possibilities for cultivation and relieving the acute food situation. At about the same time he chased Mahdists away from Halfiya and cleared the river on both banks. This gave great security for the transport of foodstuffs.

Early in September, however, the Mahdists scored a series of triumphs. The "Fighting Pasha" was lured out to al Aylafun, 20 miles from Khartoum on the north bank of the Blue Nile. At dawn al Tahir Muhammad Badr al Ubaid and Mudawi Abd al Rahman came in from Umm Dubban and slaughtered half the Pasha's army and seized a thousand Remington rifles. This was Gordon's most serious reverse. The following day the Mahdi's ablest commander, Abd al Rahman wad al Nujumi arrived to take over command of operations. The only chance for Gordon now was with outside assistance.

Gordon decided to take advantage of the still high Nile and send one of his steamers down to Egypt with senior members of his staff to impress upon Cairo and London the gravity of the situation. The only other Englishmen with him, his deputy, Colonel John Stewart, and the *Times* correspondent, Frank Power, left on 10 September in the steamer *Abbas*. It was never to reach its destination, but was captured between Abu Hamad and Merowe. All were killed and the many letters and papers seized were sent to the Mahdi who quoted them in humiliating extracts to Gordon.

To raise morale and foster the hope that a Relief Expedition was well on its way, steamers were sent to Shendi at the end of September to greet the Expedition which Gordon learned had been dispatched. They were to wait for nearly four months.

In October the Mahdi himself arrived and settled himself at Abu Sa'd just south of the present White Nile bridge on the west bank. As the level of the Nile went down, Gordon's chances slipped away. North Khartoum was taken again by the Mahdists. Gordon doubted the loyalty, not only of Salamat al Pasha, but also of the Khartoum notables. As communications became

Col. John Stewart in his "home" uniform of the 11th Hussars.

interrupted the food situation became acute. Tuti Island became a fortified granary and periodically searches were made for hoarded grain.

Gordon's last communication with the outside world was on 14 December. The city could hold out, he said, for ten days at the most. In fact it was to last for six weeks. The final month saw Gordon's policy changing to preparing for the eventuality of defeat. He still retained hope of reliefs but the military odds became more and more stacked against him.

On 5 January the fort at Omdurman fell after the commander, Faraj Allah Pasha Raghib, had resisted gallantly for two months. The Mahdi was so impressed that Faraj Allah was made a commander in the Mahdist army and came to serve with honor in later Mahdist wars with Ethiopia. On the 18th Gordon announced that one day's service for his soldiers would count as one year's service. On the 19th, several officers, un-persuaded by a 350-fold increase in their wage packet, slipped out and joined the Mahdi. Gordon invited other doubters to leave while they could. A steamer was rigged up ready to leave Khartoum with prominent citizens.

On the 20th news reached the Mahdi that the Relief Expedition had clashed with a Mahdist army sent out to face them at Abu Tilayh (Abu Klea) twenty miles west of al Metemmeh. The result seemed to be indecisive, for the Mahdist commander, Musa wad Hilu, was reported to be killed. The Mahdi seemed to panic and was tempted to withdraw with his army, now numbering about 100,000, west to Kordofan. Wiser councils prevailed, however. It was pointed out that Khartoum was desperate. Spies and deserters numberless bore witness to that. It appeared that the British too had suffered serious losses, including one Colonel. News then came of a further clash at Abu Kru during which a British major general, Sir Herbert Stewart, was killed. Whatever threat the British relief expedition might present, and they seemed mortal after all, decisive action was necessary. The Mahdi was persuaded to launch an assault. The timing was thus determined by the approach of the Relief Expedition. The assault and the approach were so linked that it is nonsense to talk about the Relief Expedition being "too late."

Gordon was well aware that the weakest point of the defenses was the western part between the Kalakla fort and the White Nile. The river, which determined so much of the character of the siege of Khartoum, also determined its fall. In August, when the river was in full flood, the water came to within a few yards of the Kalakla Fort. On the west of the city the river was seen as an adequate defense. As the waters receded the old ditch, shallow and easily passable, reappeared. The Mahdists were pressing in and harassed working parties who sought to deepen and widen the ditch. By mid January there were about 1,000 yards of inadequate ramparts. The ditch was only two meters deep. Although it was muddy still it was not sufficient to prevent a determined assault.

Strangely enough, Gordon, though aware of this vulnerability, expected the assault to come at the Masallamiya and Burri gates. Accordingly there were more troops there. However, he was aware of the sympathies many of his Sudanese soldiers might have with the Mahdi, and placed only Egyptian regular soldiers on the stretch between the Kalakla fort and the White Nile. This stretch was patrolled by two battalions of four companies each, each company containing 105 men. A squadron of irregulars including some Shaiqi was placed between the two battalions.

On Sunday 25 January the Mahdi crossed the White Nile. He addressed his soldiers. Indeed, in the words of one of them, he "Harangued us, mounted on his camel. Part of what he said, before the final oath of allegiance, was that the enemies of God had dug the ditch surrounding Khartoum very wide and deep, and had placed in it iron teeth, each with four iron spikes on three of which it stood, leaving the fourth spike upright to pierce the feet of men or the hooves of horses. Then he said, "Swear allegiance to me unto death!" and was 'silent for a moment, when the whole army with one voice shouted three times "We swear allegiance to you unto death."

Soon after midnight the assault started. The Mahdist forces concentrated their attack on the weak point of the defenses. Some carried bedsteads to throw down on the soft mud to facilitate their crossing the ditch. One soldier walked into the mud up to his knees, and his comrades leapfrogged over him to the city side, pushing the soldier into the mud up to his waist. One man, Babikr Bedri, crossed at a point so shallow and dry that he was inside before he realized it. Even so the resistance from the defenders was fierce. "Our part of the line," recalled one Sudanese soldier, "was also heavily attacked, and though we went on firing our rifles until they were too hot to hold, they finally poured over the ramparts by sheer force of numbers and anyone who remained standing was killed."

Punch prematurely celebrated Gordon's relief with a triumphant cartoon, but soon printed this one, "Too Late!"

The attackers poured in at three points by the weak ramparts, by the Masallamiya Gate and by the Burri gate, which was stormed. They tended to move inside the ramparts to a point near the Masallamiya Gate, and then headed for the town. There followed a general massacre and looting of the city. General Gordon was among those killed. The details of his death are uncertain and there is dispute about the identity of his killer. Accounts of the storming are so charged with emotion, used in later years in an attempt to excite public opinion against the Mahdist state and in favour of a campaign for the re-conquest of the Sudan, that they are of limited historical value.

Among those who were killed were Europeans, Sudanese, and Egyptians. Let us consider two. Martin Hansel was an Austrian and had been Vice Consul since 1862. He was a talented extrovert and a trained typographer. He used to play the piano and organ regularly at the Catholic mission, and probably performed on the fission piano that can be seen today in the Khalifa's House museum. He could play the fool. In advanced years he married an 18 year old half caste Abyssinian girl and used to join in wedding dances in an uninhibited way. General Gordon rather disapproved of him. He was reported to have been ready to make accommodation with the Mahdists—not an unreasonable stand for a diplomat to make. However, he never had the chance, and was killed in the general massacre.

Another who lost his life was Fayyid Muhammad. He was a holy man from Egypt, the leader of the Ahmadiyya sect. He was thrown to his death in a well 91 years ago. His tomb is still venerated and can be seen about 50 yards away on Shari' Jami'a, between the British Council and the roundabout by the Sudan Socialist Union.

But many survived the storm. Some of the soldiers defending the ramparts threw themselves among their slain comrades and waited for a safer hour. Let us consider the fate of two survivors.

Pietro Agati was an Italian bricklayer who came to Khartoum in the 1850's. He survived the siege of Khartoum and lived in Omdurman with a Sudanese wife and family. He practiced his craft for the Khalifa, building his house in Omdurman. He was unwilling to be repatriated when the Anglo-Egyptian force re-conquered the country in 1898 and lived on to 1918, dying in his 90's at the Roman Catholic mission in Omdurman.

After the killing and the pillage, Khartoum became a place of residence for the senior Emirs. The Mahdi died in June 1885 and the Khalifa shifted the centre of gravity of the state across the river. Khartoum became abandoned, and Omdurman was the capital.

The Gordon Relief Expedition; whose imminent arrival was the trigger for the final assault, reached the city on 28 January, two full days after the fall. They made no attempt to land but retreated north, pursued by a Mahdist force. Other Egyptian garrisons in the Sudan surrendered and, apart from Wadi Halfa and part of the coast by Suakin, the Mahdists were in complete control of the Sudan.

The story of the siege and fall has been seen mainly from the point of view of Gordon and the defenders. My own account has, regrettably, followed this general approach. The death of Gordon caused acute pain to many people in England who attempted to find a scapegoat.

Mr. Gladstone, the "Grand Old Man," (the GOM), was accused of indifference to Gordon's fate. He became known as "M.O.G."—the "Murderer of Gordon." An attempt was made—and still is—to attribute moral responsibility for Gordon's death either to Gladstone, individuals in the Relief Expedition, or to Gordon himself. It is curious that the fall of Khartoum, can still be seen so emotionally.

The guilt notion begs a number of questions. It is doubtful whether Gordon would have permitted himself to be rescued. He declared that he would refuse to go, affirming his responsibility for the people of Khartoum. It is uncertain what would have happened after relief. Was it planned to abandon the Sudan suddenly? Or to set up a successor regime? Or to take on the new Mahdist empire? It seems that people continually failed to understand the dynamic of Mahdism and repeatedly underestimated its appeal. It was seen as an impersonal force, and not as a collection of individuals with their own interests, moral dilemmas, and divided loyalties determining their behavior.

The idea of the Relief Expedition being too late strikes me as being particularly misleading. I have stressed that their approach precipitated the fall. Had they been one week earlier it is probable that the fall would have been one week earlier. Moreover, the Expedition reached Khartoum with considerable speed. It took them five months to come from Cairo. They came in the face of hostile tribes and with Mahdism expanding. It took Kitchener two years to come to Khartoum in 1896-98. He was far better equipped. Enormous developments had taken place in European weaponry in the interval, while the standard of the Mahdists' weapons remained the same. Armed tribes in northern Sudan gave Kitchener considerable support, and Mahdism no longer had such momentum as it had had in 1884-85.

We are still ignorant about many aspects of the siege. There has been little new material that changes the story as it was known in the 1890's. There is a shift in emphasis and a more widespread appreciation both of what Mahdism was all about, and of the dilemmas of Gordon. The drama of the siege made Gordon's death and the collapse of Egyptian rule in the Sudan like the last scene of Hamlet, needing only the curtain to be drawn. We must remember the continuity of history. People went on living in Khartoum and Omdurman. Their grandchildren are with us today. Indeed, for the Mahdi and his Khalifa, having gained control of the Sudan, their problems were just starting.

On Gordon's Death
By Douglas Johnson

The traditional image of Gordon's end. "When the legend becomes fact, print the legend."

The most frequent account of Gordon's death is that he was stabbed while making "A gesture of scorn" to his attackers. Slatin claims that the Mahdi actually wanted his death, while Wingate does admit the possibility that he was killed by a member of any one of a number of tribes that had a grievance against him dating from his first tenure as Governor-General.

Ismat Zulfo writes in-Karari: "Who slew Gordon? Most accounts, including the Sudanese, suggest that the killer was the Emir wad Nubauri, Emir of the Bani Jamar: for it was he whom the Mahdi publicly charged with the task of taking Gordon alive.

It is most likely that the account of Ali al Mahdi is nearest the truth. He is the only person who interrogated an eye-witness of the event. He said:

"I was told by Shaykh Ibrahim Ali Sabir al Maghrabi who was a clerk with the standard of Mirghani Suwar al Dhahab that the man who killed Gordon was Mursal al Haj Hamuda. This Mursal was standard bearer to the Emir Mirghani.

Ibrahim related to me: 'At dawn our standard reached the Palace. Mursal was near me and saw a man standing on an upper floor looking through the window. It was Gordon busy looking at his defeated army. Mursal thought he was armed and wished to shoot before he was himself fired at. He shot the man who fell on the staircase. Mursal did not know that he had killed Gordon.' At once Ibrahim Ali Sabir entered the palace, went up to the upper floor to confirm that the man struck was Gordon. He was wearing his official uniform with all the decorations and was gasping for breath.

'Abd al Qadir walad al Kuku, the *gadi* of Hamuda's battalion came in and asked me: "Who is this?" I told him, "Gordon." He said, "How do you know?" I said, "I used to know him when he toured Kordofan. He used to shave his chin but leaving hair on his cheeks." I then took my knife and cut off his head. When Mursal learned that Gordon Pasha had been killed he hid himself, asking those with him to conceal the matter.

Gordon's actual killer was unknown. '"When Shaykh Ibrahim 'Ali Sabir told me this, we sent two men with him to ascertain the truth from Mursal or his chiefs, but they did not find him for he was killed at Karari. When they questioned his chief he was afraid and troubled, asking them: 'We heard from Mursal himself that he killed Gordon' and had erred in so doing. But he knew not—and he was killed at Karari.' He then asked, 'What is your purpose in this?' They replied, 'Only to get at the truth.'"

A sentimentalized—and sanitized—version of Gordon's "Martyrdom."

Whatever the truth, one thing is certain: The Mahdi had absolutely no wish for Gordon to be killed. His strict orders were that he be taken alive. This is clear from the killer's fear of his deed being known. He remained hidden throughout the period of the Mahdi and the Khalifa, and made his comrades swear not to divulge his secret (Zulfo, **Karari**, Khartoum, 1973, pp.83-84).

The Gordon Relief Expedition:
The Desert Route and The Camel Corps, 1884-85
by Doug Johnson

General Sir Garnet Wolesley, A thinking man's soldier.

General Wolseley always considered himself an innovator and sought in his campaigns to produce some startling tactical innovation with which to carry on his battles. In the Sudan campaign of 1884-85 he tried two—a River Column of whale boats (similar to the Red River Campaign of Canada where he won his fame), and a flying Desert Column of camel mounted troops.

Of course the idea of a camel corps did not originate with Wolseley, but the Sudan was the first time a camel corps figured into the major plans of the British Army. Its object was to cross the Bayuda Desert from Korti to Metemmeh in order to place a small but effective force close to Khartoum to either reinforce it or relieve it entirely while the bulk of the British Army rowed its weary way up the Nile. The Desert Column was to be a self-sufficient force of cavalry, artillery and infantry. Though not all infantry involved belonged to the Camel Corps, the four regiments that comprised the newly raised unit were to be the backbone of the force.

The first contingent of the Camel Corps was raised in Dongola and was composed of the Royal Sussex Regiment and a wing of the Mounted Infantry. It was known as Major Marriott's Camel Corps (Colville, Vol. I, pp. 109-111). Volunteers were seconded from regiments serving in Egypt as well as some home regiments, and the first batch of these volunteers began to arrive at Alexandria on October 7, 1884. On October 26, 1884 the Camel Corps was officially divided into four regiments. They were:

- Guards Camel Regiment: 23 officers, 403 men; 1st, 2nd, 3rd Grenadier Guards, 1st and 2nd Coldstream Guards, 1st and 2nd Scots Guard, 100 Royal Marine Light Infantry (RMLI).
- Heavy Camel Regiment: 24 officers, 430 men; 1st and 2nd Life Guards, Royal Horse Guards, 2nd, 4th, 5th Dragoon Guards, 1st, 2nd (Scots Greys) Dragoons, 5th and 16th Lancers.
- Light Camel Regiment: 21 officers, 387 men; 3rd, 4th, 7th, 10th, 11th, 15th, 18th, 20th, and 21st Hussars.
- Mounted Infantry Camel Regiment: 26 officers, 480 men; 1st South Staffordshire (38th), 1st Royal West Kents (50th), 1st Black Watch Highlanders (42nd), 1st Gordon Highlanders (75th), 2nd Essex (56th), 1st Sussex (35th), 2nd Duke of Cornwall's Light Infantry (46th), 3rd King's Royal Rifle Corps, Rifle Brigade, Somerset Light Infantry, Connaught Rangers, Royal Scots Fusiliers.

The Light Camel Regiment was left at Korti and was used to guard supplies. The final composition of the Desert Column was:
- 2 squadrons, 19th Hussars: 8 Officers, 127 Other Ranks
- Guards Camel Regiment: 19 Officers, 365 Other Ranks
- Heavy Camel Regiment: 24 Officers, 376 Other Ranks
- Mtd. Inf. Camel Regiment: 24 Officers, 359 Other Ranks
- 1st Royal Sussex: 8 Officers, 250 Other Ranks
- Naval Brigade: 5 Officers, 53 Other Ranks
- 1/2 of 1st Bty., 1st Bde./ Sou. Div., Royal Arty., 4 Officers, 34 Other Ranks
- 1/2 26th Co, Royal Engineers. 2 Officers, 25 Other Ranks

(List from Colville, V.II, p. 254)

All of the above numbers are approximate as many men were used on convoy and garrison duty, and rarely did the entire Column move together. Rather they were sent in two or three waves from one point to another. Fifty men of the Essex Regiment relieved the Mounted Infantry Camel Regiment at El Howeiya Wells so that the Mounted Infantry could join the rest of the Column, and 150 of the Royal Sussex were stationed at Gakdul, leaving only 100 to travel with the rest of the Column (Ibid., pp. 8, 14). The total strength of the Desert Column was 98 officers, 1,509 NCO's and men, 296 natives and interpreters, 8 Egyptians, 2,778 camels, 155 horses, and two mules (Ibid., p.6).

All of the Desert Column, except the 19th Hussars, were mounted on camels. This included the Royal Sussex, the Naval Brigade, the Royal Artillery, and the Royal Engineers in addition to those designated as Camel Corps.

The Naval Brigade had one five-barreled Gardner gun with four camels to carry it; one for the barrels, one for the wheels and elevating gear, one for the trail, and one for the ammunition. The Camel Battery of the Royal Artillery had three 7-pdr Screw Guns. Each gun, plus two boxes of ammunition, was carried on six camels with one native driver allotted to every two camels.

The staff of the Desert Column consisted of Sir Herbert Stewart as Commander-in-Chief, with Colonel Burnaby as second in command. Wilson took over command after Stewart was mortally wounded at Abu Kru. The Guards Camel Regiment was commanded by Lt. Colonel E. Boscawen; Heavy Camel Regiment by Lt. Colonel R.A. Talbot; the Mtd. Inf. Camel Regiment by G. H. Gough; the Royal Sussex by Major Sunderland; 19th Hussars by Lt. Colonel P. Barren; Naval Brigade by Capt. Lord Charles Beresford; Royal Artillery by Capt. G. Norton, and the Royal Engineers by Major Darward.

Major General Sir Herbert Stewart

General Sir Charles Wilson

After leaving Gakdul before Abu Klea, the Column marched out with 300 men of the Heavies, 367 of the Guards, 360 of the Mounted Infantry, 100 Royal Sussex, 3 troops (90 men) of 19th Hussars, 30 men and 3 guns from Royal Artillery, 30 men and one Gardner Gun of the Naval Brigade, and 25 Royal Engineers.

At Abu Klea the square was broken momentarily and the Column suffered heavy losses. Colonel Burnaby himself was killed, so Charles Wilson became second in command. At Abu Kru, four miles from the Nile, Stewart was mortally wounded and though he did not die until some time later, Wilson assumed entire command.

At the Nile the column met four of Gordon's steamers which contained over 100

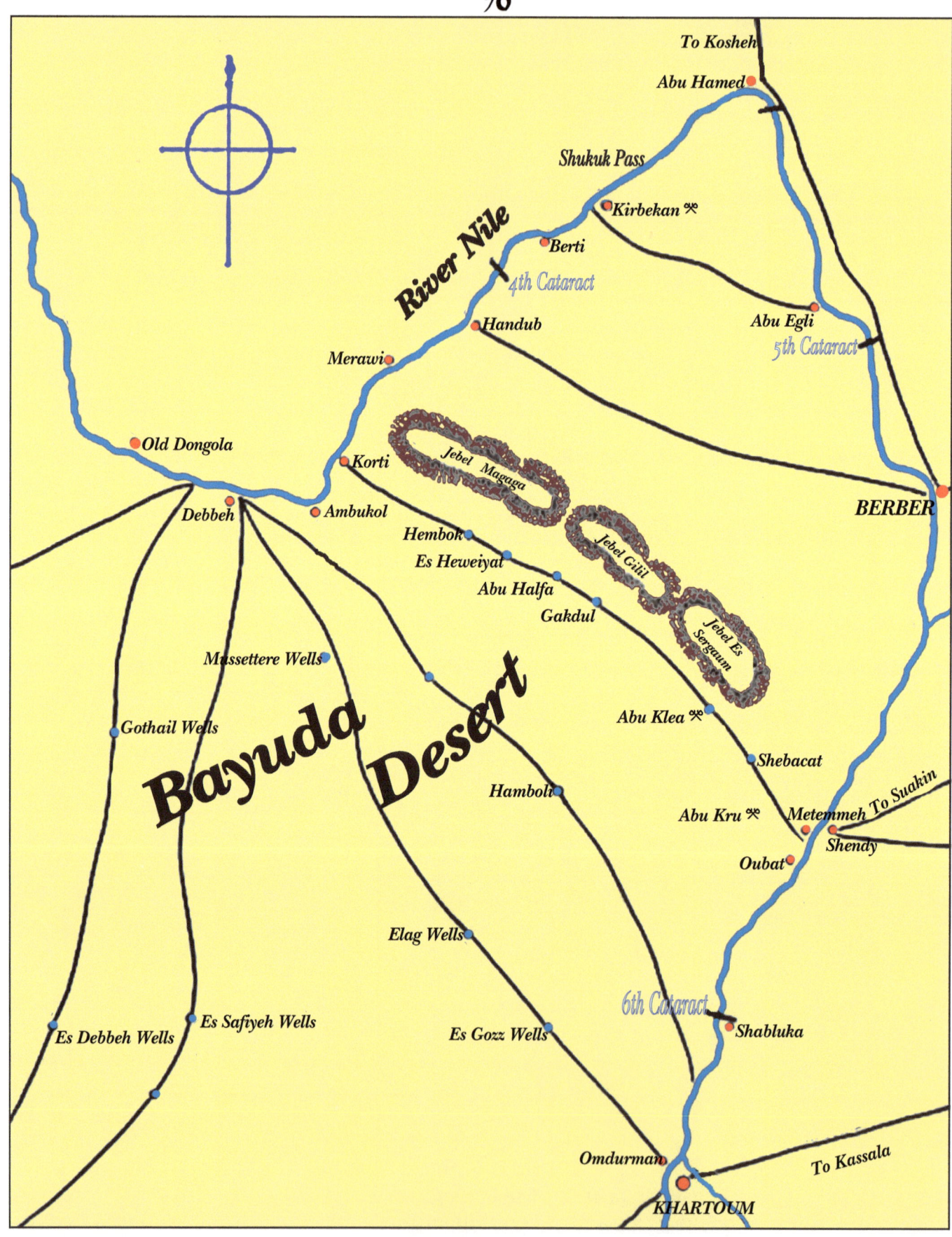

The route of the Camel Corps from Korti to Metemmeh across the Bayuda Desert was ultimately dictated by the availability of wells along the way. Of course, the Mahdists knew the wells, making it easy to choose where to fight the "Turuks" when they were most in need of water. But in Metemmeh four of Gordon's steamers were waiting, ready to make speed for Khartoum, the 6th Cataract at Shabluka notwithstanding.

of his irregular Black Sudanese riflemen (who also sported a small brass mountain gun). Taking two of these steamers, along with portions of the Naval Brigade, the Sudanese, and 20 of the Royal Sussex, Wilson and Beresford tried to steam up to Khartoum before it fell. They were two days late.

Redvers Buller was sent with the Royal Irish Regiment and the West Kents to take command of the Desert Column. He left Korti on January 29, 1885, and though ordered to attack and take Metemmeh, he decided his force was too small and began withdrawing them. An earlier attack on the Mahdist town by Wilson had failed. In the meantime Buller had left the West Kents to guard the wells on the route back and six companies of the Royal Irish joined the Desert Column at Gubat (Royle, II, p.307). The Light Camel Corps arrived at Abu Klea on the 20th of February and Sir Evelyn Wood and three companies of the West Kents arrived at Gakdul on the 17th. The Desert Column withdrew from the Sudan on foot, including even the 19th Hussars, who had only a few horses left.

Tactics of the Camel Corps

Despite what was depicted in the film *Khartoum*, the Camel Corps never used their camels for cover! Nor, as some war gamers might be tempted to do, did they ever fight mounted as cavalry. From the beginning they were conceived of as a mounted infantry force, and fought as mounted infantry.

In a memorandum dated 27th October, 1884 and signed by Redvers Buller, the following guidelines were issued:

"The soldiers of the Camel Regiments will fight only on foot. They are mounted on camels only to enable them to make long marches. The camel is a good traveler; but he is a slow mover. He cannot be managed as easily as a horse, and he cannot be mounted, or dismounted from, with great rapidity. The men of the Camel Corps must therefore trust solely to themselves and their weapons when once they have dismounted. This cannot be too strongly impressed upon the men. If we have to fight in the Sudan, we must expect to meet an enemy far outnumbering us, and who may at first charge recklessly home, apparently regardless of the intense fire we bring to bear upon him.

...The attack formation for infantry of our Drill Book is not intended to be employed against an enemy like the Arabs of the Sudan. It is designed to enable infantry to advance with the least possible loss over ground swept by a heavy fire from guns and rifles of an enemy as well armed and disciplined as ourselves, against whom an advance in close order would be impossible.

In acting against Arabs who are indifferently armed and bad shots, the open formation of the drill book is not necessary." (Colville, II, p.240).

Contrary to the portrayal in the movie *Khartoum*, when under attack the Camel Corps dismounted and lashed its camels' knees together, thus eliminating the need to keep "horse-holders" back per regular mounted infantry. The camels were placed in "a compact formation under guard" (see graphic) and the main force would march away to battle so as to keep the camels from being brought under fire. (Colville, V.I., p.102).

At Abu Kru, however, the Column was caught unaware and had to hastily construct a *zariba* of boxes and saddles keeping the camels inside of the square itself.

The Royal Engineers were brought along to

The Camel Corps's square being perfected by drills with fellow British troops prior to leaving Korti.

help construct earthworks like the stone forts surrounding the wells at Gakdul, as well as to work the pumps used to bring the water out of the wells. Occasionally they built smaller squares for the camels or wounded away from the main square, and often times the Naval Brigade's Gardner gun was placed in these smaller squares.

At Abu Klea the Column made the mistake of sending out skirmishers to cover the square. The Mahdists advanced so fast, and the square had to hold fire until the skirmishers got into the square, that only a few volleys were fired before the Mahdists engaged the British in hand-to-hand fighting. The cavalry was reserved for scouting. The guns were usually put in the corners of the square, or placed in smaller fortified *zaribas* outside of the main square.

Uniforms and Equipment

The official order concerning equipment for the Corps, issued on 4 August, 1884, included the following: waist kit, bandolier of 50 rounds, rifle, sword bayonet and scabbard, water bottle, and haversack.

The uniform was as follows: White helmet with white *pagri*, grey frock, yellow-ochre cord breeches, blue puttees, and boots. A Glengarry was carried in the *zulleetah* (saddle bag) (Colville, V. I, p. 239). Though spurs were issued, they were never used.

There were, however, variations to the

uniforms. The Guards and Heavies came over on the same boat, and to distinguish each unit they sewed the initials of their regiments on the right arm of their jackets. Red cloth was used and some examples are "RHG" (Royal Horse Guards—The Blues), "5L" (5th Lancers) or "1GG" (1st Grenadier Guards). In the last case the number was sewn above the letters "GG."

Even before marching off to the Sudan the Guards dyed their helmets coffee color and used brown leather belts. The exception to this was the contingent of RMLI who arrived in camp in "spotless" white helmet, kits and pouches (Gleichen, p.61). Though described by Gleichen as wearing regulation grey, Reynolds states that the RMLI of the Camel Corps wore khaki jackets and Bedford cord breeches (Reynolds, V. 35, p.390). The confusion may be due to the fact that the actual color of what was officially designated "khaki" was closer to grey than it later became. One Marine officer insisted on wearing his red coat and was later wounded by Mahdist rifle fire (Gleichen, p.174).

It is not clear when a tan khaki began to be worn. One picture of the Battle of Abu Klea by Y.D. Wollen in the National Army Museum (NAM) in Chelsea shows soldiers in an all khaki uniform with dark blue puttees, they also are wearing a khaki *pagri* with red stripes crossing it diagonally all the way around. A black and white picture in Marling shows what appears to be an all khaki uniform (photo opposite p. 132, Marling).

By the end of the campaign the Camel Corps was pretty rag-tag. On return to Gakdul some were wearing black serge trousers, some with puttees and others tied up under the knees (Gleichen, p. 243). On return to Egypt from Dongola in June, 1885 they were wearing khaki tunics and trousers, but probably without puttees. Many patched their pants with red saddle leather or with sacking. Few had boots, and some wore red Arab slippers (Gleichen p. 289).

Stewart was described as wearing a "shiny Guards' helmet" with an orange silk *pagri* (Symons), but Gleichen says he wore a yellow *pagri*. One picture from the Graphic reproduced in Preston's book shows a man that may be Stewart with a colored *pagri* and a brass spike in his helmet.

Based on the "G" just visible on the right arm, this is a Guardsman of either the "RHG" or "GG".

Royal Sussex:

All troops stationed in Egypt prior to the Sudan campaign were issued with grey serge uniforms (Gretton, p. 260). One photograph of the Royal Sussex shows the men wearing a variety of clothing; full khaki uniforms, khaki jackets with blue trousers, grey shirts with either blue or khaki trousers (Sandes photo opposite. p. 114). The helmets appear also to be khaki. Puttees were not always worn.

Royal Irish:

The Royal Irish marched out from Korti with Buller wearing khaki cotton drill jackets, trousers and helmet covers, grey woolen puttees, rolled greatcoats, wooden water bottles, haversacks, waist belts and braces and pouches. They were armed with the triangular socket

Illustration possibly Representing the Royal Irish Fusliers' khaki uniform.

bayonet and had a leather hand-guard sewn around the stock and barrel of their rifles. By the time they returned to Korti their boots were falling to bits, and their uniforms were patched with any material that was available (Gretton, pp. 274, 280, 285).

Naval Brigade:

A picture in Reynolds (V. 35, p.200) shows the Naval Brigade of the Desert Column in their regulation blue seaman's collar bordered in white, white straw hats with blue hat bands tied with the ends hanging over the back brim. A thin red arm-band is worn around both upper arms. The gaiters and waist-belt are brown, the haversack is white and the bayonet is in a black scabbard with a brass tip. Officers wore double-breasted frock coats and straw hats.

Wollen's painting in the National Army Museum (NAM), however, shows the Naval Brigade in all white uniforms, white helmets with blue *pagris*, and blue seaman's collars.

Gleichen shows the Naval Brigade with white helmets without *pagris* and either all blue or all white uniforms. The officer is wearing a frock coat with regulation naval cuff insignia. The officer is shown with a sword, and it should be noted that the bayonet the Naval Brigade used was a specially contrived cutlass with brass cutlass hilt that could be attached to the rifle as a bayonet. It is likely that any variation of white and blue uniforms were worn, with either straw hats or sun helmets.

19th Hussars:

19th Hussars, here in a more gray than blue jacket.

The Hussars were mounted on the same grey Syrian Arab horses, about 18 hands high, that the Egyptian Cavalry used (Biddulph, p. 247). The *Illustrated London News* (ILN) depicts them in white helmets, blue jackets, khaki breeches, blue puttees, brown belts and white haversacks. They may have occasionally worn blue trousers with yellow seam stripes, as such trousers turned up among Gordon's Sudanese at Korti after they had pilfered some of the British soldiers' kits (Gleichen, pp. 210-211).

Royal Artillery (RA) and Royal Engineers (R.E.):

Both the Artillery and the Engineers were dressed in the grey khaki uniform issued in Egypt. One photo of an R.E. Officer shows him in full khaki with no puttees, and with his helmet a darker shade with than his uniform (Sandes, photo opposite. p.114). The R.A. were armed with three 2.5" rifled muzzle loading screw guns, each carried by five camels (Headlam, pp. 211, 218-19).

Native Drivers:

There were some 120 drivers attached to the Column. They wore a red turban, a blue jersey that reached almost to the knees, white haversack, and "a brass ticket," though it is unclear just what a brass ticket was (Gleichen, p.107).

Gordon's Sudanese:

The officers of this irregular force were Egyptians and wore the regulation Egyptian uniform with red fez. The troops themselves wore red fezzes and white *jibbas*. They were armed with Remington rifles, spears, a cartridge belt worn around the waist, and sometimes bayonets attached to the cartridge belt. On the march back to Egypt they picked up many things from the British camp and some pictures show them in blue jerseys (with a white "5L" sewn on front) and blue infantry pants (Gleichen, pp. 210-11).

Saddles:

Saddles were various and often of poor quality. Though the Mounted Infantry Camel Regiment was issued with the best, most fell apart after hard use. Two *zulleetah* (saddle bags) were worn, one on each side. They were white with a broad red border. A brown leather *Namanqua* rifle bucket was worn on the off side over a leather water skin (*gubeleh*). A long stiff leather Egyptian water bottle (*mussek*) was worn on the left side. In front, a tan 30 pound bag of corn was strapped (three days rations for the camel— this sometime later was replaced by a net-bag of grass. All of this was covered with a red saddle cover. The head stall was black leather. The saddle cover for the Camel Corps, Naval Brigade and all other troops was always red, though I have been unable to locate the peculiar pattern shown in the movie *Khartoum*.

Note the saddle being carried.

Conclusions

In making rules for war games one should keep in mind that the Camel Corps fought on foot. They should, when mounted, move faster than infantry but somewhat slower than cavalry, and perhaps have a bigger decrease in movement when dismounting and mounting. Perhaps it should take longer for them to go from marching order to a square formation with the camels in a different square or in the center of the main square. Saddles and boxes can be used for cover—but please, never the camels themselves—they suffered enough from the British soldier without adding that! As the camels were lashed securely, one needn't hold back the usual one out of every four men to secure them as the normal Mounted Infantry—the entire force can be placed on the firing line.

Guards Camel Corps as mounted.
Note on left camel grass fodder net bag.

Abu Klea--The Other "Broken Square"

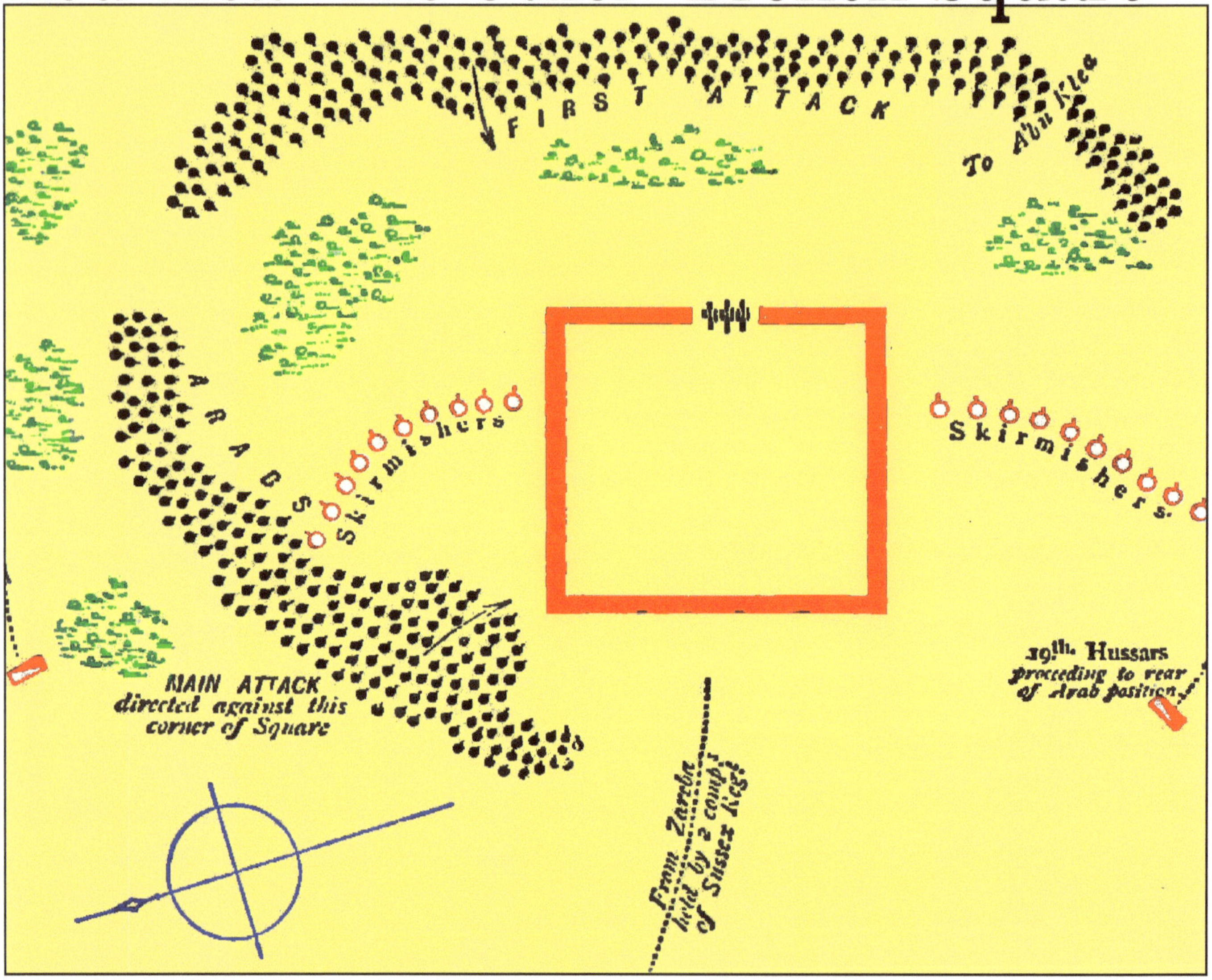

The Red Coats are wrong, but this still gives a fair impression of just how close this action was.

*"A day with Fuzzy on the rush,
Will last a healthy Tommy for a year...."*

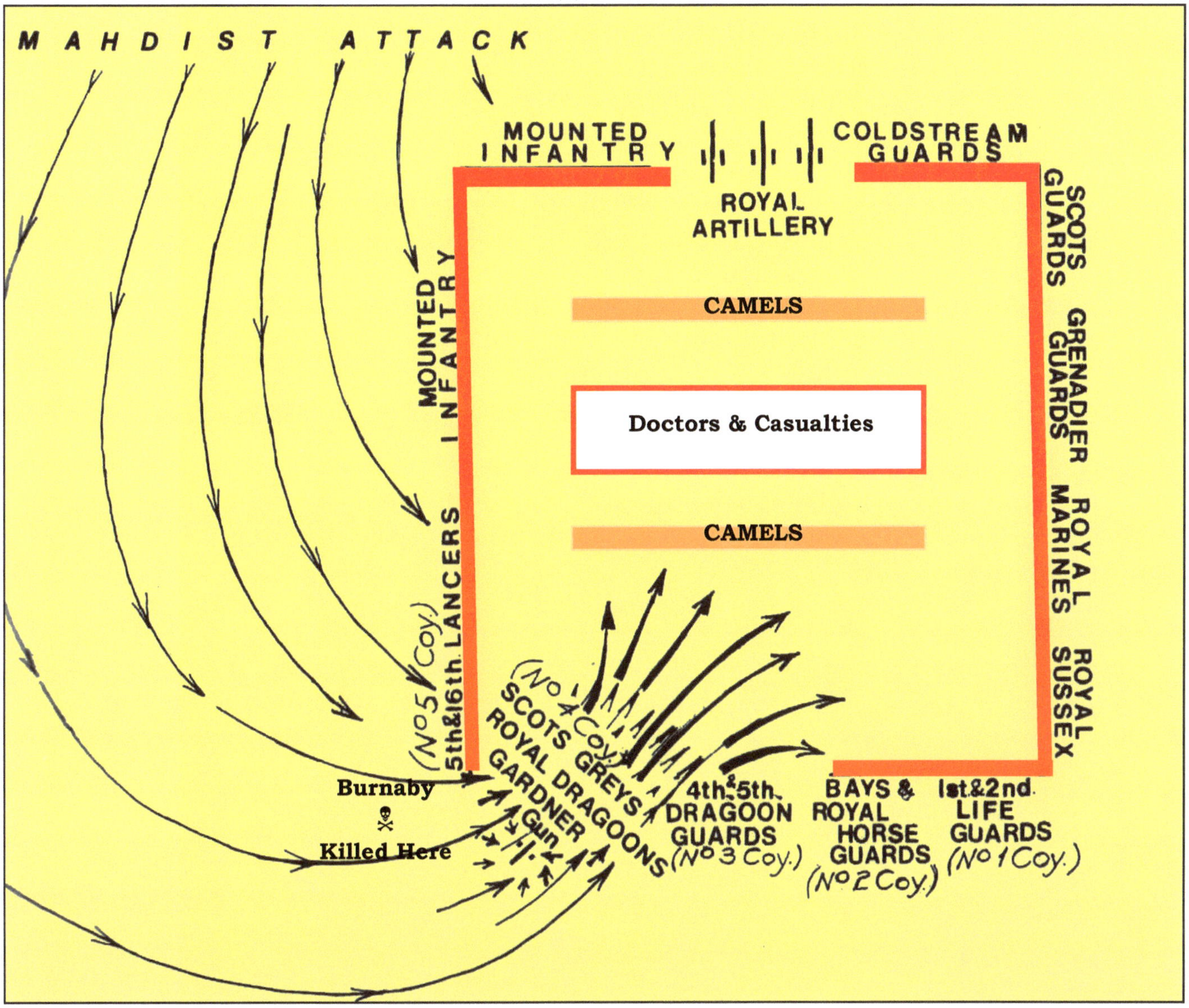

The Ansar flags are not right for this battle, but William B. Wollen's famous painting speaks for itself.

The Gordon Relief Expedition: The Nile Route, 1884-85

By Douglas Johnson

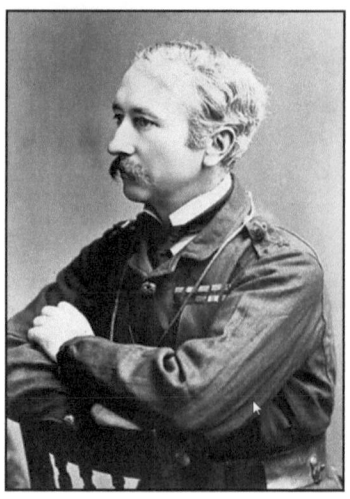

Wolseley

When Sir Garnet Wolseley arrived in Cairo on 9 September 1884, he had at his disposal from the British garrison in Egypt 1 cavalry regiment, 1 horse and 1 field battery, 1 camel battery, 2 garrison batteries, 2 Companies of Royal Engineers, 11 1/2 battalions of infantry and 1 battalion of Royal Marines. In addition to this, another infantry battalion was on the way from India, one from the West Indies, and two more Royal Engineer (R.E.) Companies from England (Colvile I: 52-3). It was from these troops, with only a few additions, that the Gordon Relief Expedition was drawn.

Two routes were under consideration for the advance to Khartoum: From Suakin to Berber (or some other point along the Nile), or from Egypt to Khartoum following the route of the Nile.

Lt.-Gen. Sir F. Stephenson, commander of the British garrison in Egypt, preferred the Suakin-Berber route. It was shorter, it had frequently been used by the Egyptian army, and it contained a number of sources of water during the latter half of the year (Colvile I: 32-4). Wolseley preferred the Nile route, claiming that the water

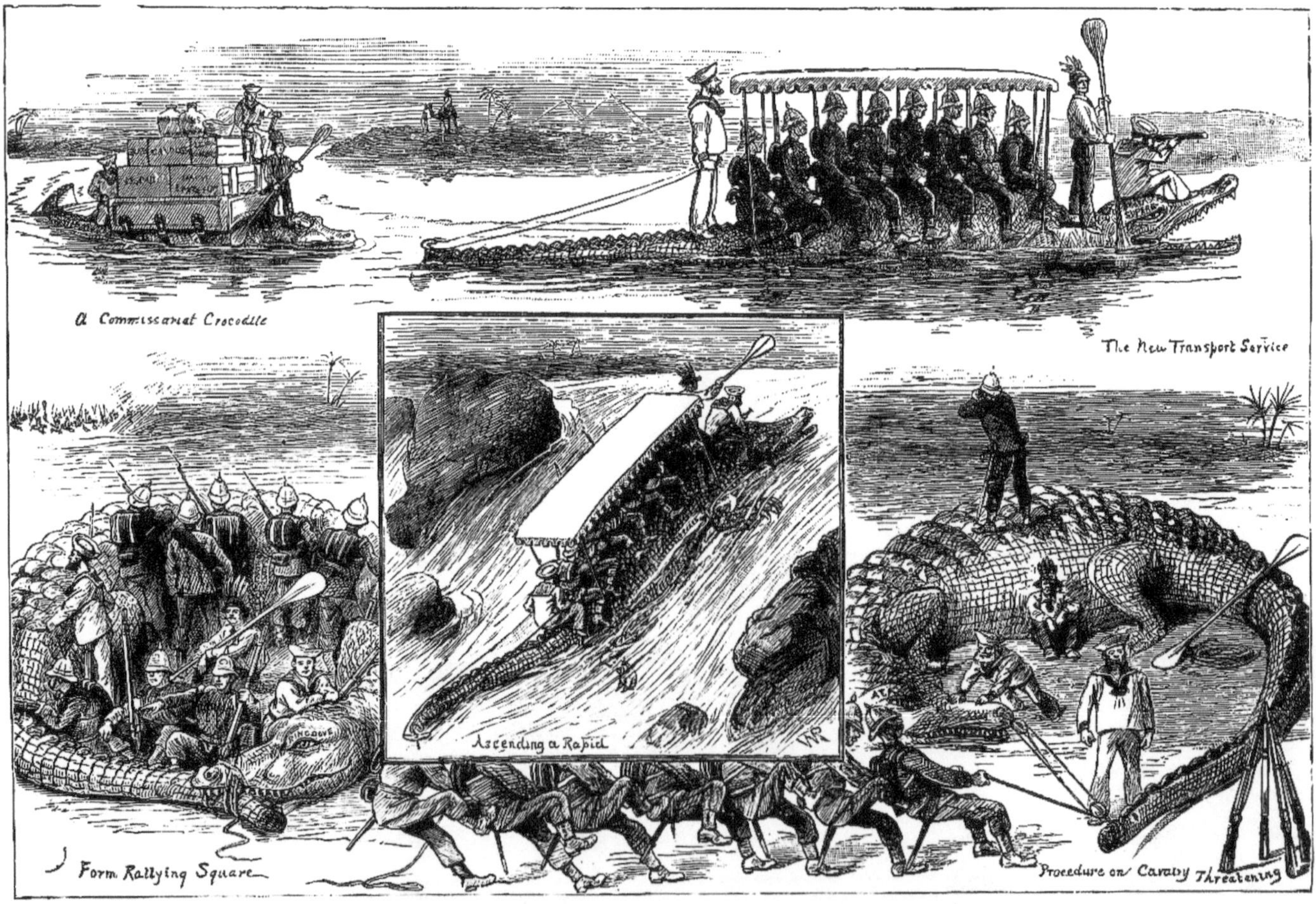

THE NILE EXPEDITION FOR THE RELIEF OF GENERAL GORDON—THE TRANSPORT DIFFICULTY SOLVED

E. de S. H. Browne | Rev. J. T. Hartley (Champion 1879, 1880) | C. W. Grinstead | Miss Maud Watson (Lady Champion) | H. F. Lawford (Irish Champion, Winner of Wimbledon Gold Prize, 1884) | W. Renshaw (Champion 1881, 1882, 1883, 1884)

The Graphic's suggestion of September 20, 1884 for making practical use of the omnipresent Nile Crocodiles to solve the transport problems of the Gordon Relief Expedition.

supply between Suakin and Berber was problematic, and that an advance by river in small boats (*a la* the Red River Expedition) would be faster and safer. In the end it was Wolseley who chose the river route, and it is possible to argue that his experience in Canada may have led him astray.

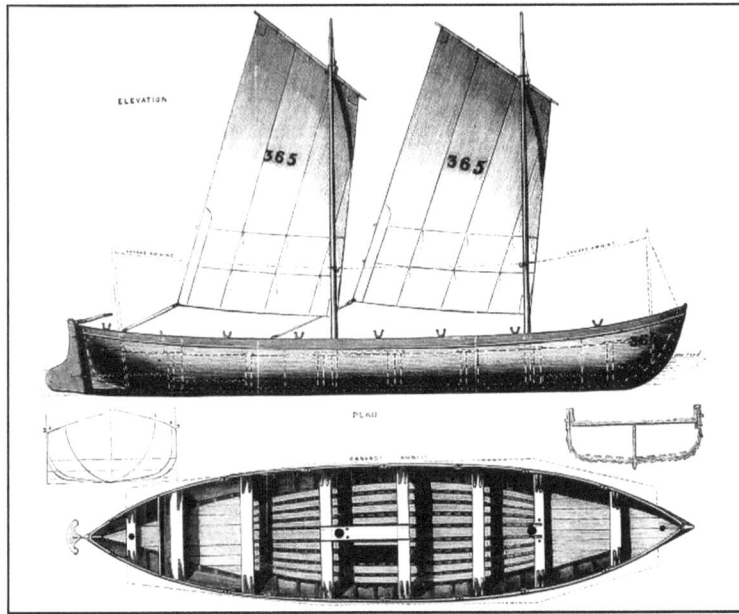

The 800 small whalers he had specially constructed in England were light, and it was possible to get them through or around the rapids and cataracts of the steadily falling river. They were, however, cramped, taking only 10 men each (plus one man at the rudder and perhaps another on the bow), they could carry few supplies and gave the men little room for movement. Their masts were only 10 feet tall; thus far too short to catch the breezes that blew above the banks of the river. This meant that the soldiers in them had to row upstream most of the way. By contrast the, locally built sailing *nuggars* commonly used along the Nile had 80 foot high sails which caught every sigh in the breeze, allowing them to sail where the whalers rowed. They could also carry 150 men and three months' supplies comfortably. They frequently sailed through the shallower rapids, though all boats had to be hauled through the cataracts. One *nuggar* carrying Egyptian soldiers sailed from Dal to Akasha in three days, while it took a convoy of whalers to travel the same distance in 23 (Ternan; 50-1). However, these craft could not be carried around the rapids, the way the whalers could, and it was decided that they would be unable to boat through the cataracts after October. Some 296 native craft were deployed along the river as far as Meroe (including 48 *nuggars*), but they were not used for the advance to Berber and Abu Hamid. The progress of the whalers was painfully slow. They had not even reached their first objective—Berber—by the time Khartoum fell.

To guide the whalers through the river, Wolseley imported 266 West African Krumen (whom he had first used in the Ashanti Campaign) and an *ad hoc* detachment

Wolseley's whalers stroking up the Nile.

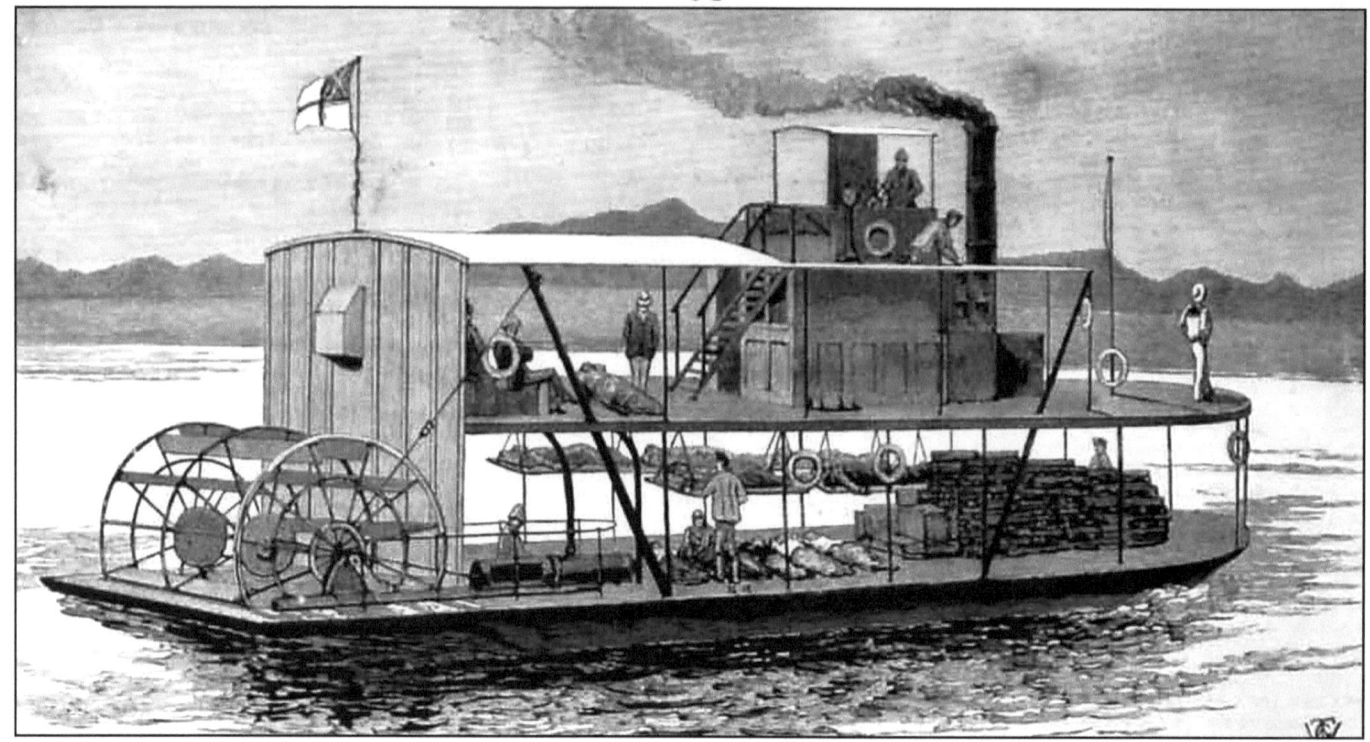
One of the hurriedly ordered Nile steamers for the Gordon Relief Expedition designed and built by Yarrow.

of 380 Canadian voyageurs. Some 396 Egyptians and Nubians were used to man the native boats, and 847 Egyptians and Nubians were assigned to the whalers. Another 25 officers and 784 NCO's and men of the Egyptian Army were placed in the whalers or along the lines of communications (Colvile I: 66-7). Only a few of the Canadian *voyageurs* were experts on the river—some being veterans of the Red River Expedition, but a considerable number were lumberjacks or city dwellers—"dead beats" as Col. Butler, another veteran of the Red River, called them. In his opinion they gave a very mixed performance (Butler: 143, 177-8).

There were 36 steamers used along the lower reaches of the river (including two new Yarrow boats, the *Lotus* and the *Water Lily*). These never saw action, but some were armed with one or two Nordenfelt or Gardner guns. Of the 800 whalers, 600 went up to Korti, while 200 were used for convoy work from Sarras to Dongola (Colvile I: 72, 129).

Narratives of the Nile Column make very dull reading, except to those who love messing about in boats. The concentration of troops south of Egypt was a long process. By 18 November, 1884, there were some 10,260 British troops in the Sudan or along the frontier, distributed as follows:

At Dongola (1355): 45 HQ, 440 Mtd. Inf. Camel Regt., 820 Royal Sussex, 50 Details.
Between Dongola & Dal (970): 320 Guards Camel Regt., 600 South Staffords and 50 R.E.
Between Dal & Gemai (1955): 670 Duke of Cornwall's Lt. Inf., 620 Essex and 225 Black Watch, 370 voyageurs & Krumen, 70 RN Between Halfa & Dongola: 300 19th Hussars
At Halfa, Sarras & Gemai (1895): 450 Black Watch, 85 R.A., 300 R.E., 225 Hvy. Camel Regt., 135 Lt. Camel Regt., 100 RMLI, 150 Commissariat & Trans-port Corps, 170 Bearer Co. & Moveable Field Hospital, 60 Departmentals, 220 sick.
Between Halfa and Assouan (1370): 720 Gordon Highlanders, 230 Heavy Camel Regt.,

250 Lt. Camel Regt., 70 Transport Co., 50 19th Hussars, 50 R.E.

At Assouan (1840): 750 Royal West Kents, 750 Royal Irish, 120 Sick, 50 Gordon Highlanders, 120 Essex, 50 sundries, 500 Cameron Highlanders, plus details 75 details (Colvile I: 129-30).

In addition to this, the Egyptian Army on the Nile by 1 January, 1885 was distributed as follows:

South of Halfa: 5 Btns. Infantry (20 British officers, 99 native officers, 2381 NCOs & men), 5 troops of cavalry (1 British officer, 14 native officers, 345 NCOs & men), 1 camel battery (1 British officer, 4 native officers, 115 men), 1 camel Co. (2 British officers, 5 native officers, 154 men).

At Assouan: 1 Btn. Infantry (2 British officers, 24 native officers and 451 NCOs & men), 1 troop cavalry (5 officers, 65 men), 1 artillery battery (5 officers, 93 men).

(Colvile I: 227)

With the exception of the camel battery and the camel Company, the Egyptian Army units were confined entirely to support roles.

The entire expedition assembled at Korti during December 1884 and January 1885. On 27 December Wolseley issued an order sending out two preliminary columns, the Desert Column and the Nile Column. The Nile Column was to occupy Abu Hamid, Berber and other points along the Nile, collect supplies and forward them to the Desert Column as it proceeded to Khartoum (Colvile II: 82). The rest of the expedition assembled at Korti would follow by river. The Nile Column was under the command of Major-General Earle (Chief of Staff) with Col. (Brigadier-General as from 7 January, 1885) H. Brackenbury as principle Staff Officer and Second-in-Command, and Lt.-Cols. Alleyne and Colvile, Major Slade and Col. Sir W. F. Butler. The force consisted of:

- 1 Squadron 19th Hussars
- 1st Btn. (38th) South Staffordshire Regt., 2nd Btn. (46th) Duke of Cornwall's Light Infantry (D.C.L.I.)
- 1st Btn. (42nd) Royal Highlanders (Black Watch)
- 1st Btn. (75th) Gordon Highlanders
- 1 camel battery Egyptian artillery (six 7-pdrs)
- 1 Co. Egyptian Camel Corps
- Headquarters and 400 camels of the 11th Transport Co.

The 2nd Btn. (56th) Royal Essex Regt. was originally assigned to the line of communications between Meroe and Abu Hamid, but this order was subsequently cancelled (Colvile II: 81).

The first detachments left Korti on 28 and 29 December and consisted of the S. Staffords (545 all ranks), two boats of the 26th Co. R.E., and half a troop (26 all ranks) of the 19th Hussars. The first concentration point was Hamdab, which Earle reached on 4 January, 1885. It was there that the rest of the troops assembled, including the D.C.L.I. which, undermanned as all regiments were, had been filled up with men from the R. West Kents. Wolseley now ordered Earle to take two battalions to advance through the Manasir country (where Stewart had been murdered), letting the rest of his troops follow to Abu Hamid where they would then march on Berber. Earle would take with him the guns of the camel battery of the Egyptian artillery (the only artillery with the Nile Column) and some 310 Sudanese troops from the Mudir (Governor) of Dongola's command (the Mudir was the last Egyptian official with any authority left in any of the provinces of the northern Sudan).

Throughout 22-3 January the troops at Hamdab practiced forming squares on the broken rocky bank of the river, a maneuver they were fortunately not, required to made during their advance. By the end of the 23rd the last of the British troops arrived at Hamdab (except for part of the Gordon Highlanders and the D.C.L.I.), and the Mudir's troops, under his *vakil* (deputy) Ahmad Effendi Suleiman, assembled on the bank opposite Hamdab.

Earle began his march on 24 January, 1885. Col. Butler commanded the advance guard both on the river and on land. He had with him 1 squadron of the 19th Hussars (about 60 men) and one Company of the Egyptian Camel Corps (about 40 men) to patrol to the front and on the right flank of the column (and the left bank of the river). On the left flank (right bank of the river) Col. Colvile took command of the Mudir's troops who, carrying their baggage on their own donkeys and camels, and foraging for themselves rather than being supplied from the boats, were able to move quickly and keep pace with the rest of the column. Col. Alleyne took command of the main boat column, which consisted of the S. Staffords, the Black Watch, 2 boats of the 26th Co. R.E., half the Field Hospital, and a repairing party. A number of *voyageurs* under Lt. Col. Denison were assigned to the column, along with an extra boat containing a naval detachment of 1 officer and 11 men. The mounted troops, baggage (11th Transport Co.), the Mudir's troops and the Headquarters all set out by land. The D.C.L.I., Egyptian artillery and two Companies of the Gordon Highlanders came up to Hamdab after the advance force departed. As the advance force abandoned each subsequent camp, they were replaced by the two rear battalions and the Egyptian artillery. In all, the column totaled about 2400 men in 217 boats, though it never concentrated in one place until after the battle of Kirbekan (Colvile II: 87, 89. Butler: 266, 292-4).

It was hard going. The boats stowed their masts and sails and had to row upstream. The small horses of the Hussars were already exhausted before the advance began and had to cover broken ground all the way. Scouting by the Mudir's troops was confined to those few officers who had riding camels (occasionally one of the baggage camels was pressed into service). Throughout the advance detached Companies of infantry had to march ahead overland to secure positions for the main column, and then march back to their own boats to retrace the same distance by river. Mahdist cavalry scouts shadowed the force from their first day out of Hamdab (Colvile II: 89-92. Butler: 294-5).

Both flanks made fleeting contact with the Ansar on 27 January. An Ansar force estimated at between 3,000-5,000, but with only 300 rifles and limited ammunition, was reported camped at Berti. The Nile Column established an advance base at Ghamra, seven miles south of Berti, on 31 January, only to find that the Ansar had withdrawn the previous day (Colvile II: 88, 92). Butler moved to Berti with the mounted troops and half the Black Watch on 1 February, and the remainder of the column was ordered up to Ghamra, but it took them some three days to struggle through the Rahmi cataract to reach the new *zariba* at Berti. On 12 February they were stretched along the river as follows:

- 1/2 Black Watch   in Rahmi Cataract
  HQ, mounted troops, guns, S. Staffords,
- 1/2 Black Watch, Convoy   at Ghamra
- The Mudir's Troops   Urn-Kumb'atat Is. (opposite Ghamra)
- 1/2 D.C.L.I.   Warrak
- other 1/2 D.C.L.I.   Um Habwa Cataract
- Gordon Highlander   Kab an-Nat   (Colvile II: 93)

While the force continued concentrating at Berti, Butler made another advance camp ("Castle Camp") a few miles upstream, and the Black Watch and S. Staffords moved there. On 5 February Butler madee a reconnaissance around *Jebal* (Mt) Kirbekan just below the mouth of the Shukuk Pass. Returning to the camp that day, Butler received orders to halt all forward movement. The next day Brackenbury reached his camp with the news that Khartoum had fallen. The troops were not told. The same day a Mahdist force advanced out of the Shukuk pass and reoccupied Kirbekan.

From 8 February, Earle strengthened the main camp at Berti while he waited new orders. He now had 2,966 officers and men, 140 horses, and 580 camels, in addition to 300 or so of the Mudir's men. Opposing him at Kirbekan were about 1000 Ansar with 150 rifles (Colvile II: 96 7).

On 8 February, Earle received orders to continue this advance to Berber. On the same day, Earle ordered the Gordons up to Berti while the S. Staffords and mounted men advanced out of "Castle Camp." The next day the Black Watch followed them while the Mudir's troops now crossed to the left bank of the river to prepare to occupy the Manasir country in the rear of the advancing British. The S. Staffords, Black Watch, two guns of the Egyptian artillery, and the mounted troops were now brought together at a *zariba* facing Kirbekan, while the D.C. L. I. and the Gordons remained at Berti (Colvile II: 100-1).

Butler had scouted around Kirbekan on 8 February. "There were the Arabs at last," he later wrote. "On the red granite groups near the river, and on the white streaked crest of Kirbekan the white tunics of the Mahdi's soldiers were plainly visible" (Butler: 326). Jebal Kirbekan itself was a jagged black rock arising out of the yellowish sand, "More like a moonscape than anything on earth" (Hamilton: 177). It was 300 feet high, 600 yards long, and came to within 200 yards of the river. "When viewed obliquely it had the appearance of a gigantic wall built across the desert (Colvile II: 102). On top the Ansar had built low stone breastworks. Their force completely blocked the way to Abu Hamid.

Earle was determined to dislodge the Ansar from the mountain. A few days before the battle he reminisced with Butler about the Crimean battles of his youth, especially Alma, "The last battle of the old order'" (Butler: 324). The assault on Kirbekan was to be a similar line battle. "None of your Abu Klea or Metemmeh squares," snorted Ian Hamilton in his memoirs. We would have been shot to bits by their riflemen had we tried sheep tactics against shock tactics (Hamilton: 178).

It was not to be a frontal assault, as Butler had found a way around the flank. Assembled in front of Kirbekan, Earle had 1169 men of all ranks including the staff:
- 19th Hussars   5 officers   78 men
- S. Staffords   23 "   533 "
- Black Watch (7 Cos. only)   20 "   417 "
- Egyptian Artillery   (2 guns)   2   22"
- Egyptian Camel Corps   6   42 "
- Medical Staff   7   12 "   (Colvile II: 104)

The force was collected in and around the *zariba* in front of Kirbekan on 9 February. On the 10th they deployed as follows:
- 1 Co. Black Watch in the *zariba* with the baggage and boats.
- 2 Cos. S. Staffords and 2 guns E.A. under Col. Alleyne on two low hillocks between the *zariba* and the mountain.
- 6 Cos. S. Staffords under Col. Eyre in 1/2 Btn. columns at intervals of two Companies.

- 6 Cos. Black Watch under Col. Green in the same formation.
  The Field Hospital and reserve ammo camels in between, moving with the left column. 19th Hussars in front. Egyptian Camel Corps covering the left flank.

(Colvile II: 104)

At 7:15 AM the column left the *zariba* with Butler leading the front. They marched obliquely along the Mahdists' front, but keeping behind low hills and ridges. In order to confuse the Mahdists about the ultimate direction of the flanking movement, Butler detached the Camel Corps and sent them towards the granite knolls to engage the enemy on the main ridge. The Camel Corps opened up a rapid fire, as if in prelude to a frontal assault. At about the same time (8:30 AM) the infantry reached the gap between the hills, from which they were to start their rear attack. The artillery, seeing them in position, opened fire on the Ansar, hitting the summit of the hill with their first shot (Butler: 334-5. Colvile II: 104).

As the infantry rounded the eastern spur of the mountain, they came under fire, particularly from a group of Ansar occupying a low spur. One Company of the Staffords was sent to occupy the spur, another to rocks on the left to keep down the fire from Jebel Kirbekan, and the column continued its advance under increasing fire from the summit of the mountain. Col. Eyre was sent with two Companies of the S. Staffords to storm the hill, but they were pinned down by heavy fire about a third of the way up the mountain, and Col. Eyre was shot and killed.

By this time two Companies of the Black Watch had been sent to occupy the ground between the mountain and the river to prevent the Ansar from retreating to the bank. Three Companies of the S. Staffords and four Companies of the Black Watch were then sent to attack four low hills where a strong body of Ansar were found. A heavy fire was brought to bear on these hills as the two advance companies of the Black Watch finished clearing the bank. When the main troops were in position in rocks 400 yards from the hillocks, Earle sent two Black Watch companies and one S.

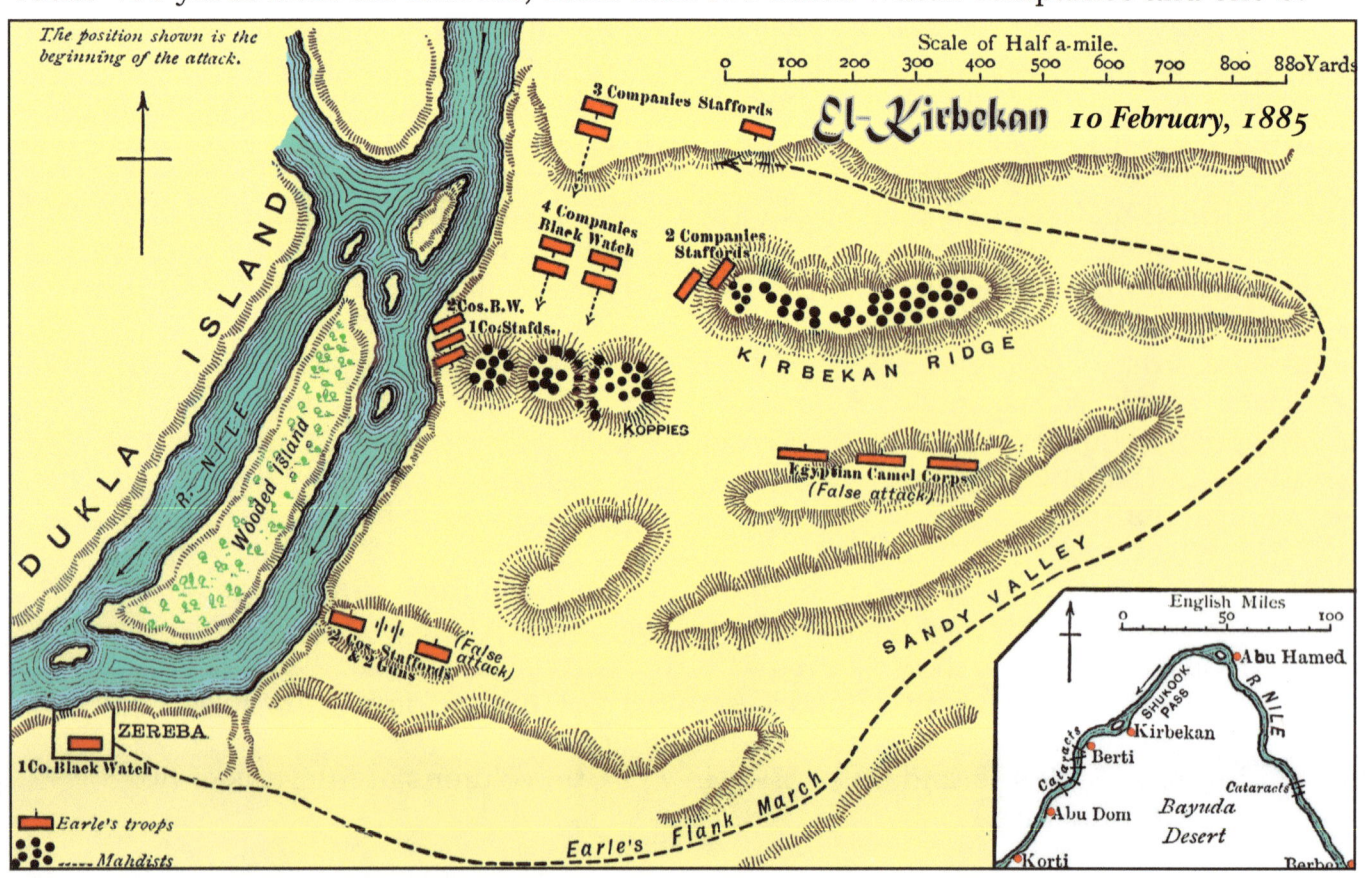

Battle of Kirbekan as seen from the position of the Egyptian battery.

Stafford company along the bank to storm the hillock nearest the river. This done, the other hillocks were now enfiladed, but the Mahdists had good cover. One company of Black Watch under Col. Green was charged by spearmen but repulsed them, with the loss of Lt. Col. Coveney. The Highlanders then charged and took the remaining hillocks. A few men remained defending a small stone hut, and it was while the Black Watch were attempting to dislodge them that Earle himself was shot and killed. The thatch of the hut was then set on fire and the occupants burned to death.

The house where Earle met his fate.

Brackenbury now assumed command. The two Companies of S. Staffords were still pinned down a third of the way up Kirbekan. They were under heavy fire and down to only four rounds per man. One reason why they had not already been swept away by a Mahdist counterattack was the presence of the Egyptian Camel Corps along the base of the mountain. For four hours they had poured continuous fire into the Ansar on the summit. Brackenbury now sent the rest of the Staffords to the relief of the two Companies in trouble. They climbed the mountain in broken rushes, bayoneting the Ansar at the top, who fought to the very end. The position was finally taken at 12:30 PM. The Egyptian Camel Corps won the grateful praise of the S. Staffords and of General Brackenbury (Colvile II: 105-8, 279-80).

The total British losses were 3 officers and 7 men killed (two of whom were Camel Corps), 4 officers and 43 men wounded. The Ansar lost about 200 killed out of a force of 800 or so men actually present at the battle. Among those killed were the three main Amirs of the force: Musa wad Abu Hijal, Ali wad Hussain, and Hamid al-Kalik. Some 41 donkeys and camels, 58 rifles, 4 fowling pieces, 2 flintlock muskets, 1 revolver, 22 swords, 53 spears and 10 flags were captured at Kirbekan (Colvile II: 108-9, 279-80. Royle II: 321).

Butler took a few Hussars to the main Ansar camp (now abandoned) at the mouth of the Shukuk Pass above Kirbekan, but his force was too small and too exhausted to try to seize the other end of the pass. Two Companies of Black Watch were left on the field as the rest of the force returned to the *zariba*. Earle, Eyre and Coveney were buried side-by-side on the river bank at sunset.

Of the loss of three senior officers Butler wrote, "A week ago this would have seemed a trifling price to pay for any rock or ridge that brought us nearer to Khartoum, but now it is different. Now there was no Khartoum—there was nothing behind that black range whose bare possession would have been dearly won at the cost of the humblest life lost that day..." (Butler: 342). Wolseley was equally despondent. "Our other losses were trifling," he noted in his diary after learning of the deaths of Earle,

Eyre and Coveney, "but they all mean so many men less for our final coup, & these Arabs can afford to lose 10 for every one Englishman either killed or wounded (Preston: 142-3).

The next day (11 February) the two Black Watch companies on the battlefield were relieved by a wing of the D.C.L.I., two other Black Watch companies and 2 companies of the S. Staffords. Another wing of the D.C.L.I. and the rest of the artillery and convoy arrived at the *zariba*. The Gordons reached "Castle Camp" the same day, and the *zariba* at Kirbekan on the 12th. From then until 21 February the column continued its advance through Manasir country, this time with the D.C.L.I. and Gordons leading and the S. Staffords and Black Watch bringing up the rear. The Shukuk Pass was secured and Hebba, the village where Stewart was murdered, was destroyed on 21 February. There was no further serious fighting (Colvile II:111-21).

On 21 February Wolseley postponed the advance, and on 24 February the column was ordered back to Meroe. The force now consisted of :

- 19th Hussars   96 all ranks
- 26th Co. R.E.   22 "
- S. Staffords   566
- Black Watch   582 "
- D.C.L.I.   575 "
- Gordon Highlanders   511
- Naval Brigade   12 "
- *Voyageurs*   66 "
- Egyptian Artillery   90 "
- Egyptian Camel Corps   97 "
- Egyptian Cavalry   7 "   (Stacey: 241)

They began the return journey on 25 February, this time much helped by the current of the river. The column was under orders not to stop if fired on from the river banks. Two men were stationed in the bow of each boat to return fire if necessary. If under serious attack, the boats were to head for the nearest shore and deploy under the covering fire of the riflemen in the bows. No such attack materialized. The column stopped briefly at Berti to await reinforcements and then continued to Meroe, which they reached on 5 March. On 7 March Brackenbury started the return to Korti, leaving the Black Watch, 1 troop 19th Hussars, the Egyptian Camel Corps, and a detachment of Royal Engineers at Meroe as a rearguard. Some 6000 Ansar followed the column as far as Berti but advanced no further (Colvile II: 124-32. Royle II: 324-69).

The withdrawal from the Sudan continued throughout June, 1885. By 26 June the troops were distributed as follows:

Dongola: 1st Btn. R. West Kents, 1 Squad. 19th Hussars, 2 guns 1/1 Southern Division R.A.
Hafir: 2 Cos. S. Staffords, 1 Squad. 19th Hussars, 2 guns 1/1 S. Div. R.A.
Fatma: 2 Cos. S. Staffords
Kubuda: Baker's Gendarmerie, 9th Sudanese Btn. Egyptian Army, 600 total
Shaban: 4 Cos. S. Staffords
Kaibar: 500 Egyptian troops (whaler crews)
Kaibar-Abri: Squad. 19th Hussars, 2 guns 1/1 S. Div. R.A.
Abri & Dal: 2 small Egyptian garrisons
Akasha: 500 Egyptian troops, 300 1st Btn. R. Sussex
Halfa-Akasha RR: 400 Egyptians

Halfa:	Mtd. Inf. Camel Regt., 4 Cos. 2nd Btn. D.C.L.I., 2 Egyptian Camel Batteries, Egyptian Camel Corps
Halfa-Assouan:	1/2 Lt. Camel Regt.
Assouan:	1st Btn. Yorkshire Regt., 4 Cos. R. Sussex, HQ, 26th Co. R.E.
North of Assouan:	Black Watch, 2nd Btn. Es-sex, 1st Btn. Gordons, 1st Btn. R. Irish Guards Camel Regt., 1/2 Lt. Camel Rect., 1/2 D.C.L.I., Heavy Camel Regt. (Colvile II: 174-6)

On 27 June, Wolseley handed over command of troops in Egypt to Sir F. Stephenson. On 5 July Dongola was evacuated, on 21 July Brackenbury handed over command of the frontier to General Grenfell (Sirdar of the Egyptian Army), and on 9 September the Gordon Highlanders were the last of the Gordon Relief Expedition to leave Alexandria for home (Colvile II: 219-21).

The strength of the Gordon Relief Expedition was such that it could contemplate only the relief of Khartoum, not the conquest of the Sudan, or even of a significant portion of the country north of Khartoum. It could advance only so long as Gordon held enough men in the garrison of Khartoum to prevent the Mahdi from opposing the expedition with enough men either to defeat it or stop it. Once Khartoum fell, the expedition was not in a position to face the entire Mahdist Army. Both the Desert and Nile Columns won pyrrhic victories, and while the losses they suffered were not large in themselves, they were large enough to slow down and finally prevent a final advance in force. The Mahdist strategy in this respect, was successful. The Mahdists had hoped that they could destroy the Desert Column, but they sent insufficient forces to the north to do this. Nevertheless they did prevent both columns from joining up and advancing to Khartoum. It was a defensive strategy, but it worked well enough.

The Infantry

The infantry were issued with the standard red serge Mediterranean frock coat, which probably did not have regimental facing colors, and blue serge trousers (Syons: 99-100). Pictures of troops at the beginning of the advance show them wearing red coats, blue trousers, white helmets and belts; officers often went without gaiters or puttees (ILN 17 Jan. 1885, p. 40 and 24 Jan. 1885, pp. 92-3). It was intended that the men would march and fight in red, and they wore their red uniforms on church parades as well (Keltie & Melven: 456, Archer IV: 160). They were issued with both buff and black valises, but used the black valise (Colvile It 231). Belts and haversacks were white, but the Egyptian service water bottles were made of brown leather with brown straps, and were a square, almost rectangular shape (displays in the Scottish United Services Museum and the Royal Highlanders Museum).

However, fatigues were worn more often than red coats. Gray flannel shirts were issued (Symons: 100), and these, along with trousers or trews (in the case of the Highland regiments) were worn in the boats. The Royal Irish Regiment usually rowed clad only in their greatcoats, or in the nude, to save their specially designed uniforms for the final march to Khartoum (Gretton: 265).

Black Watch: The Black Watch had been issued gray serge frocks in Egypt, but in the boats wore gray shirts and tartan trews (often patched with various materials such as sail cloth) with their white spats underneath their trews. When the trews wore out they were replaced by "gray suits." At Kirbekan the Black Watch wore their kilts, red doublets with blue facings, white helmets and red hackles. The doublets, too, became ragged and patched towards the end of the campaign (Keltie & Melven: 449, 455-6. ILN

7 Feb. 1885, p. 139, sketch by Melton Prior).

South Staffordshire Regiment: The Staffords, too, wore red coats at Kirbekan. Contemporary sketches do not make it clear whether the coats were plain without facing colors, or whether the Staffords wore coats with their standard white facings. It is likely that the facing colors were absent. They also wore white helmets and white *pagris*, blue trousers without gaiters or puttees (Grant III: 89, 185, Butler: picture opposite p. 342, Brackenbury: 145).

Royal Engineers: While on duty, the R.E. wore fatigues like the infantry. One picture shows them in gray shirts, blue trousers with red seam stripes, and no puttees or gaiters (Melton Prior in ILN 31 Jan. 1885, p. 106).

Gordon Highlanders: The official history of the Gordons states that the regiment worked in fatigues while in the boats, but marched and fought in Highland dress (Gardyne: 264). The only "engagement" they were involved in was the burning of Hebba, but they never fought in a battle. However, it appears that for a few days towards the end of February they wore kilts and red doublets with yellow facings.

Canadian *Voyageurs*: The men dressed in dark gray Norfolk jackets, trousers and broad-brimmed felt hats; the officers were dressed in outfits of a lighter shade of gray. Some men worked in jerseys and moccasins (Stacey).

Uniform Key
(1) 19th Hussars (2) Egyptian Camel Corps
(3) Mudir's Troops (4) Black Watch
(5) British Infantry, work order

Mudir of Dongola's Troops: These were dressed in the old white uniform of the Egyptian infantry, with red fezzes, some having leggings and others not, some having boots and the rest barefoot. Some also wore white turbans wrapped around their fezzes. All were armed with Remington rifles and sword bayonets (Colvile II: 293-4. Butler: 278. ILN 28 Feb. 1885).

Egyptian Artillery: This was the only artillery for the entire Nile Column (Headlam III: 216). The uniform would also have been the old white Egyptian army uniform, though not necessarily as ragged as the Mudir's troops.

Mounted Troops
19th Hussars: The 19th were all mounted on small gray Syrian Arab horses used by the Egyptian cavalry (Biddulph: 247). They are shown in various illustrations wearing blue jackets, khaki trousers, either white or khaki helmets with *pagri* and brass chin scales, white belts and haversack. They are shown variously wearing knee boots, blue

puttees and even long blue stockings. They sometimes carried net bags of grass on the left rear side of the saddle (ILN 17 Jan. 1885, pp. 68-9, 24 Jan 1885, pp. 92-3, 31 Jan. 1885, pp.110-1, 7 Feb. 1885).

Egyptian Camel Corps: A sketch by R. C. Woodville (ILN 1 March 1885) shows an Egyptian Camel trooper in a dark jacket with facings of a different color (also dark). This appears to be another of Woodville's creations. The Camel Corps at Suakin had been dressed in the standard white Egyptian uniform with red fez, armed with the Remington rifle (Haggard: 305). In all probability. this was the same uniform as used on the Nile Column.

Other Units
Royal Marine Light Infantry: 100 Marines were stationed on the Nile between Halfa, Serras, and Gemai at one time (Colvile I: 129-30). They wore red coats with dark blue collars, shoulder straps and cuffs, a white helmet with no *pagri*, and blue trousers (Reynolds 35: 390). This may have been the same unit which eventually joined the Desert Column, giving up their red coats for gray-khaki.

Royal Irish Regiment: The Royal Irish Regiment had acquired the reputation as the best dressed regiment in India and intended to maintain that reputation in Egypt. They were appalled by the gray uniforms worn by troops already stationed in Egypt in 1884. which was described as "a very hideous gray serge very similar to that worn by convicts which was worn apparently exactly as it had been issued from the store." The Royal Irish brought with them a uniform designed by their former commander and kept it carefully until they were safely disembarked from their boats at Korti. On 28 January 1885, they were sent with Sir Redvers Buller to reinforce the Desert Column at Gubat. It was then they put on their uniform, which was "a khaki colored frock and trousers of cotton drill, a helmet covered with the same material, gray woolen puttees, a woolen shirt, socks and ammunition boots, spine protectors, cholera belts, and drawers had been issued, but were not in general use among the rank and file; all hands carried haversacks, wooden water bottles and rolled greatcoats.

The officers wore "Sam Browne" belts, which supported their swords and field-glasses, revolvers and cartridge pouches; the non-commissioned officers and men were equipped with braces and waist belt, pouches containing 70 rounds of ammunition, three edged bayonets, and Martini-Henry rifles (which) were fitted with leather hand-guards, tightly laced round the stock and barrel behind the back-sight, to enable the men to get a firm grip of their weapons." (Bretton: 260, 274-5).

References
Archer, T., THE WAR IN EGYPT AND THE SUDAN, Vol. IV, London, 1886.
Biddulph, J., THE NINETEENTH AND THEIR TIMES, London, 1899.
Brackenbury, H., THE RIVER COLUMN, Edinburgh, 1885.
Butler, W. F., THE CAMPAIGN OF THE CATARACTS, London, 1887.
Colville, H.E., HISTORY OF THE SUDAN CAMPAIGN, 2 vols., London, 1889.
Gardyne, C. G., THE LIFE OF A REGIMENT; THE HISTORY OF THE GORDON HIGHLANDERS, Vol. II, London, 1929.
Grant, J., CASSELL'S HISTORY OF THE WAR IN THE SOUDAN, Vol. III, London, ca. 1886.
Gretton, G. Le M., THE CAMPAIGNS AND HISTORY OF THE ROYAL IRISH REGIMENT FROM 1684 TO 1902, Edinburgh, 1911.

Haggard, A., UNDER CRESCENT AND STAR, Edinburgh, 1895.

Hamilton, I., LISTENING FOR THE DRUMS, London, 1944.

Headlam, J., THE HISTORY OF THE ROYAL ARTILLERY, VOL. III, CAMPAIGNS (1860-1914), Woolwich, 1940.

ILLUSTRATED LONDON NEWS (ILN), 1884-5.

Keltie, J.S., and Melven, W., HISTORY OF THE SCOTTISH HIGHLANDS, HIGHLAND CLANS AND HIGHLAND REGIMENTS, Vol. V., Edinburgh, 1887.

Preston, A., IN RELIEF OF GORDON; LORD WOLSELEY'S CAMPAIGN JOURNAL OF THE KHARTOUM RELIEF EXPEDITION 1884-1885, London, 1967.

Royle, C., THE EGYPTIAN CAMPAIGNS 1882-1885, Vol. II, Landon, 1886.

Sandes, E. W. C., THE ROYAL ENGINEERS IN EGYPT AND THE SUDAN, Chatham, 1937.

Stacey, C. P., RECORDS OF THE NILE VOYAGEURS, Publications of the Champlain Society, Vol. 37, Toronto, 1959.

Symons, J., ENGLAND'S PRIDE, London, 1965. Ternan, T., SOME EXPERIENCES OF AN OLD BROMSGROVIAN, Birmingham, 1930.

Battle of Kirbekan, February 10, 1885: A costly victory in a lost campaign.

Wilson's Dash to Khartoum:
The Last Heave to Save Gordon
By Gerry Webb

Major General Sir Charles Wilson

Over the years I have read quite a few accounts of the Gordon Relief Expedition of 1884-85. The final, failed attempt to reach Khartoum by Nile steamers usually receives short shrift, often with veiled or open criticism of the acting commander, General Sir Charles Wilson.

Wilson's own account of the expedition, *From Korti To Khartoum*, written shortly after the events took place, is an amazing story, even allowing for personal bias, and gives a fair appreciation for the difficulties faced and the heroic efforts made by the men on the spot.

It is also—and more pertinently—rich ground for the war gamer.

I will not dwell here on the Desert Column's crossing of the Nile "Loop" to Metemmeh, or events prior to Wilson's departure down the Nile towards Khartoum. These are more widely known and the bibliography gives references for further reading. Suffice to say that precious days were lost before departure and this is where Wilson comes in for much criticism. Wilson's own account outlines his decision to scout the Nile in both directions and to try to gain some intelligence of enemy forces and intentions. By this stage the Desert Column was deep in enemy territory, having sustained heavy casualties and with many wounded, with it's original commander, Stewart, mortally so, and with a tenuous supply line dependant on a rapidly dwindling number of camels.

Given the circumstances it is perhaps remarkable that an attempt to relieve Khartoum was made at all. Four steamers had been sent four months earlier by Gordon to meet the relief column. They linked up with the British force at Metemmeh, and in consultation with the sole surviving naval Officer, Capt. Charles Beresford (Wolseley's naval ADC), Wilson decided to take the two largest and best protected boats, *Talahawiyeh* and *Bordein* in the dash to Khartoum.

Gordon's flotilla of four steamers reaching Metemmeh in order to meet the relief expedition.

The boat captains advised him that in twelve days they would not be able to pass the cataracts due to the falling level of the Nile. Omdurman, across the Nile from Khartoum, was known to be held by the enemy, and there were several batteries along the river they would have to fight past while attempting to get upstream. Prudent precautions for overhauling the engines, selecting crews, loading supplies and strengthening defenses took up valuable time. As Wilson wrote:

> "The original plan was for Beresford to man two of the steamers with the naval Brigade, mount his Gardner gun on one of them, and after overhauling them, take me to

Capt. Charles Beresford

Khartoum with about fifty men of the Sussex Regiment. This was now impossible; all of the naval officers were killed or wounded except Beresford, who was himself unable to walk, and many of the best petty officers and seaman were also gone."

Wilson allowed for the possibility that the remaining steamers might have to fight, and so left Beresford with them. Given the situation of the desert column, Wilson "...Did not feel justified in taking more than an officer and twenty men as an escort." Wolseley had sent red coats specifically to be worn by the troops entering Khartoum, but these had been lost or looted. Enough were raised from the Guards and Heavies to equip the small Sussex contingent.

"We were going to fight our way up the river and into Khartoum in two steamers of the size of 'penny' steamers on the Thames, which a single well-directed shell would send to the bottom: with crews and soldiers absolutely without discipline; with no surgeon; and with only one interpreter, the faithful Mohammed Ibrahim, still suffering from a flesh-wound in the side."

Wilson

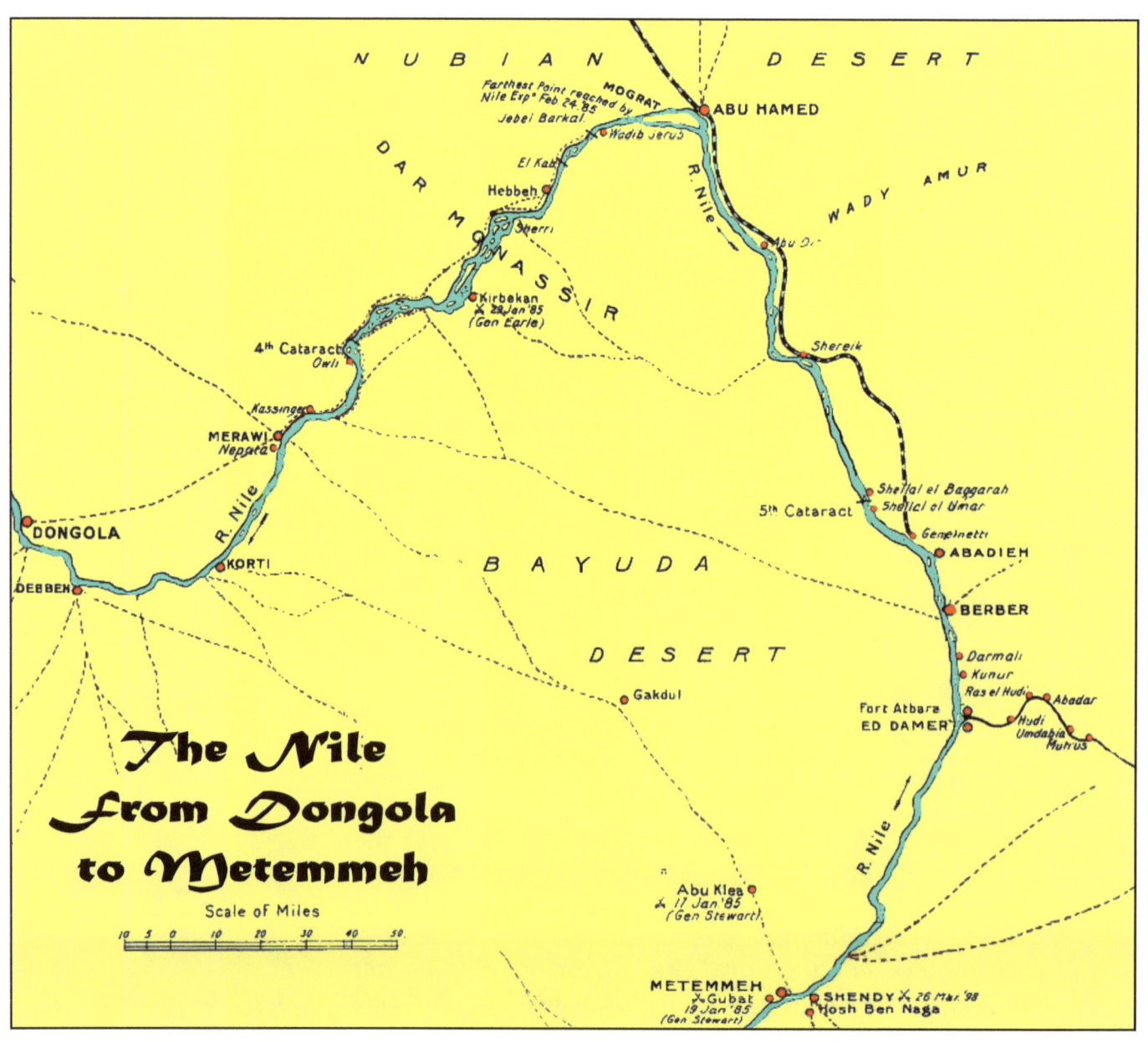

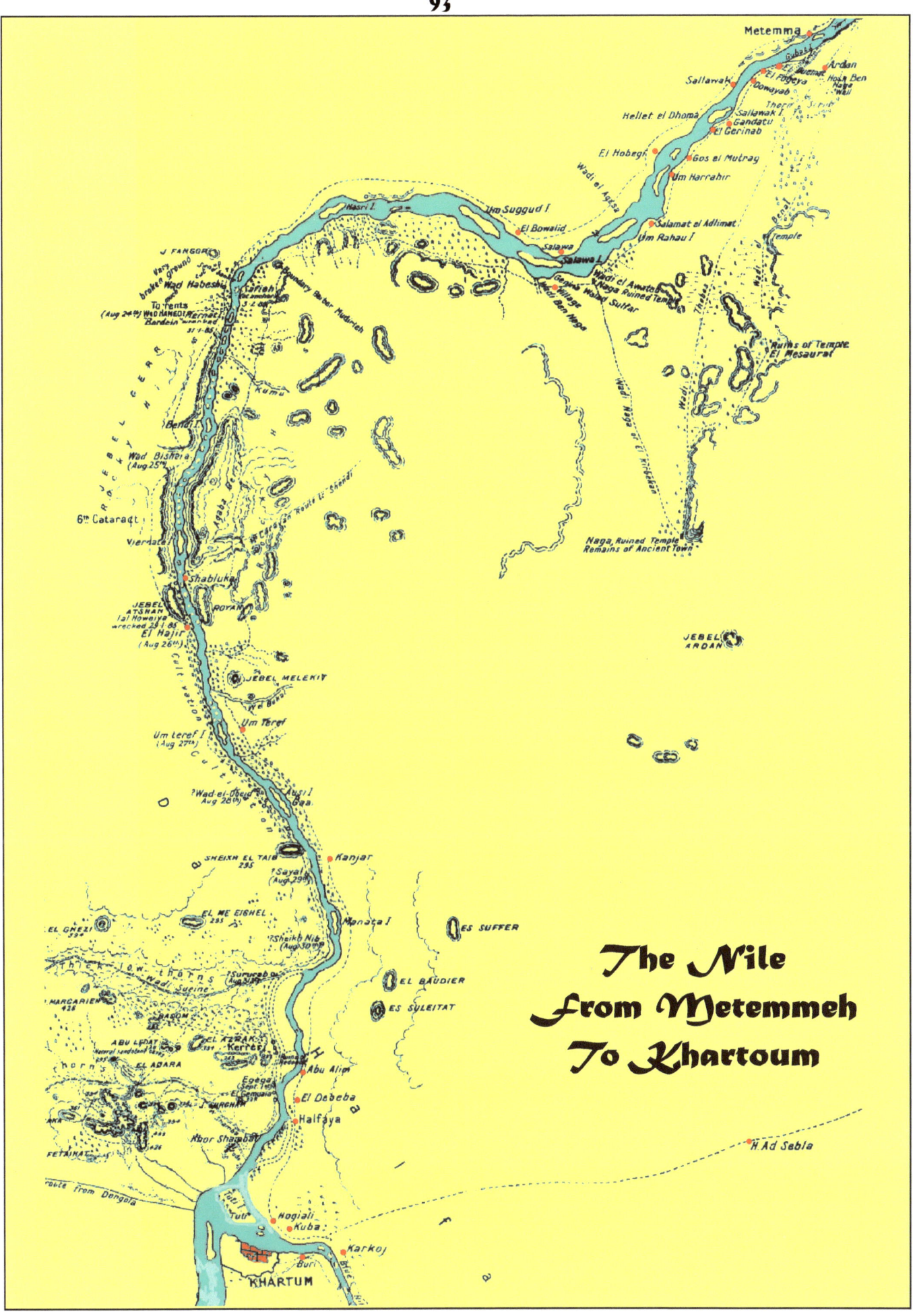

January 24th

The steamers departed at 8:A.M. Wilson aboard the *Bordein* with half the Sussex men and 110 black troops, plus the crew, while Captain Trafford, commanding the Sussex detachment, was aboard the *Talahawiyeh*, with the remaining Sussex and 80 black soldiers. *Talahawiyeh* also towed a large dismasted *nuggar*, or native boat, with 40 to 50 additional soldiers and a large supply of *dura* grain for Khartoum.

About 10:30 a native was taken aboard who told of a battery with a gun ahead. Rounding a corner, the battery was seen and troops were landed, Gascoine with some of the black troops from Wilson's boat, and Trafford and Wortly with black troops from the other boat. The battery was empty, with fresh marks from gun wheels. Locals said the gun had been withdrawn after the Emir of Shendy had heard the boats had gone towards Shendy. Luckily, Wilson's earlier reconnaissance had paid off by accident.

Like all the gun positions encountered it had three embrasures—to fire up, down and across the river. A little farther up river a large enemy mounted force was sighted on the left bank, and a few ineffective shots were fired at the boats. Stray shots were fired from the left bank throughout the day.

At about 12:30 a halt was made at a deserted village to take on wood. The native troops were ill-disciplined while ashore and Wilson had the *kurbash* (whip) administered.

The boats kept going until dark and tied up on the right bank near Gos el Bessabir.

January 25th

"I lay awake for a long time last night thinking over the situation, and how Gordon will receive the news, and what effect it will have on affairs at Khartoum. Buller's calculation was that Earle would be at Shendy on 5th March, and Lord Wolseley at Metemmeh on the 2nd March: more than a month to wait, and Gordon had given up hope in December. The outlook is not bright: my only hope was that, with the steamers and the few Englishmen, we might make a sortie before I left which would shake the enemy and bring in provisions."

Wilson

In the morning there was another stop for wood and more enforced discipline with the *kurbash*. Fueling was difficult and time consuming. Houses had to be pulled down, and the tools for cutting up logs were poor. Another strong, and fortunately deserted, position was passed at Jebel Tanjur. About 5 miles further along, another strong position at Wad Habashi was also abandoned. "The enemy had made a small work in the sand with three embrasures, and a long rifle-trench on each side: a nasty-looking place, which we were glad to find unoccupied." Rocks on the river and a narrow channel would have made an opposed passage very difficult. Next was the Shabluka Cataract, consisting of open stretches with dangerous rocks and rapids.

A Nuggar being hauled up a cataract of the Nile

Just before sunset the *Bordein* struck a rock at the last rapid. Though the crews worked by moonlight they could not get her off. *Talahawiyeh* got through safely and lay at an island for the night.

Throughout the day stray shots from the West showed the local tribes were hostile.

January 26th

Work started at dawn, but it took hours of hard work with hawsers, engines and anchors before *Bordein* finally came free of the rock.

A rare surviving photo of the Bordein, though before being armed and protected for military use.

The worst part of the rapid was ahead, and despite the best efforts of both Captains, *Bordein* ran aground again. The Nile had thrown up an unexpected sand bar in the main channel. *Talahawiyeh* passed safely on the other side of Hassan Island but it took until sunset for *Bordein* to be got free and join the other boat. The whole day of enormous effort had got them only three miles further up the Nile.

Fortunately there were only a few scattered shots from the bank during the day.

During the evening, friendly locals came aboard and reported than there had been heavy fighting around Khartoum for fifteen days. Gordon was winning, and the British advance was dreaded.

> *"Evidently, as we thought, the Mahdi was fighting hard to get into Khartoum before we got there, and Gordon gallantly holding his own. We little dreamt all was then over."*
>
> Wilson

January 27th

Beyond the cataract the boats passed through a gorge no more than 300 yards long and 3 or 4 miles long. Wilson ordered full speed, and told the Sussex men to reply to enemy fire with volleys, but again there was no opposition.

Near Jebel Royan the boats stopped again on the left bank to take on wood. A few shots were fired at long distance, and the *kurbash* was needed again to stop looting, but fueling was completed.

Then came another cataract, this time the boats passed through successfully. After 2 P.M. the scattered firing became more frequent. The boats moored for the night on the left bank opposite Tamaniat, and wood was again taken on board. During the day a passer by had shouted news that Khartoum had fallen and Gordon was dead. Similar reports had been circulating locally for months, so the news was not believed.

The Bordein reaches Khartoum—"Too late!"

> *"We dined together in high spirits at the prospects of running the blockade next day, and at last meeting General Gordon after his famous siege."*
>
> Wilson

January 28th

The boats started at 6 A.M., and at 7:30 A.M. passed another abandoned enemy strongpoint at Jebel Seg et Taib. Soon after passing Abu Alim they could see Khartoum in the distance over the trees on Tuti Island. Another report of Gordon's death was shouted from the right bank.

Scattered shots had been fired at the boats all morning, but as they neared Fighiaiha the real fight began. At Halfiyeh the enemy opened up a heavy fire with four guns and many rifles, from a range of 600 to 700 yards. The crews replied, and both boats came through safely.

They could now see Government house at Khartoum, but could not see the Egyptian flag which Gordon was reported to have always kept flying.

Beyond Shamba two enemy guns opened fire from the right bank, with heavy rifle fire from both banks. Then the boats were in range of the guns at Omdurman. Wilson initially thought Gordon's men still held Tuti Island, and brought his boat within 70 yards to ask for news, but was driven under cover by rifle fire. Hoping that Khartoum might still be holding out, the boats pressed on after a short delay.

Immediately the boats came under intense fire from at lease 2 guns in Omdurman, 3 or 4 from Khartoum or Tuti Island, a machine gun and continuous musketry.

> *"We kept on to the junction of the two Niles, when it became plain to every one that Khartoum had fallen into the Mahdi's hands; for not only were there hundreds of Dervishes ranged under their banners, standing on the sand spit close to the town ready to resist our landing, but no flag was flying in Khartoum and not a shot was fired in our assistance; here, too, if not before, we should have met the two steamers I knew Gordon still had at Khartoum. It was hopeless to attempt a landing or to communicate with the shore under such a fire."*
>
> Wilson

The expedition had failed, but this was only half the story. Wilson's force was now deep in enemy territory, and a rapidly falling Nile studded with rocks and treacherous cataracts offered the only possible escape route.

Wilson's Return From Khartoum

Wilson tuned back with *Bordein*, and called to *Talahawiyeh* (which had run aground off Tuti Island) to follow. Below Omdurman, a Dervish showed a white flag and beckoned, but he was ignored since the firing never let up.

There were some close shaves. A Sudanese soldier on the *Bordein* left cover to throw burning debris overboard. Wilson said he would have had the Victoria Cross if he had been an Englishmen. He was shot shortly after. The small boat towed behind *Bordein* was sunk by a shell, and *Talahawiyeh* was struck by a solid shot and a bursting shell, but no one was hurt.

The Sudanese crews and soldiers were despondent. They had lost their wives, families and all they possessed in Khartoum. The Sussex men remained very steady. By the time the boats got clear they had been under fire for four hours, fortunately for them the enemy were poor shots. That night they halted at an island, and Wilson sent out spies disguised as Mahdists. He learned that Khartoum had fallen during the night of January 25th-26th, through the treachery of the commander of the regular garrison,

Faraj Pasha, and the *mudir* of the town, Ahmad Bey Jalabi. The spies also reported that Gordon was dead, and the Mahdi had given Khartoum up to three days' pillage.

January 29th

Wilson's expedition kept busy caring for their wounded. He held a conference with the captains and *reises* of the boats, and they discussed the difficulties ahead. The Nile was much lower than usual, even for this time of year, and the boats were heavily laden with supplies and iron plate armor.

The morning was spent on repairing and patching the many bullet holes in the steamer hulls. These looked to have been made by a Nordenfelt machine gun. They got moving at 7 A.M. but *Bordein* struck a sandbank at 8:30 and was freed after half an hour. Before running the first cataract a large quantity of the *dura* grain supply was thrown overboard to lighten the load.

The captains and *reises* took the boats through the first cataract one at a time, without incident. They moved on, but at about 4:30 pm *Talahawiyeh* struck a submerged rock opposite Jebel Royan and began to sink. *Bordein* halted at a small island just downstream. The *Talahawiyeh* crew managed to transfer the men, two guns, rifles, rations and some small-arms ammunition into the large *nuggar* they were towing, and joined the *Bordein* just before sunset.

There had been no serious opposition that day, just a few shots from both banks. In the evening Wilson consented to meet a messenger, who brought a letter from the Madhi promising protection for the Egyptian and Sudanese boat crews, and an invitation to the English to become Moslems. Wilson declined to reply, but his Egyptian commander, Kashm el Mus, urged him to use a ruse, pretending to negotiate to prevent the Mahdists from destroying the boats at the gorge and cataracts ahead. Wilson wanted nothing to do with this, but finally allowed him to do as he wished, as long as the British were not involved in the deception.

Other locals came aboard with news, and Wilson now had the added problem of treachery to contend with. His Egyptian and Sudanese crews were being offered safety in return for surrender, many must have been tempted. His loyal deputy Ibrahim went amongst the men and prevented any secret conversations. Wilson posted sentries to prevent desertion, but despite this one man escaped from their island camp.

January 30th

The *nuggar* was fitted with large sweeps, and went ahead thought the next cataract, scouting the passage for *Bordein*, which passed safely. They then passed through the gorge, which was again undefended. Before the next and most dangerous cataract, they stopped to lighten the boats as much as possible. Again the *nuggar* passed through safely, but a strong headwind pushed *Bordein* onto rocks, and it was only with a mighty effort they managed to get her off. The next cataract was very narrow and rocky, but *Bordein* passed safely stern first, lowered down on hawsers attached to anchors or rocks. The boat moved by inches, controlled by the hawsers and the engine running forward. It was a slow and anxious process, and the boats anchored for the night soon after, in mid-stream to prevent night attacks.

January 31st

Bordein was lowered down the next cataract in the same manner as the previous day. Then *Bordein* and the *nuggar* stopped for wood, as the supply was very low, all the reserve as well as empty ammunition cases had been burnt. Wilson prepared to run past the expected batteries at Wad Habashi, but the *Bordein* never made it that far.

Lt. Wortley and General Wilson on Mernat Island from a sketch by the latter, rendered by war correspondent, Melton Prior.

Just after passing the next cataract safely, she struck a submerged rock and began to take in water rapidly. The captains managed to reach a sand spit at the end of a small wooded island and ran her aground there. Fifty yards beyond lay the larger island of Mernat. Despite all efforts the *Bordein* was finished. Men, guns, ammunition and stores were landed on the island.

As soon as it was dark, Wilson sent Wortly in a small boat downriver to bring help from Gubat. He took a crew of four English soldiers and eight natives, and safely passed the Wad Habashi battery, despite having three volleys fired at them from the two guns now positioned there. Wortley's boat reached Gubat at 3am the next day, having covered nearly forty miles in just over eight hours.

Wilson had planned to march towards Gubat by night, but could not get his demoralized native troops to move.

February 1st

Wilson arranged most of his forces on Mernat Island but left a detachment of 20 men on the smaller island to prevent the enemy from occupying it. The Nile had fallen so low there was a steep bank, 25 to 30 feet high, protecting the perimeter of Mernat Island. The force built a *zariba* of mimosa thorn bush, and within this, a shallow trench. Outside the defenses they cleared the grass as a protection against fire.

At night, pickets were posted fifty yards in front of the *zariba*, (they would not go further), plus a line of sentries within. Wilson calculated he could depend on the loyalty of just over half his men, plus the Sussex detachment.

February 2nd

During the day, some local messengers tried to encourage desertions, and one officer, Abdul Hamid did slip away with a group of the men. That night, the pickets refused to leave the *zariba* at all, so the line of sentries within was strengthened. The British officers decided to march to safety down the right bank of the river if no help arrived.

February 3rd

Gunfire heralded the arrival of a gunboat, which engaged the enemy fort three miles downstream. Gascoigne raised flags on the grounded *Bordein* to show their position to the relief force. This drew fire from the enemy on the left bank of the river, and Wilson's force replied with Remington rifle fire and shells from their four guns. Wilson noted that the act of firing tended to raise the morale of native troops.

Wilson and his officers could indistinctly see the battle. He decided to break up the *zariba* immediately, and march down the right bank of the river to link up with the relief force. This order caused wild and confused scenes as the native troops sought to save themselves and their possessions aboard the remaining *nuggar*. The enemy began a sharp fire into the *zariba* and several men were hit.

Guns and stores were taken aboard the *nuggar*, and the men crossed from the end of Mernat Island to the right bank using the one remaining small boat. The crossing was a slow process, but well covered and planned. The force then marched the three miles to the battle, and the few enemy horsemen encountered were scattered by a protecting screen of skirmishers.

They were able to signal the gunboat, the *El Safia*. It had suffered a damaged boiler and was anchored while still engaging the enemy fort. *El Safia* signaled it would be able to make repairs during the afternoon and evening and would pick up Wilson's force the next day. He ordered one gun brought from the *nuggar* and had it engage the enemy fort. The native riflemen and the Sussex men also engaged the enemy embrasures at 1100 yards. Gascoine volunteered to go over to the steamer in a small boat, and took two naval artificers and some native crewmen.

Despite a hot fire, he returned with news from Beresford who commanded the gunboat. Repairs would be complete by sunset, and Beresford requested continuing fire support to take attention away from his stranded vessel. Wilson had only sufficient ammunition for the one gun, and some of that was wet, but the crew used it to good effect. The enemy replied with badly aimed solid shot.

Wilson's *nuggar* also ran aground and the enemy began firing on it. He sent most of the force on to find a place where they could be picked up, and to build a *zariba* there. He remained behind with the gun and thirty men to draw fire away from the *nuggar*. It re-floated just before sunset, and Wilson rejoined the main force, after spiking and abandoning the gun. During the night the *nuggar* ran aground again, right in from of the centre embrasure of the enemy battery.

February 4th

The steamer *El Safia* got under way after dawn and engaged the enemy fort yet again. It then assisted the *nuggar* to get free, and Wilson sent men to fire from the bank in support. The *nuggar* had been aground within 400 yards of the fort, and was hit repeatedly by rifle fire, but all artillery fire missed her.

El Safia had almost made it past the battery the day before when her boiler was struck and she lost power 200 yards beyond the enemy fort. Her Gardner gun and a small artillery piece kept up such a hot fire on the enemy parapet that they could not use their guns to effect.

Wilson's force was picked up by *El Safia*, which headed downstream to friendly territory. They took fire several times from the left bank, and ran aground again briefly. They stopped once more to collect wood for fuel and reached their base at Gubat at about 5.30pm.

So ended Wilson's attempt to reach Khartoum. It had failed, but the efforts and risks had been epic. Despite the loss of two steamships to the treacherous Nile, the force remained largely intact, and had fought its way to Khartoum and back against terrific odds.

Order of Battle
Wilson's Force to Khartoum
Two steamships, *Talahawiyeh* and *Bordein*.

Bordein carried 110 black troops plus crew, *Talahawiyeh* had 80 black soldiers plus the towed *nuggar* with 40–50 further troops. One Officer and twenty men of the Sussex regiment, divided between the two steam vessels, plus at least 2 small rowing boats, towed behind.

The native troops consisted of Sudanese regulars, ex-slaves and Shaigyeh Bashi-Bazouks. Wilson noted that the Sudanese were armed with Remington rifles and spears, and considered bayonets useless in action against spear-armed opponents.

Officers were Egyptian, Circassian and Turkish Bashi Bazouks.

Wilson listed the following detachments in his defensive position on Mernat Island:

- Captain Trafford and the Royal Sussex detachment
- Shagiyeh Bashi Bazouks commanded by Kashm el Mus
- Gunners from the *Talahawiyeh*
- Mahdi Agha and Bashi Bazouks
- Sailors of the *Bordein*
- Ali Agha and Bashi Bazouks
- Shagiyeh Bashi Bazouks and slaves commanded by Abd ul Hamid (deserted Feb. 2nd)
- Sailors of the *Talahawiyeh*
- Captain Gascoigne, Bakhit Agha and Sudanese regulars
- Gunners from the *Bordein*

Protection for these original Nile steamers was improvised, mostly relying on lumber planks erected around as much of each vessel as possible, and with the odd boiler plate section set up around the exposed boilers. The helmsman's position was protected as much as possible in the same manner, but most of this "armor" provided only bullet proofing. Direct hits by solid shot, and especially explosive shell, could be devastating.

The steamboats carried large quantities of *dura* grain to re-supply Khartoum, loot, ammunition, wood for the boiler, bedding, women, a few babies and a herd of goats for milk.

Beresford's relief force from Gubat; One steamer, *El Safia*, armed with at least one small artillery piece and a Gardner gun. It was crewed by Naval Brigade under the command of Keppel, and Mounted Infantry commanded by Bower. Native troops also likely, numbers of these detachments unknown.

Mahdist Forces

Full numbers are unknown, but the batteries along the river contained one or two guns. The main army with large numbers of guns, riflemen and sword and spearmen were in the Khartoum, Omdurman, Tuti Island area. Wilson noted the following enemy guns during the final attempt to reach Khartoum.

Halfiyeh: Four guns and many rifles
Beyond Shamba: Two guns on the right bank of the river, heavy rifle fire from both sides
Omdurman: At least two guns
Khartoum and Tuti Island: Three or four guns, a machine gun, and continuous musketry.

Smaller detachments and mounted scouts were encountered at several points along the river, and scattered sniping was common throughout Wilson's voyage.

Another army was believed to be in the area and was expected to attack the British position at Gubat.

Gun batteries consisted of earthwork parapets with embrasures for the guns pointing across, up, and down the river. These batteries were often supported by rifle trenches.

Gaming the Actions

There are several ways to approach this, and and others will have their own ideas. The first is to have players on both sides involved in a map campaign, with the Steamers trying to reinforce/re-supply Khartoum and the Mahdists trying to prevent this.

A further option would be for all the players to be on the same side, against an umpire-controlled enemy or one run by charts and die rolls, as is the way with the rules *Science vs Pluck: Or "Too Much For The Mahdi."* The Mahdists did not oppose the expedition very well so this may be more satisfying and realistic. The danger is that a modern day and better informed Mahdist player will block the river with massed guns or some "hind sight" stratagem and the campaign will be all over too quickly. If Mahdist players are used they could have different objectives, since commanders in the North drew off their forces to protect their own villages, despite the wishes of the Mahdi. It was also clear from local reports that the Mahdists who had faced the Desert Column and Camel Corps were much demoralized by their defeats, impressed by British firepower, and not anxious to repeat the experience.

Finally, particular incidents from the expedition could be used to set up "one off" games rather than a campaign. For a large game steamships can attempt the final run against massed fire to relieve the Khartoum garrison. Smaller games could involve running the gauntlet past a battery, or landing troops to clear a position. The rules, *Boilers And Breechloaders*, may be just the thing here.

The biggest logistical problems faced by Wilson were lack of wood for fuel and lack of water under the hulls. The steamships had to stop constantly for fuel. Wood was scarce, difficult to cut up and difficult to load. An expedition scenario should include long delays caused by the fuel problem, and perhaps longer delays passing rapids, rocks and cataracts. The British commanders have to race against the falling level of the Nile, get to their destination and return quickly, or be stranded in enemy territory.

Food and ammunition did not seem to be a problem for Wilson's force, since it carried large quantities to re-supply Khartoum. Wilson only ran low on artillery ammunition at the end, when his steamships were gone and he was reliant on the *nuggar* for transport.

Miniatures

The native forces commanded by Wilson had been effectively river pirates and free agents for the past five months, so an irregular appearance is appropriate. Wilson noted that a few of the officers managed to retain their blue coats but most of the men were in very tattered apparel, and some had nothing but a long cotton shirt and a cartridge belt. Wilson described their appearance as "very quaint." There was even a sergeant in Mahdist uniform. He had surrendered at Abu Klea, and was an excellent shot.

Model gunboats are available from many sources, including the new ones from The (Virtual) Armchair General. My own is a resin model with cast metal barricades from Merrimack Miniatures.

Terrain

The main requirement is of course the Nile—"It was the reason for everything....". The modeled river will need to be wide enough to allow model steamers to pass shore defenses at a reasonable distance, yet narrow enough at other points to restrict passage. There were also the numerous islands, good places to tie up for the night or to defend.

The large engagement at Khartoum/Omdurman would be a sight to see on the tabletop, and may need to be scaled down, or fought in sections.

In the past, I've played river actions where the whole table is considered water, with banks, batteries or whatever represented along the sides of the table. This does look better than having beautiful model steamers with massed crews jammed into tiny creeks. It also helps to have a "rolling" terrain, where the scenery at the table edge is moved to represent the progress of the ships.

Tactics

The Mahdist forces heavily outnumbered the British and Egyptians, in both troops and guns. Wilson's forces managed to maintain fire superiority over their opponents, and kept their heads down and aim poor by firing on the enemy embrasures and parapets. Rules should take this into account, as well as the "uneven" shooting of the Mahdists. When *Jihadiyya* Riflemen are encountered (only with the Mahdists immediately around Khartoum, or with those forces facing the Desert

A scene on the Nile typical of many steamer's experiences while navigating between one or both banks occupied by the Ansar.

Column) they would be very like the Egyptian Regulars for fire effects, while all others would show very poor marksmanship indeed.

Perhaps a game could be built around these firefights, with the boats firing first and causing a heavy minus on the fire factors of the shore defenses and riflemen. The fire may also negate return fire completely, since the Mahdist gunners will have their heads down. This could be an exciting game, as the British and Egyptians may be unable to cover everything, and will have to choose where to commit their firepower.

Bibliography
From Korti to Khartoum, Sir Charles Wilson' (William Blackwood and Sons, Edinburgh and London, Seventh Edition, 1886.)

Useful readings for the overall expedition include:
The Journals of Major General Gordon at Khartoum, Darf Publishers Limited, London, reprinted 1984
England's Pride, Julian Symons, White Lion Publishers, London, 1974
In Relief of Gordon, Lord Wolseley's Campaign Journal of the Khartoum Relief Expedition 1884-1885, Hutchinson of London, 1967

The endless and back-breaking work of hauling vessels up stream through the cataracts of the Nile.

The Wars In The Eastern Sudan Part 1: The Rise of Osman Digna
By Doug Johnson

Introduction: Egypt On The Red Sea

Since classical times the Red Sea coast has been one of the Sudan's main links to the wider world of the Middle East and the Indian Ocean. In the mid-Sixteenth Century it became part of the Ottoman empire, administered from Jeddah on the Hijaz. The Red Sea ports of Suakin and Massawa did not pass into Egyptian control until long after the Turco-Egyptian conquest of the Sudan.

Egypt first conquered the province of Taka and established a military garrison at the foot of Jebel Kassala in 1840. Muhammad Ali leased Suakin and Massawa from the Ottoman Sultan in 1846-9, but it was not until 1865-6 that they were granted outright to the Khedive Ismail. From its base in Massawa Egypt tried to control the Sannaheit area (around Keren in present day Eritrea) and it was also from Massawa that Egypt expanded into Somalia in the 1870's and launched its two disastrous

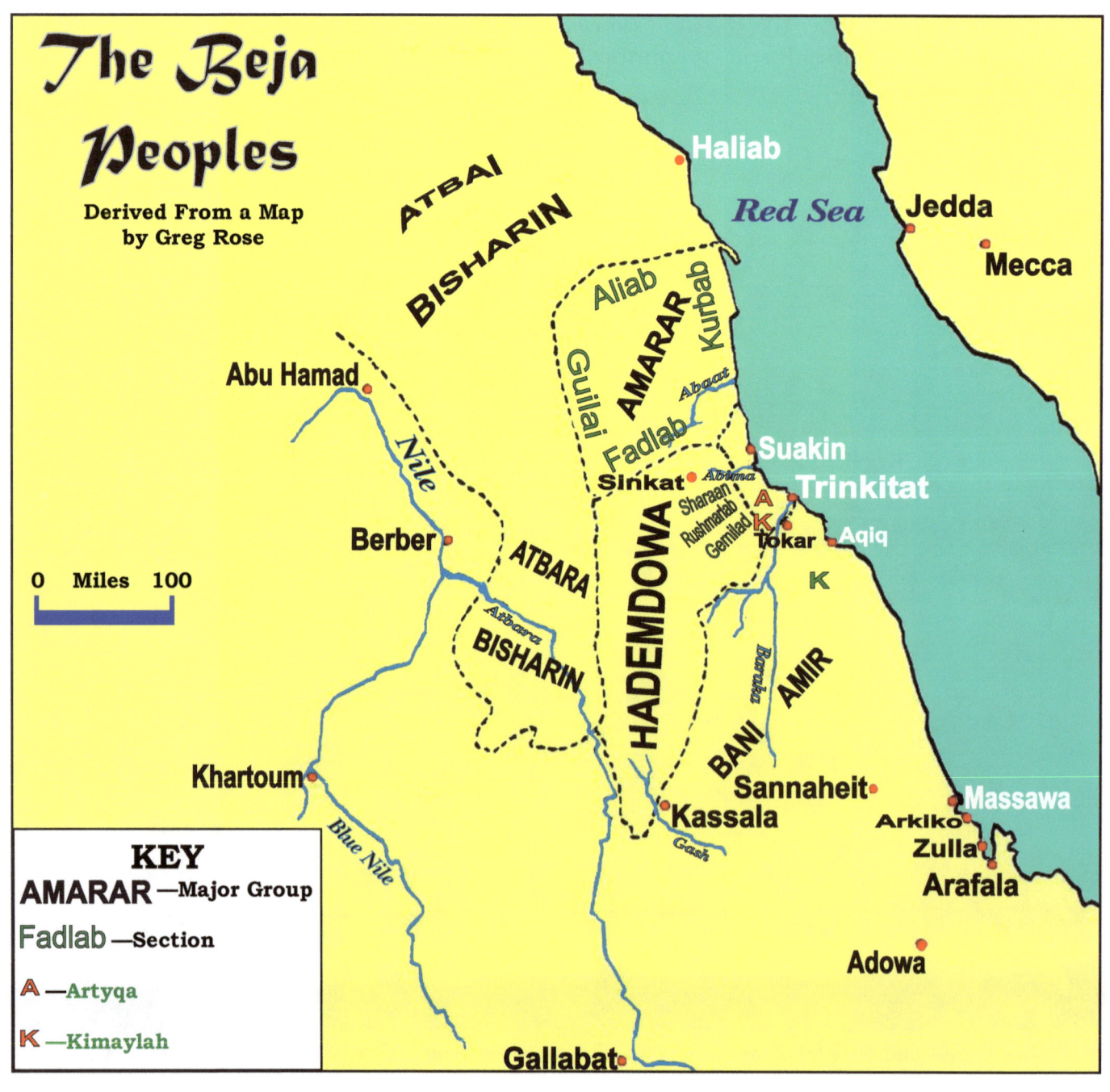

invasions of Abyssinia in 1875-6.

In 1882, before the British occupation of Egypt, the Sudan was reorganized into three *Hukumdirias*, governor-generalates, independent of each other and reporting directly to Cairo. The governor-generalate of the Eastern Sudan included Suakin, Taka (Kassala and Gallabat) and Massawa (the proposed capital). Somalia (including Harrar and Berbera) was also attached to the new Sudanese ministry in Cairo. Events in both Egypt and the Sudan that same year were to overtake this reform and render it void.

The Beja

The Beja peoples who inhabit the Red Sea coast from Eritrea to the modern border between Egypt and the Sudan all speak dialects of To Badawie, share many cultural traits, and are for the most part nomadic, raising either cattle or camels. It would he difficult to speak of the different Beja groupings as "tribes" in the most commonly understood sense. Each group (especially the Hadendowa and the Beni 'Emir) is a mixture within itself.

The Beja country is divided into four distinctive areas. The coastal area between the Red Sea hills and the sea, known as the Gwineb, stretches from the Tokar delta to Haliab in the north. The northern and western plains, or Atbai, runs from the western slopes of the hills to the Egyptian border. It is a desert of firm sand and pebbles, with wells built on rocky outcrops and a few well-watered drainage channels after the rains. Further south, flanking the east bank of the Atbara river is the Tamarab, a better watered plain marked by curved ranges of sand dunes. Some of the most prized grazing areas are found in a small triangle of flat land south-west of the Atbara. Rains come to the coast mostly in November-February, to the Atbai mainly in July-October. The Atbara is in flood from June-October, and grass for grazing usually dies back in March or April.

The inhabitants of the Atbai are mainly the Bisharin (or Bishariyin). They are divided into two main groups: the Um Ali and the Um Nagi. The Um Ali are further segmented into the Aliab, Amrab, Hamadorab and Shatirab, the last two occupying the northern coastal plain and the hills. The Um Nagi contain the Ariyab and Nafaab Mansurab, who live west and south of the Atbai and on part of the Tamarab; and the Adeloyab, Hamadab, Ibrahimab, Wailaliab, Batran, Garab, Mushbolab and Madakir sections, who live on the Atbara and in the southern half of the Tamarab. The Bisharin are mainly camel herders, and they and their neighbors the Amarar were renowned for their breed of camels, unlike the Hadendowa, who are mainly cattle keepers.

The Atbai Bisharin were largely untouched by Turco-Egyptian administration, though they had many trading contacts with Upper Egypt. The Hamadorab and Shatirab on the coast prospered from their grazing and their trade with Egypt and Arabia but were largely beyond the range of Turco-Egyptian control, as they continued to be beyond the effective range of both Mahdist and Egyptian influence throughout the 1880 and 1890's. Egyptian influence was felt mainly on the Atbara where the newcomers intervened in the 1840's and deposed the Hamadab paramount *shiekh* with their own choice from the Ibrahimab section. Still, the Egyptians collected little tribute from the whole of the Bisharin throughout their reign (Sanders 1933: 135-8).

The largest and most expansive group of the Beja during the nineteenth century were the Hadendowa. They grew in numbers and expanded their territory by conquest, intermarriage and the absorption of smaller groups, becoming a diverse mixture of peoples or, as one British administrator described them in this century, "A haggis of Beja elements" (Owen: 183). They frequently clashed with the eastern-most sections of the Bisharin over grazing, and also had an intermittent feud on with the Bani 'Emir.

Their great leader of the nineteenth century was Musa Ibrahim, the nephew of Muhammad Din who was defeated by the Turco-Egyptians in 1840. Musa was placed in power by the Egyptians and consolidated Hadendowa hegemony from Kassala to Suakin. Egyptian rule over the Hadendowa was never easy. The Hadendowa did provide transport, but they were unwilling to pay tribute. Those living in the hills retained their autonomy from the Egyptian garrisons at Erkowit and Sinkat. Musa Ibrahim died in c.1884, but by that time he had already been succeeded in practical affairs by his son, Muhammad Bey Musa (Owen:191-5).

The Hadendowa numbered some 100,000 at the time of the Sudan's independence in 1956 and would not have numbered more than this during the Nineteenth Century. Their main sections are: the Wailaliab, Samarar, Gemilab, Hakolab, Bushariab, Meishab, Shara'ab, Samaramdowab, Gar'ib, Kalolai, Hamdab, Beiranab, Buglinai, Tirik, Emirab, Shaboidinab, Gurhabab and Rabamak. Being a very diverse and segmented people, they did not all take the same attitude to either the Mahdiyya or the Egyptians.

Between the Bisharin (who were less than 50,000) and the Hadendowa lie the Amarar, a group of less than 70,000 people, who are divided into three main groups: the Fadlab, Esharbab and Otman. The Otman are further divided into the Aliab, Guilai, Kurbab and the Nurab who now live around Tokar.

In the early part of the *Turkiyya* the Amarar lived mainly in the *khors* and western slopes of the Red Sea hills. During the *Turkiyya* they were able to emerge into the plains between Khor Arbaat and the Atbara through judicious inter-marriage with the Bisharin and Hadendowa. Their occupation of the plains was also facilitated by the growing estrangement between the Atbai and Atbara Bisharin groups, following the installation of an Egyptian-backed *shiekh* on the Atbara. The Amarar, too, engaged in transport work for the Turco-Egyptian government (Sanders 1933: 139; Paul 1971: 101).

The most easterly group of the Beja, the Bani 'Emir, provided the new Turco-Egyptian government with its greatest support. The Bani 'Emir are even less of a "tribe" than the Hadendowa, consisting of a small group of "aristocrats," the Nabtab, to whom were attached a large number of serfs, slaves and a number of small groups of independent peoples. The Bani 'Emir are mostly bilingual in To Bedawi and Tigrinya, a language spoken by many peoples in the neighboring area of Ethiopia. They did not resist the Turco-Egyptians, but instead paid a tribute and provided auxiliaries for Egyptian expeditions into Sennaheit and Massawa throughout the 1850's and 1860's. They had a paramount leader, the Diglal, whose power was extended into non-Bani 'Emir areas by the Egyptians, and who was also able to strengthen his own position against that of the Nabtab aristocrats during the same time by attaching more and more clients to himself (Nadel: 54, 61, 63, 73-4; Paul 1950: 226, 230; Paul 1971: 17). Throughout the *Mahdiyya* the Bani 'Emir, of all Beja peoples, were the most consistent in their opposition to the Ansar and in their friendship first to the Egyptians and later to the Italians.

The Egyptian Army on the Red Sea in 1883

The Egyptian Army on the Red Sea in 1883 was a mixture of regular and irregular soldiers. The regulars consisted of Egyptian troops and Sudanese (black African) slave soldiers. The Sudanese soldiers, serving for life, were a more professional military body than the Egyptian conscripts. It is for this reason that they were considered more reliable and adept fighters in the Sudan than the Egyptian peasants.

The irregulars consisted of two groups: The Bashi-Bazouks and local "friendlies."

*Osman Digna
(aka "Uthman Diqna")*

The Bashi-Bazouks were cavalry recruited from the Albanians, Circassians, Kurds and Slavs who had been the nucleus of Muhammad Ali's army prior to the conscription of Egyptian peasants and the formation of Sudanese slave regiments. The local irregulars were usually raised by their local shiekhs to help in tax collecting and slave raids. The *shiekh* was responsible for paying and outfitting his men, who each owned their own musket and mount. The irregulars were under the governor of each province, and not under a central command. The Deli-Bashi (or Dalil-Bashil) was the commander of the irregular mounted corps. A squadron of about 400 men was divided into *buluks*, companies of varying size, under a *Buluk-Bashi* or *Sanjak*. By the 1880's the officers in irregular corps were also given regular army ranks, a *sanjak* usually corresponded to a *Yuzbashi* (Captain) (Hill 1959: 27-8, 47)

Wingate (50-1) gives the size of the Egyptian force in the Eastern Sudan in 1883 as: Somalia garrisons, 4,572; Massawa, 2,442; Suakin, 1,800; Abyssinian Frontier, 4,304. Over half the troops were in Somalia and Eritrea, and the majority of those troops actually in the Sudan were strung out along the Abyssinian border, making it impossible to concentrate when they were needed.

Osman Digna And The *Mahdiyya*

The British administrators who governed the Beja after the Re-conquest were never quite sure why the Beja had joined the *Mahdiyya*. They seemed insufficiently motivated by Islam in any of their daily occupations to become "Allah-inflamed fanatics," a view that Osman Digna seems at one time to have shared (Paul 1971: 106-7). Some put it down to ill-timed cheating by the Turco-Egyptian authorities, some to the Beja's "natural enjoyment of a scrap," and all agreed that a great deal of blame fell on Osman Digna (Paul 197:106; Owen: 196).

Osman Digna was equally inscrutable to the British. He, along all other Mahdist Emirs, was best known to the British public throughout the many battles of the *Mahdiyya*. He served more than twenty years in captivity afterwards. His erstwhile enemies and captors had a chance to get a good look at him, but none really claimed to understand him. To the representatives of the Anglo-Egyptian regime the *Mahdiyya* was a tyranny, its justice harsh, its leaders cruel. Osman Digna was no exception. He was described as "An ill-conditioned, ill-disciplined youth, always ready to join in any disreputable disturbance that might be there," he was unrelentingly stern and quick to anger, "He ruled by fear, not love; his adherents were only kept in check by self-interest" (Jackson: 192-3).

The British, too, found the Beja difficult to rule, and there were some administrators who developed a begrudging sympathy for Osman's sternness, admitting that it may have been justified. The Beja, they decided, could be respected and even admired in some ways; they could not be loved. Two years before the Sudan's independence one

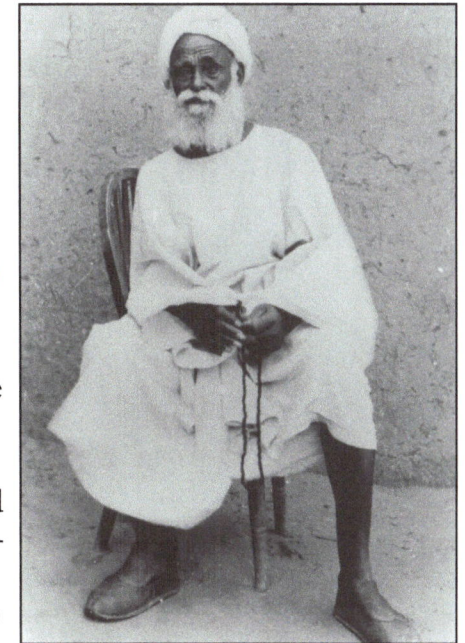

Osman Digna in old age after long imprisonment.

British administrator summarized Osman Digna in this way:

> "He was not popular with his own people, and he had none of the qualities which command respect among an independent and warlike race, for he seems to have had neither courage nor affability, nor generosity, nor even by their standards, a sense of honor. On the contrary, he was mean and churlish, and after his first experience of hand-to-hand fighting at Sinkat never again took an active part in battle, but developed an uncanny flair for judging the right moment at which to quit a stricken field. His reputation for harshness and treachery still lives, and he was, as reported in Wylde, 'Of a morose and taciturn disposition.' Yet for all that he had some unexplained gift to leadership, and was a great and unabashed liar, with great powers of persuasion; and in this, and a certain dour sagacity and formal fixity of purpose, must lie the secret of his success in holding together an always formidable fighting force, for long the only one in the country to have to contend with opponents both better trained and better armed" (Paul 1971: 107).

This does not, perhaps, fully explain the unexplainable. Many modern Sudanese have a higher regard for the man than the British had. He was, as even his captors admitted, well versed in the Koran and Koranic law and meticulous in hearing and judging cases himself, unlike many other Emirs (Jackson; 173). His military shrewdness is also appreciated rather more highly now than it was in the preceding century. One Sudanese officer from the Staff College in Omdurman explained to me some years ago Osman's virtues as an organizer and as a commander, pointing out that he seldom made the mistakes of other Emirs, who were prone to underestimate the Anglo-Egyptian enemy and commit insufficient forces to battle. He used two examples: Osman's advice to Mahsud prior to the battle of Atbara (Osman's withdrawal before the slaughter he thought justified), and his ambush of the 21st Lancers at Omdurman, the only bright spot for the Ansar in that unhappy battle.

Certainly we will see that the cumulative military effect of Osman's battles in 1884-5 was to make it impossible for the British to contemplate holding an extended enclave or to use the coast as a base for further penetration into the Sudan. One British officer at Suakin in 1885 was convinced that Osman was a Frenchman trained by French officers! (Parry: 32-3)

Osman Digna (or "Uthman Abu Bakr Digna" in strict transliteration), was born of a local merchant family of mixed Kurdish and Hadendowa descent. He has been described as being a lighter shade of brown than most Beja:

> "Thick-set and of middle height, he was taciturn and morose in expression and seldom indulged in laughter.... His eyelashes were thick and his fore-head had a habit of wrinkling up when he became angry. His nose, partially aquiline, fell away and was inclined to be snub.... His sharp-cut features must have given him, as a young man, a somewhat hawk-like appearance." (Jackson: 170).

His motivation for joining the Mahdi has been described by most British authors as resulting from the ruin of his slave-trading business by Royal Navy anti-slave patrols in the Red Sea. Yet his own religious convictions, which he kept all his life, and his fervent adherence to *sufi* doctrines must be seen as having at least equal weight in his motivation. The appeal of the *sufi* brotherhoods and the excitement of the Mahdi's revival seem also to have had greater influence among the Beja than most British authors have allowed.

As all serious students of the *Mahdiyya* now know, popular Islam in the Sudan

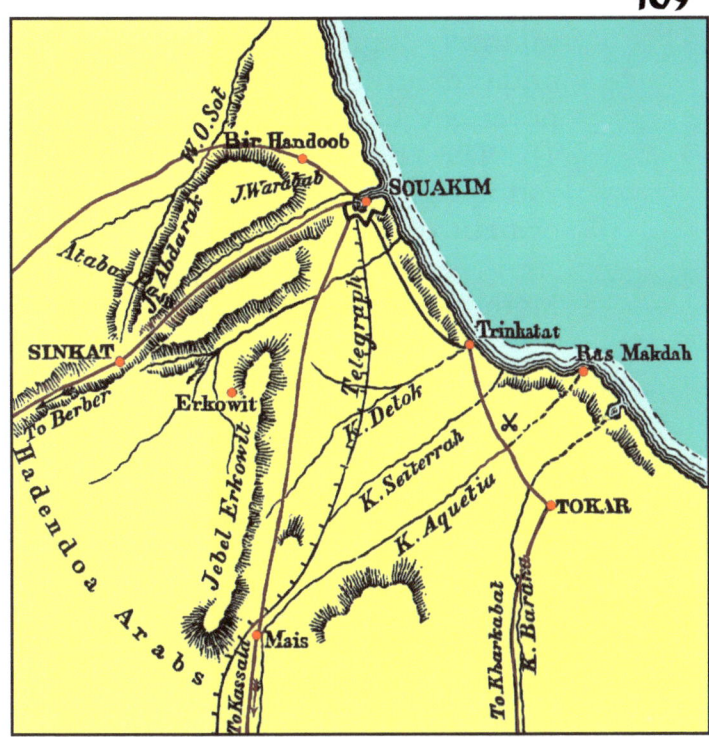

in the Nineteenth Century was dominated by various *sufi* brotherhoods. One, the *Khatmiyya*, led by the Mirghani family from their headquarters in Kassala, had the active support of the Turco-Egyptian government. The *Khatmiyya* remained opposed to the *Mahdiyya*, and this helps to explain the decision of the Beni 'Emir around Kassala to reject the Mahdi. The other large sect active on the Red Sea coast was the Majadhib, led by *Shiekh* al-Tahir al-Tayyib al-Majdhub. The Majadhib had tremendous influence among the Beja, especially the Hadendowa (Holt: 82).

Osman Digna went to see the Mahdi after the fall of El Obeid in January 1883. In May that year the Mahdi appointed him Emir and on 8 May Osman set off to return to the coast. He arrived first amongst the Bisharin and administered the Mahdist oath to the Aliab section of the Um Ali. The head of the Amarar, nazir Hamad Mahmud, refused either to accept or reject the Mahdi, but Muhammad Adam Sa'adun and Onar Isa Magit of the Abd al-Rahmanab section of the Guilai Otman Amarar did join Osman. The Amarar split over the *Mahdiyya*, and many actively supported the government.

Osman then traveled to Qubab, administering the oath to people on the way. At Qubab he met *Shiekh* al-Tahir al-Tayyib al-Majdhub and handed him a letter from the Mahdi, which the *shiekh* took, "Kissed it and placed it on his eyes and forehead. He took the oath of allegiance, praising God for it...." The allegiance of *Shiekh* al-Tahir automatically brought in many of the Hadendowa to Osman's side, the first to join being the Bushariab (Shaked: 128-9; Holt: 82; Owen: 197; Sanders 1935: 207-8).

Osman also sent letters to the leaders of the Khatmiyya, but they quietly continued to adhere to the Egyptian government. In August Osman reached his family home at Erkowit. This brought him to within striking distance of the Egyptian garrison at Sinkat, under Muhammad Tewfiq Bey.

The First Battles

Muhammad Tewfiq Bey... Not enough like him.

Of all the Egyptian officers in the Sudan in 1883, Muhammad Tewfiq Bey was one of the most—if not *the* most—able. He was a Cretan, educated in the French school at Cairo. He had reached the rank of Qa'immaqam (Colonel) by the time he was appointed governor of Suakin in February, 1883. He was the type of soldier British officers would have warmed to, had they known him, for "He was a cultured man and a good sportsman with the rifle" (Hill 1967:276).

He spent the entire first phase of the war, some six months, besieged in Sinkat. Sinkat is about 4,000 feet above sea level, built on a plain surrounded by hills. It had only two or three moderate sized stone barracks, on the west side of which ran a *khor*. At the outbreak of the *Mahdiyya*, Tewfiq seems to have had only 70-100 men at Sinkat. He sent for reinforcements of 200 cavalry, 2000

Sinkat, a lonely bastion among the Hademdowa.

infantry, 3 quick firing cannons and 6 mountain guns, which he never got (Colvile:18; Jackson: 30-1). The area immediately surrounding Sinkat was either friendly or neutral. The recently appointed "Bey" of the Fadlab Amarar, *Shiekh* Mahmud Ali Bey, came with some 400 men and induced Amin Fafair, of the Shara'ab Hadendowa, to remain loyal to the government. In the first battle around Sinkat, though, both these sections stayed out of the fighting (Jackson: 29-31; Hill 1967: 225).

On 5 August, 1883 Osman Digna and *Shiekh* al-Tahir joined forces outside Sinkat and marched to within rifle range of the garrison. There a parley took place, using some of the *shiekhs* of the Khatmiyya as emissaries. Tewfiq prolonged the negotiations as long as possible while his men fortified the barracks and deployed in front of the fort. When Osman realized he was being tricked, he attacked, launching his assault from the western *khor*. He had come to Sinkat with something like 1,500-2,000 followers, most of whom came as spectators. Only about 300 men joined in the battle (Jackson: 31; Hoyle: 100; Paul 1954: 132). Osman's men were armed with spears, a few swords and clubs. The Egyptians held their fire until the Mahdists were ten yards away. Only a few men, led by Osman's brother, Ahmad Digna, penetrated the defenses. Ahmad was killed, but the Mahdists broke through the barrack doors more than once. Osman himself penetrated the defenses and was severely wounded. He was carried away by his men and the battle was over, after about an hour's fighting. In the return to Erkowit Osman had to be tied to a bedstead carried by a camel.

Government accounts said that the Mahdists lost 65 men killed (20 inside the fort) and about 200 wounded, while government losses were 7 killed and 11 wounded. Osman admitted to 60 killed but claimed to have killed 57 enemy (Shaked: 13-1; Jackson: 31-2; Halt: 83).

British authors have made much of the fact that after being wounded at Sinkat Osman never again led his troops into battle, clear proof of his cowardice. The same point could be made of Kitchener, following his wound at the battle of Gammaiza in 1888, and in all fairness the same conclusion should be drawn, because the evidence is equally circumstantial in both cases. No British author has made the same logical step concerning Kitchener, so perhaps we should also look for other reasons for Osman's subsequent actions. We can find then in the outcome of the battle. Osman's forces, small in number and ill-equipped, broke through the fortifications several times and withdrew only when Osman himself was wounded. His death would have brought the *Mahdiyya* in the east to a temporary halt. Much depended on Osman's survival, not just the outcome of individual battles, but the entire war in the east. Osman would have seen this clearly after Sinkat and could only do what most sensible generals since the time of Hannibal have done: direct the battle from some vantage point that enabled him to co-ordinate the movements of his troops. Osman's British opponents did the same.

The next month Tewfiq mustered some reinforcements and was able to sortie out in search of Osman with some 200 men and two guns, accompanied by *Shiekh*

Mahmud Ali Bey of the Amarar. Osman sent a force under his nephew, Muhammad Musa Digna, to intercept them. Tewfiq made a *zariba* at Qubab (not Handub as Wingate later wrote) on 14 September, and Muhammad surrounded his that night. The next morning Muhammad attacked, but he was unable to penetrate the *zariba* and had to withdraw. Muhammad Musa Digna was himself wounded, and he claimed to have lost 27 men and to have killed only 8 of the enemy. Government sources claimed 70 Ansar killed. Tewfiq was unable to pursue and had to return to base, the winner of a pyrrhic victory, leaving the Ansar in possession of the country outside Sinkat (Shaked: 131-2; Jackson: 34; Holt: 841.)

Sinkat was now strongly fortified with a trench surrounding the barracks, sandbags and an earthen parapet. Cannons were placed in each corner, and a thorn *zariba* ringed the lot (Shaked: 132-3; Sartorious: 61). By now there was a new governor of the Red Sea at Suakin, Fariq (Lt.-General) Sulaiman Pasha Niyazi. Sulaiman was a Circassian who had served under Muhammad Ali and had fought in the Crimea. He had been financial officer at Massawa during the disastrous Abyssinian war of 1875-6. In 1883 he was made commander of the Egyptian Army on the White Nile and won a victory against the Ansar in April. He was removed from command at Hicks' insistence and was transferred to the Red Sea to get him out of Khartoum. His attempts to buy off Osman Digna only added to the alienation of the Beja from the government (Hill, 1967: 349-50).

At the end of September he visited Tewfiq at Sinkat, where he put an end to Tewfiq's plans for active operations against the Beja. While Sulaiman was at Sinkat, Osman ordered Ali Tallab ibn Muhammad to besiege the town. Sulaiman, uncertain about his return to Suakin, ordered 150 gendarmes, under Bimbashi (Major) Muhammad Effendi Khalil, up to Sinkat to escort him back. On 16 October some 150-200 Gar'ib Hadendowa from Ali Tallab's force ambushed the gendarmes while they were marching, with their rifles slung on the baggage camels, through Khor Abint. The Egyptians were massacred, with only eight to twenty-five men escaping, leaving the Ansar in possession of 150 rifles and 30,000 rounds of ammunition (Jackson: 36; Royle: 100). (1) This defeat startled Sulaiman Pasha into a precipitate retreat to Suakin.

Tewfiq was left in Sinkat with 600 men, mostly Bashi-Bazouks (Wylde:128), but with no orders to advance against the Ansar (Paul 1954: 133-4). The besiegers were soon joined by a further 750 men under Ali ibn Hamid, and gradually the inhabitants of the town melted away, either reaching Suakin or joining Osman's forces, until no locals were left in the area and the Ansar completely surrounded the town (Shaked: 134).

On his return to Suakin, Sulaiman Pasha turned his attention to Tokar, the penal settlement on the road to Kassala. Tokar was also a center for cultivation and the main source of food for the Egyptians at Suakin, and for this reason was more important to the Egyptians than Sinkat (Shaked: 133). Tokar is set in a depression where water collects, and the wells are always full. There was one two-story government house built by the local governor in the 1870's, and the soldiers, used mostly for tax-gathering, lived in mud huts. The surrounding area was inhabited by several different groups of Beja, including Hadendowa, Amarar, and Bani 'Emir, who bred camels for the government (Junket: 62-3; Sartorius: 62).

At the end of October Osman appointed al-Khidr ibn Ali as commander of the Tokar district and sent him to take the town. Al-Khidr was welcomed by Musa ibn al-Fiqih, leader of the Artayqa, a Beja group who had migrated to Tokar from Suakin at the beginning of the 19th Century (Shaked: 135-6; Paul 1971: 141). The Egyptians at

Tokar, numbering not much more than 600 men, women, and children, refused to surrender and fortified the barracks and surrounding mud huts with a strong parapet (Shaked: 136; Wingate: 117; Sartorius: 62). Al-Khidr then sent 'Abdallah ibn Hamid to the coast to prevent reinforcements coming up.

The man Sulaiman sent to relieve Tokar was Lira (Brigadier) Mahmud Pasha Tahir. He had been governor of Kordofan in 1874-8 before being relieved and imprisoned for dishonesty. He was later reinstated and made sub-prefect of police in Cairo until he was promoted Liwa and sent to Suakin as commander of Egyptian troops in October 1883. He took with him Commander Lynedock Needham Moncrief, the British Consul at Suakin who had earlier served with the Royal Navy in the Zulu War (Hill 1967: 227, 241).

On 3 November, Mahmud Pasha left Suakin on the steamships *Tor* and *Gabariyya* with between 500-550 men and one gun. They arrived at Trinkitat on the 4th and set out for Tokar on the 5th. They posted no flank guards and were attacked at Andetteib, which later became known as And al-Tayb, or El-Teb. 'Abdallah ibn Hasid's force appears to have been between 150-200 men, and they were armed mostly with spears and sticks. Mahmud Pasha was one of the first to flee, and the majority of his force also escaped. In all some 150 soldiers were killed, including 11 officers, 142 men and Commander Moncrief. They also left behind their cannon, some 300 rifles and 50,000 rounds of ammunition. Both Mahdist and government sources give the Mahdist losses as about two dozen men (Shaked: 136; Jackson: 38-9; Royle:101; Wingate: 94; Holt: 84-5).

On the same day as the 1st Battle of El Teb (or the "1st Battle of the Coast," as the Ansar called it) the Egyptian District Officer at Tokar returning from Kassala was ambushed and killed by the Kimaylab Beja under al-Hajj ibn Hasan, who were on their way to join al-Khidr at Tokar (Shaked: 136). Suakin was now cut-off from the three main Egyptian garrisons of Sinkat, Tokar and Kassala. Its already small garrison on the Red Sea had been unable to follow up its victories and had suffered disproportionately from its losses. It was now too weakened, too spread out. and too demoralized to regain the offensive. The defeats of October and November, coinciding with Hick's defeat in Kordofan, forced the Egyptian government to commit itself to further action along the Red Sea. Mahmud Tahir was removed and eventually court-martialed for negligence.

Sulaiman Pasha Niyazi was replaced as governor by Mirliva (Major-General) Husain Pasha Wasif in early 1884 (Hill 1967: 350). The garrison at Suakin was reinforced in late 1883-early 1884 by troops for a new expeditionary force under Valentine Baker, Commandant of the Gendarmerie.

The Egyptian troops overwhelmed by Beja warriors at the earliest of several bloody battles at El Teb, November 5, 1883.

Footnote:
Colville (18) puts the Egyptian force at 158. The official Mahdist history (Shaked:134] claims the victory was won by 60 inexperienced boys! Halt (84)

puts the date of the battle as 26 October, due to an error in Osman Digna's manuscript. Shaked (133, n.56) has corrected this error and adopts the date used by most British sources.

Beja Costume, Arms and Tactics

Illustration by Greg Rose

The Beja in 1883 wore clothes and hairstyles which had been common to nomads in the Sudan over a wide area from the Ethiopian to Egyptian borders and from the Red Sea coast to the deserts of northern Kordofan before the Egyptian Occupation of 1820. The style gradually changed along the Nile under Egyptian influence, and this transformation was accelerated under the *Mahdiyya*. Hairstyles and clothing were not part of a "tribal" costume, as some recent articles have assumed. Contemporary illustrations in the works of the travelers William Junker (1890) and Ernst Marne (1879), especially those based on the photographs of Richard Buchta, clearly show the similarity of styles throughout the Red Sea. The illustrations of hairstyles and costumes in this article are based on those sources, plus other contemporary sketches in Grant.

The most common hairstyle was that frequently described by Europeans as resembling the "Club" in a deck of cards. The hair was drawn out to cover the ear, then divided into two by a horizontal parting. The upper mass was raised into a top-knot while the lower half was either fanned out and left frizzy (Style "A"), or plaited into small tresses and covered with mutton fat (Style "B"). A thin wooden skewer, used in hair-dressing, was usually tucked in the top half of the hair. Hair could also be cut short or tucked up entirely behind the back of the head (Style "C').

The usual Beja costume was the *tobe*, a long narrow strip of cotton cloth with a colored border, usually wrapped around the waist, leaving the torso exposed (Dunker: 57). Short cotton drawers, and sometimes long, loose trousers were worn underneath. The *tobe* very often resembled a short skirt. One loose end was often draped over one or both shoulders, or even unfolded like a cloak, very like the Ethiopian *shamma*. Occasionally a collarless shirt, with either short or long sleeves, was also worn under the *tobe*, but this seems rare in the 19th Century. Leather amulets and strings of wooden beads were usually worn around the neck. Feet were either bare or sandaled, with a simple leather sole tied with a thong around the ankle and big toe.

The Beja were armed with thin curved mimosa clubs, spears, swords, daggers and shields. The spear blades were a variety of shapes, usually long and narrow. Beja swords were (and are) straight and double-edged, carried in red leather scabbards suspended by a loop from the left shoulder. The sword belt often had tassels of various kinds, and both scabbard and belt were usually ornamented with tooled designs. Swords were much prized and were passed on from father to eldest son, or more often carefully selected and purchased.

The different parts of the handle and the different styles of blade are all named. The handle is *alqaim*, the protuberance at the end of the handle is *al-toma*, the cross-piece is *al-barsham*, and the tassel at the end of the handle is *al-jidla*. There are four main blade styles: Sulaimani Da'ud has three parallel grooves down the blade, the center groove going all the way to the point; Sulaimani abu Shabaish is the same, but with the part of the blade nearest the handle being engraved with scrolling; al-Jar has a single groove from the handle to the point; Dukkari abu Dubban) has a short central groove, and carries three marks known as dubbana, nugara, and 'asad (Clark: 18).

Daggers came in many styles, either straight or curved, but all double-edged. Handles were made out of yellow mimosa wood or black ebony. Scabbards were either brown or red leather. The short, straight daggers were usually worn on the upper left arm. The Bani 'Emir seemed also to have some of the more curved daggers in sheaths attached to ornamented red leather waist-belts (Thomas).

Beja shields are a distinctive shape, not used in other parts of the Sudan. They are round with a conical central boss, into which a leather handle is lashed. On a diameter at right angles to the handle, two holes are cut out of the shield edge (Thomas: 65-6). These shields are often described as being made out of rhinoceros hide, but the rhinoceros is a rare (if non-existent) animal in this part of the Sudan. Same may have been made of hippopotamus or giraffe hide, but a good many were probably made out of cow hide.

The Beja *tobe*, drawers and shirt were sometimes white, but became gray or beige with use. Douglas Giles' famous paintings in the National Army Museum show a variety of terra cotta colors. Sword scabbards and waist belts were almost always red leather; sandals, shields and amulets were a variety of shades of brown. Aside from the embroidered band on the loose end of the *tobe* (often dark red, but probably any color which could be obtained from a vegetable dye), no patches were worn on the *tobe* at this stage.

The Beja usually fought on foot, but some also rode camels. The Hadendowa, being cattle breeders, were not known as great camel men. The best cattle breeds came from the Bisharin and Amarar. Two of the most famous were the Ba Nagir and Kiliewau, bred by the Hamadorab and Aliab Bisharin. The Bishari camels of the Atbai desert were considered the best in the Sudan, being strong and bred for endurance and pace, able to maintain a comfortable cruising speed of 5 m.p.h. The Kurbab Amarar also bred a smaller but handy "all-purpose" camel. Beja camel riders have been noted since at least medieval times for their skill in riding, handling their camels in battle as skillfully as horses. A good rider could ride at full tilt, standing on his camel, brandishing his sword or carrying a howl of milk without spilling a drop (Paul 1971: 147).

Camel saddles were made of wood and covered in leather, but when in place a sheepskin or blanket usually covered them. Two types of saddlebags were used: the leather *khur*, laid across the seat of the saddle with a pouch hanging on either side, and the *jurab*, often made out of gazelle skin and resembling the shape of the torso of the animal. It was slung from the front and back pommel of the saddle and was preferred to the *khurg*, which could not carry much weight (Acland). There was also a type of conical spear quiver, usually made out of soft dark brown leather and tassled at the bottom and at places along the seam (Thomas). This quiver was probably slung on one or other of the saddle pommels, as was the shield when traveling. The camel was guided by a simple leather head rope.

The Beja used the same tactics in 1883 that they were to use against the British in 1884-5, and against the 21st Lancers in 1898: One later British administrator described their method of fighting this way: "Firearms they never cared about and still have no interest in; sword and spear, shield and camel stick, an approach under any available cover, and a rush of tremendous velocity were their methods of offence..."

(Owen: 197).

Their cover was provided not only by the undulating ground and a series of low rises, but by the thick, tall mimosa bush, which was able to keep hundreds of persons hidden from an enemy only a few yards away (Sartorius:181). When attacking they would first throw their mimosa club at their enemy's head, or at their horses' feet, and then close in with spear or sword, aiming always for some vital part like the head, throat or chest. They made little use of the large numbers of rifles and ammunition they captured. During this stage of the war they fought under their own section leaders in their own sections.

References

Acland, P.B.E. (1932), "Notes on the Camel in the Eastern Sudan," SUDAN NOTES AND RECORDS (SNR) 15/1.

Clark, W.T. (1938), "Manners, Customs and Beliefs of the Northern Beja" SNR 21/1.

Colville, H.E. (1889), HISTORY OF THE SUDAN CAMPAIGN, PART I, London. HMSO

Brant, J. (c.1886), CASSELL'S HISTORY OF THE WAR IN THE SOUDAN, London.

Hill, R. (1959), EGYPT AND THE SUDAN, London, Oxford University Press.

Hill, R. (1967), A BIOGRAPHICAL DICTIONARY OF THE SUDAN, 2nd Edition, London, Frank Cass.

Holt, P.M. (1970), THE MAHDIST STATE IN THE SUDAN 1881-1898, 2nd Edition, Oxford, The Clarendon Press.

Jackson, H.C. (1926), OSMAN DIGNA, London, Methuen.

Junker, M. (1890), TRAVELS IN AFRICA DURING THE YEARS 1875-1878, London, Chapeau and Hall.

Marno, E. (1879) REISEN IN DER EGYPTISCHE AEQUARTORIAL-PROVINZ UND IN KORDOFAN IN DER JAHREN 1874-76, Vienna.

Nadel, S.F. (1945), "Notes on Bani Emir Society," SNR 26/1.

Owen, T.R.H. (1937), "The Hadendowa," SNR 26/1.

Parry, E.G. "An Officer Who Was There" (1885), SUAKIN, 1885, London, Kegan, Paul, Trench and Co.

Paul, A. (1950), 'Notes on the Beni Amer," SNR 31/2.

Paul, A. (1954), "Tewfik Bey," SNR 35/1.

Paul, A. (1971), A HISTORY OF THE BEJA OF THE SUDAN, 2nd Edition, London, Frank Cass.

Boyle, C. (1886), THE EGYPTIAN CAMPAIGNS 1882 TO 1885, VOL. II, London, Hurst and Blackett.

Sandars, G.E.R. (1933), "The Bisharin",: SNR 16/2.

Sandars, G.E.R. (1935), "The Amarar," SNR 18/2.

Sartorius, E. (1885), THREE MONTHS IN THE SOUDAN, London, Kegan, Paul, Trench and Co.

Shaked, H. (1978), THE LIFE OF THE SUDANESE MAHDI, New Brunswick, N.J., Transaction Books.

Thomas, E.S. (1924), CATALOGUE OF THE ETHNOGRAPHICAL MUSEUM OF THE ROYAL GEOGRAPHICAL SOCIETY OF EGYPT, Cairo.

Wingate, F.R. (1968), MAHDIISM AND THE EGYPTIAN SUDAN, 2nd Edition, London, Frank Cass.

Wylde, A.B. (1969), '83 TO '87 IN THE SOUDAN, VOL. I, New York, Negro Univ. Press. (reprint of 1888 edition).

Wars in Eastern Sudan Part 2: Baker & El Teb
by Doug Johnson

With Mahmud Tahir Pasha's defeat at Andetteib (El Teb) on 5 November, 1883 the Egyptian Government was forced to bring in reinforcements to help secure Suakin from attack.

Valentine Baker Pasha, Commander of the Egyptian Gendarmerie

Baker Pasha

The reinforcements came from two main sources: from other Red Sea garrisons in Abyssinia and Somalia, and from Egypt itself. By the end of 1883 the Abyssinian and Somalia troops were deployed as follows (Wylde: 45-7 [a complete list of Egyptian infantry units is unavailable]): The total force in Abyssinia consisted of 1,015 Egyptians, 1,918 Sudanese and 649 irregulars (some of whom were recruited locally). The largest garrisons were at Massawa and Sannaheit. Somalia totaled 1,005 Sudanese and 2,425 irregulars, some of which were old Egyptian soldiers. The garrisons at Gallabat and Kassala, both being in the Sudan, were effectively isolated from Suakin and could not be drawn on. The Somali garrisons were so far away that they were not evacuated in time to be used in Baker's campaign. That left only about 3,000 regulars from Abyssinia that could be brought to Suakin, a force too small to be effective. The main body had to come from Egypt.

In Egypt after Tel-el-Kebir the gendarmerie was raised from old soldiers in the Egyptian Army to act as a semi-military force in the provinces, guarding the border and patrolling the desert. They were given the same uniform and equipment as the old army, and up to 1883 officers were interchangeable between the army and the gendarmerie (Haggard: 24; Sartorius: 72, 77). General Valentine Baker was given command of the gendarmerie, a post he held until his death in 1887.

Baker had served in the Turkish Army during the Russo-Turkish War of 1877-8, after having been dismissed from the British Army for the attempted rape of a woman in a railway carriage in 1875. He rose to the rank of Fariq before being seconded to the Egyptian Army where he was first proposed to take overall command. The scandal of his dismissal followed him and Queen Victoria, among others, opposed his appointment. He got the gendarmerie instead.

The gendarmerie originally totaled 6,000 men, organized into companies of 50 with three officers each. There were 1,600 mounted gendarmes, 500 "Turks" and 400 "European" police (all natives of Egypt) for Cairo and Alexandria, and 3,500 other gendarmes. But in 1883 it was remodeled along the lines of the Irish Constabulary and the number of officers and horses were reduced. The Cairo and Alexandria battalions were then recruited entirely from the NCOs of the old army (Sartorius: 74, 77, 80).

Baker was reluctant to take command of an expeditionary force to Suakin but agreed to do so when it was decided to raise a supplementary force of Turkish Bashi-Bazouks as well as some *bazingers* (slave riflemen) under Zubair Rahma Pasha.

Before these troops could arrive, some 600 Sudanese from Massawa (not included in the above figures) under Col. Kassis Effendi reached Suakin and were immediately sent out along with 200 Egyptian soldiers, 50 Bashi-Bazouk cavalry and one gun under Major Izzet Effendi and Capt. Ibrahim Effendi to capture Osman Digna. (1)

The column set out on the night of 1st-2nd December and came upon a small party of Mahdists at the wells of Tamanieb in the morning. The cavalry had stayed close to the flanks of the column all the while and had done no scouting. The Sudanese infantry opened fire on the Ansar, dispersing them. The square then moved up, occupying the wells, with the Sudanese forming three sides of the square and the Egyptians forming the rear face.

While the troops were watering, some 3,000 Ansar suddenly attacked the rear face. The cavalry fled into the Sudanese in an attempt to get into the square, and then the Egyptians broke and fled into the backs of the Sudanese. The cavalry and the two Effendis retreated, but the Sudanese fought on for some hours, back to back, until almost all were killed. (2)

The situation in Suakin was critical. The gun-vessel H.M.S. *Ranger* under Commander W.E. Darwall had been sent to Suakin in November, 1883 and now became the town's main defense, moored along the causeway connecting the town to the mainland (Clowes: 350). Suakin itself contained only 300 mixed troops, mostly "old soldiers of the garrison," 2 Krupps, 3 mountain guns and some 18th Century smooth-bore cannons (Wylde: 7; Sartorius: 104). The *Ranger* was joined by the corvette *Carysfort* (Capt. Walter Stewart), the torpedo-depot ship *Hecla* (Capt. A.K. Wilson), and eventually the H.M.S. *Coquette* (Capt. Alexander Plantagenet) and the H.M.S. *Woodlark* from Aden (Clowes: 350-1). Baker's chief of staff, Col. Sartorius, arrived with the first batch of 650 gendarmes on 8 December, 1883, and Suakin, at least, was considered secure (Sartorius: 92; Royle: 104).

The force that set out from Egypt in stages underwent a number of shifts in composition. Six hundred from the Alexandria battalion were sent and 800 from the Cairo battalion, but 280 Cairenes deserted on the way and only 520 arrived in Suakin. A number of Turks were also recruited but only 100 obeyed the summons (Sartorius: 86).

Throughout the month of December various batches of gendarmes arrived in Suakin. There was a small contingent of "European" police (about 50) under Major Maletta, an Italian (Sartorius: 147). The depletion of gendarmerie in Egypt itself meant that new recruits had to be found to increase their ranks quickly. These were all "Turks" (Albanians, Circassians, etc.) living in Egypt, same 500 in all, who were first instructed in drill only after arriving in Suakin (Sartorius: 156, 167, 211).

It had been decided to augment the gendarmes by raising some 1,600 semi-regular black riflemen, or *bazingers* as they were known in the southern provinces of the Sudan, and send them to Suakin under the command of Zubair Rahma Pasha. Zubair had been an ivory and slave merchant on a far larger scale than Osman Digna and had conquered much of Bahr al-Ghazal and Darfur with his own bands of slave riflemen in the 1860's and 1870's. He had lost his prize of Darfur to the government and found himself a permanent "guest" of the Khedive in Cairo for his pains. His son had been executed by Gessi during a revolt during Gordon's first governor-generalship.

Because of his success with slave armies, it was first thought that he would be equally successful with a smaller force raised and trained in a shorter period, but then it was decided politically unwise to send Zubair himself to Suakin. It was doubtful what he would have achieved even if he had gone. His nephew, sent as an emissary to Osman Digna in December, failed completely to interest any of the Beja in coming over to Zubair and the Egyptian government.

Zubair paraded his first battalion of *bazingers* in front of the Khedive in Cairo on the 2nd of January, 1884. There were delays in their departure because of lack of transport, but finally six companies, along with their families, under the command of Khalil Ali were dispatched from Egypt on the 16th of January, arriving in Suakin a few days later (Royle: 104- 5; Sartorius: 199, 208).

The second battalion was placed under the command of a well-educated, French-speaking Turkish officer who complained both of the quality of the retired Egyptian officers and NCOs allotted to the battalion, and of the quality of the troops themselves. He protested that his men were untrained and unfamiliar with their firearms, but because Baker had requested the immediate dispatch of all men, trained and untrained, they too embarked on 20 January and arrived at Suakin by the end of the month (Sartorius: 209; Royle: 105).

In all there were some 1,200 *bazingers* sent to the Eastern Sudan, but unlike the experienced riflemen who had fought in the Southern Sudan and who were soon to join the Mahdi's army, they were *bazinger* in name only. Despite the fact that the reinforcements from Egypt were supposed to provide the main force of operations in the Eastern Sudan, their lack of training and experience forced the commanders of the new expeditionary force to rely even more heavily on the experienced soldiers they were ostensibly coming to reinforce. These fell into three main groups: the "Old Soldiers" of the Suakin garrison, the local Bashi-Bazouk irregulars, and the regular troops in the Abyssinian and Somali garrisons.

The "Old Soldiers" were never a credible force. They numbered no more than 320 by the beginning of February, were given no regular uniform, and were detailed mainly to guard the gates of the town (Sartorius: 104, 225). The Bashi-Bazouks were potentially more useful, but in fact provided no core of disciplined men around which the rest of the force could be organized. They were all Albanians and were not normally drilled. When Col. Sartorius tried to institute regular drill, they refused and had to be disarmed by four companies of the Alexandria battalion and their leaders flogged before training could proceed. Some of their numbers included young boys and old, deaf, blind and lame men who had to be sent back to Egypt. Their numbers were expanded, however, by new batches from Egypt. Some had preceded Sartorius to Suakin and more came afterwards. The last batch of 200 arrived at Trinkitat direct from Suez only two days before the 2nd Battle of El Teb. The commander of all Bashi-Bazouks was Yusuf Bey, and they were employed in a number of reconnaissance sorties around Suakin before the final march to Tokar (Sartorius: 96, 128-9, 139, 147, 151).

There was only one contingent of Bashi-Bazouks which did command respect. These were local Abyssinian hill men attached to the Massawa garrison and outposts. They were good at skirmish fighting, but as they were locally recruited in Abyssinia they were not available for the Tokar campaign, despite Baker's wish that he could have brought them along (Wylde: 109). Only 24 came as volunteers to Suakin, a token unit entirely (Sartorius: 214).

This left the regulars of the Abyssinian garrisons. They were needed desperately since Col. Sartorius decided soon after his arrival that Muhammad Tewfiq at Sinkat should be relieved before the advance to Tokar (Sartorius 137-8).

Sinkat was besieged by at least 4,000 men, though some reports put the besiegers at 11,000 (Sartorius: 137-8; Colville: 19). Against this Tewfiq had to hold the town with only 150 Bashi-Bazouks, 300 Egyptian infantry and 32 gunners (Sartorius: 107). But Suleiman Pasha assured Baker that Tokar was in more urgent need of relief, so Sinkat was left to fend for itself while the Tokar relief force was gathered together.

Baker and his staff assembled in Suakin throughout the month of December. With Baker were Major-General (Egyptian rank) Sartorius Pasha (2nd in command),

Col. Abd al-Rassak (Egyptian Chief of Staff), Lt.-Col. Fitzroy Hay (European Chief of Staff), Major Harvey, 42nd Highlanders (ADC to Baker), Lt.-Col. Morice Bey, RMLI (Paymaster), and Dr. Leslie (medical department). Sartorius was commander of the 1st division and had under him Lt.-Col. Harrington (Rifle Brigade) as chief of divisional staff, Major Izzat Effendi, and Capt. Goodall as ADC. Major G.D. Giles (the war artist) commanded the "Turkish" (Bashi-Bazouk) cavalry, while Major Holroyd commanded the "Turkish" infantry. Capt. Forrestier Walker, who had served with Hicks before the march into Kordofan, now came as the correspondent of the *Daily News* and doubled as commander of artillery, while Col. Frederick Burnaby came along for the ride (Sartorius: 85-6, 157; Haggard: 126-7; Royle: 102).

Baker had at his disposal the Egyptian gunboats *Tor* and *Gefferiah*, along with the troopships *Zagazig*, *Tantah*, *Mahallah*, *Mansurah*, and the small paddle steamer *Deb el-Bar*. The Royal Navy was represented by a squadron under Admiral Hewitt, now consisting of the H.M.S. *Euryalus* (flagship), *Sphinx*, *Ranger*, *Woodlark* and *Coquette*.

To strengthen his force Baker transferred the Sudanese soldiers of Massawa and Sannaheit to Suakin, replacing them with some of the Egyptian infantry. He could not wait for the arrival of the Harrar garrison, and Suleiman Pasha ordered the return of one batch of Sudanese troops to Massawa for fear of an Abyssinian attack (Wylde: 53; Sartorius: 153).

Fortifications

Suakin itself had to be fortified. The main town was an island, linked to the mainland by a causeway. At the end of the causeway was the market town of El Geif. Just outside the milk market was an old three-roomed stone fort, surrounded by a trench and earthwork, containing two Krupp guns, three mountain guns and some 18th Century smoothbores.

Next to the fort was a stone barrack which could hold up to 400 men. To the north of El Geif was an unfortified mud and stone barrack which could hold two companies. Beyond this was a police station, inhabited only by day. There were no defenses to the south, facing Tamai and Tokar. The army headquarters tent was pitched in the silk market, and the troops were stationed around El Geif. There were no forts guarding the wells outside the town (Wylde: 7-8).

In December, after Sartorius' arrival, a four foot deep, three foot wide trench was dug around El Geif, with a parapet of about five to six feet high. Six foot long stakes were placed in the trench. The trench connected up a series of small forts, which were detached buildings surrounded by ditches. A *zariba* of old sisasa bushes was placed around the outer edge of the parapet. Sartorius established the headquarters of the 1st Division in a small two-story building near the flag staff, with a small barrack occupied by the "European" police. Forts were placed at the wells, and at night they hung lanterns out on the town side so as not to be fired on. Baker added another series of small forts outside the lines in January 1884, and this kept the Ansar further away from the town as they did not want to get caught between the redoubts and the main fortifications (Sartorius: 126-7, 131, 186, 197).

Mahdist pressure on the various garrisons of the Red Sea continued. On 20 December, 1883 the Ansar seized part of the town outside Tokar, but Ibrahim Markavi, the garrison commander, drove them off (Sartorius: 180). On the same day, Sartorius, Major Giles and Augustus Wylde (the British consul at Suakin) made a reconnaissance against the Hadendowa with 250 cavalry. They managed to capture some 260 camels and a number of other livestock, but learned later that they had seized the herds of some of their "friendlies" (Sartorius: 149-52).

One of the Redoubts and part of the zariba around Suakin.

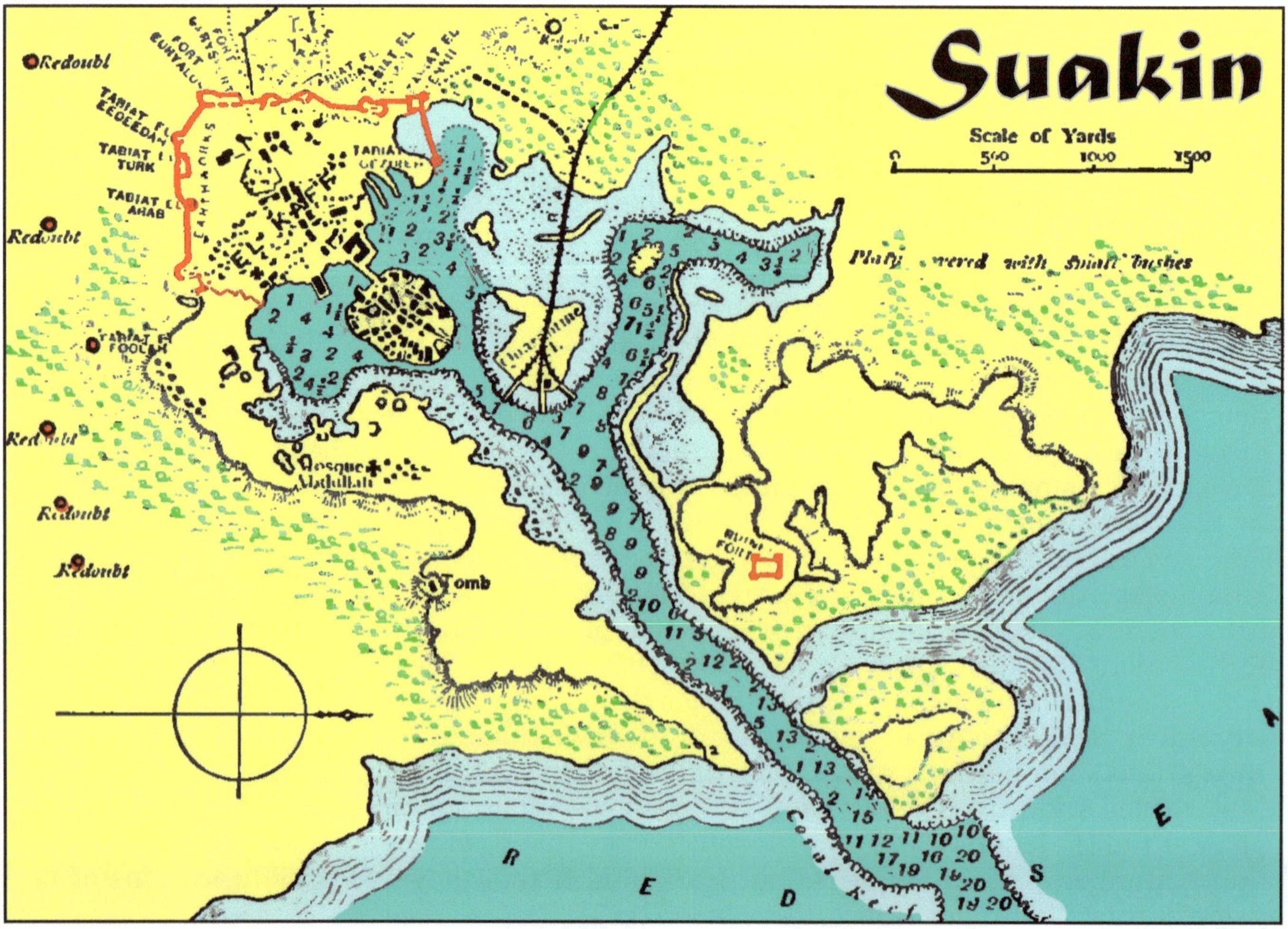

Remarkable view of the Causeway connecting Suakin with the trading center of El Geif ("El Keif") immediately opposite on the mainland. (Note the warship masts and funnel smoke at right background.)

"Quarry Fort" on the Southeast side of Suakin Harbor.

Photo identified as "West Redoubt." Note the deep trench apparently filled with thorn bush, and the section of guns (with supporting limbers) to the right.

Fort Carysfort (named after one of the warships in the harbor) located on the Eastern center of the fortifications around El Geif before Suakin.

The Royal Navy's Presence at Suakin

HMS Ranger (1880) — Composite Gun Vessel
Displacement — 835 tons   Length — 157'
Beam — 29.5'   Draft — 13.5'
Speed — 10.5 knots
Armament — One 7" MLR, Two 64-pdr MLR
Crew — 100

HMS Carysfort (1879) — Steel Corvette
Displacement — 2380 tons   Length — 225'
Beam — 44.5'   Draft — 19'   Speed — 13 Knots
Armament — Four 6" BL, Eight 64-pdrs MLR,
Two light guns, and two
Torpedoes
Crew — 265

HMS Coquette (1871) — Composite Gunboat
Displacement — 430 tons   Length — 125'
Beam — 22.5'   Draft — 10.5'
Speed — 10 knots
Armament — Two 64-pdr MLR,
Two 20-pdr BL
Crew — 60

HMS Hecla (1878) — Torpedo Depot Ship
Displacement — 6400 tons   Length — 392'
Beam — 39'   Draft — 24.5'
Speed — 13 knots
Armament — Five 64-pdr, One 40-pdr
Crew — 277

HMS Euryalus (1877) — Screw Corvette
Displacement — 3932 tons Length — 280'
Beam — 45.5' Draft — 23'
Speed — 14.7 knots
Armament — Fourteen 7" MLR,
           Two 64-pdr MLR
Crew — 375

HMS Woodlark (1871)
Wooden Gun Vessel
Displacement — 755 tons Length — 170'
Beam — 29' Draft — 10.5 Speed — 10 knots
Armament — One 7" MLR,
           Two 40-pdr BL
Crew — 90

HMS Condor (1877)
Composite Gun Vessel
Displacement — 774 tons Length — 157'
Beam — 29' Draft — 12'
Speed — 11.5 knots
Armament — One 7" MLR,
           Two 64-pdr MLR
Crew — 100

HMS Sphinx (1882)
Composite Paddle Vessel
Displacement — 1130 tons Length — 200'
Beam — 32' Draft — ?
Speed — ? Armament — One 6",
           Four 4" Guns
Crew — ?

HMS Cygnet (1874)
Composite Gun Boat
Displacement— 455 tons   Length— 125'
Beam— 24' Draft— 10.5'
Speed— 10 knots
Armament— Two 64-pdr MLR,
　　　　　　Two 20-pdr BL
Crew— 60

HMS Dolphin (1882)
Composite Screw Sloop
Displacement— 1140 tons   Length— 157'
Beam— 32' Draft— 14'
Speed— 11.5 knots
Armament—　Two 6" BL
　　　　　　Two 5" BL
Crew— 115

HMS Starling (1882)
Composite Gun Boat
Displacement— 455 tons   Length— 125'
Beam— 24' Draft— 10' Speed— 9.5 knots
Armament— Two 64-pdr MLR,
　　　　　　Two 20-pdr BL
Crew— 60

HMS Albacore (1883)
Composite Gunboat
Displacement— 560 tons   Length— 135'
Beam— 26' Draft— 10.5'
Speed— 10.7 knots
Armament—　Two 5" BL, Two 4" BL,
　　　　　　Two MG
Crew— 60

HMS Jumna (1866) -
Troop Ship
Displacement— 6211 tons   Length— 360'
Beam—49' Draft—22'
Speed— 15 Knots
Armament— Three 4-pdrs
Crew— ?

HMS Orontes (1862) -
Troop Ship
Displacement— 4857 tons   Length— 300'
Beam—44.5' Draft—?
Speed— 15 Knots
Armament— Three 4-pdrs
Crew— ?

Royal Navy vessel taking a pot-shot at a concentration of Beja warriors on the north side of Suakin.
Note the island city to the left, the causeway, center, and El Geif and outer defenses on the mainland.
Such targets of opportunity served as frequent monotony breaks—for both sides—during the siege.

About a month later, on 22 January 1884, Baker himself led some 300 cavalry on another reconnaissance and also captured a good deal of cattle, but had to retire to Suakin with the Beja camel men harrying him part of the way (Sartorius; 201).

First Battle of El Teb

By the beginning of February, Baker was ready to set out for Tokar. Colonel Iskander Bey was left in command of Suakin with 108 men of the Cairo Battalion, 68 of the Alexandria Battalion, 72 Massawa Sudanese, 639 of the 2nd Battalion of *bazingers*, 320 "Old Soldiers," 107 of the 1st Battalion of *bazingers*, 35 of the Turkish Battalion, 50 bandsmen, 186 gunners, 33 Turkish cavalry and 54 Arab cavalry (of which only 34 had horses). On 1 and 2 February the rest of the army left Suakin for Trinkitat, and on 3 February they camped at Fort Baker, some three miles inland from Trinkitat.

The entire force numbered some 1,300 Egyptian gendarmerie (divided about equally between the Cairo and Alexandria battalions), 900 Sudanese infantry (about 450 each from Massawa and Sannaheit), 500 *bazingers*, 400 "Turkish" infantry (including some 200 untrained troops sent straight from Suez to Trinkitat), 300 Egyptian cavalry, 150 Bashi-Bazouk cavalry, about 40 European police under Italian officers, 4 Krupps, 2 Gatling guns and 2 rocket tubes under Capt. Forrestier Walker. (3)

The camp at Trinkitat was left with a guard of 200 Egyptians and 300 "Shageer" (Sha'iqiya?) Arabs sent straight from Egypt and armed with double-barreled smoothbore muzzle-loading muskets. Two of the Krupps and part of the Massawa Battalion were left at Fort Baker (Sartorius; 230-1).

The force marched out on 4 February, 1884 in three battalions in echelon, companies marching in columns. The artillery (including the Gatlings) were escorted by two companies of the Alexandria Battalion and 40 European police, while the camel train in the rear was escorted by 200 *bazingers*. The Egyptian cavalry were deployed to the front and the left, while the Bashi-Bazouks were in the front (Royle: 108; Wingate: 95). (4)

In case of attack, the Cairo Battalion was to form the front face of the square, the Alexandria Battalion the right, the Sannaheit Battalion the left, and the *bazingers* the rear. The Massawa Battalion and the Turkish infantry were to form battalion squares of their own on the flanks of the main square (Sartorius: 232-3).

The march was partially obscured by occasional rain, and the column struggled across undulating ground with high mimosa bushes further obscuring their vision. At about six miles out two flags were spotted an the top of the next rise. The Krupps fired three rounds in their direction and a force of Beja camel and horsemen were noticed trying to work around the right flank. Major Giles and the Bashi-Bazouks were sent out to intercept them, but the Beja led them on across the front of the column and to the left until they found themselves among the main body of Ansar, some 1,000-1,200 men under Abdullah ibn Hasid, hidden behind the rise.

The Bashi-Bazouks became disordered and scattered and started riding back over the hill with the Ansar coming quickly behind them. The Egyptian cavalry scouts opened fire, hitting a number of Bashi-Bazouks, before they, too, were attacked by the Beja. The Egyptian cavalry now turned and fled.

Into Square

The infantry were ordered into square. The Cairo Battalion formed the front face, but two companies of the Alexandria Battalion on the right refused to move. The Sannaheit Battalion first tried to deploy to the front and then had to be wheeled back to save the left face. The *bazingers* in the rear were too mixed up with the baggage animals to form anything properly. Both the Turkish and Massawa Battalions formed their individual squares quickly. Troops began firing before the square was fully formed, covering the formation in smoke.

By the time the Bashi-Bazouks and the Egyptian cavalry began rushing into the square only the front, left and part of the rear faces were formed. The Cairo and Alexandria Battalions began to dissolve as the cavalry rode through them. The left front and left faces of the square were the first to be hit by the Ansar. The Cairo and Alexandria Battalions broke and began to run only eight minutes after the rush began; they surged against the Sannaheit Battalion and the *bazingers*, disorganized the Massawa Battalion square (which was so placed as to be unable to fire on the enemy). The Sannaheit Battalion was forced back on the Turkish square, taking part of it with them, but the Turks reformed. The guns had no time to fire before the European police escort were attacked and died fighting, almost to a man.

Sartorius and Col. Ahmad Kamal Bey tried to rally the gendarmerie, but they were carried away for 200 yards by the flood of men. Baker sent Sartorius back to the fort to try to stop the men as they passed, and he shot down many as they ran by. The Sudanese and the Turks stood for a while but then began to retreat. Only the Sudanese infantry stopped occasionally to turn and fire during the flight. The army was pursued for five miles by the Ansar. Those who survived the flight all embarked immediately on arriving at Trinkitat.

Out of a force of some 3,715 men, about 2,373 were killed. Two Krupps, 2 Gatlings, 3,000 Remingtons and about half a million cartridges were captured by the victorious Beja. The Ansar lost some men, including Muhammad ibn Ali, brother of al-Khidr, commander of the forces besieging Tokar. The Ansar were outnumbered by the Egyptians by about 3 to 1, and none of the Ansar were then armed with rifles (Sartorius: 233-41; Haggard: 128-31; Royle: 108-117; Wingate; 95-6; Shaked: 137).

Aftermath

The remnants of Baker's army returned to Suakin on the night of the 5th. On the 6th Admiral Hewitt landed a force of sailors and marines with Gatling and Nordenfelt guns to help protect the city, which otherwise had less than 3,000 scared and demoralized soldiers to defend it. On the 9th Suakin was declared in a state of

A popular impression—and not inaccurate—of the rout of the Egyptian Square at El Teb.

siege, Admiral Hewitt was given complete military and civil powers over the town, and Britain pledged herself to defending the town from attack.

All of this made little difference in the interior. On 8 February the Sinkat garrison, having eaten all its animals, spiked its guns and tried to fight its way to Suakin, taking with it over 200 women and children. The force was attacked a mile out of town and annihilated, Tewfiq Bey being killed with them. On 23 February 1884 the Tokar garrison came to an understanding with al-Khidr ibn Ali and handed over the fort. Only Kassala continued to hold out.

The first phase of the war in the Eastern Sudan had come to an end. Egypt was almost completely expelled from the coast. Britain could no longer avoid intervening.

Troops and Tactics

The British officers attached to the Egyptian Army were new to Egypt and the Sudan, and their inexperience showed in their assessments of their own soldiers and the enemy. The Egyptian Army contained a wild variety of regular and irregular soldiers, from the conscript Egyptian peasant, to the Albanian and Circassian freebooters, to the enslaved black African rifleman, to the loyal tribal levy.

It is no wonder that the authorities in Cairo didn't really know what to make of it all, and it is no wonder that Baker, like Hicks, misjudged his own men. Before 1884 the British command in Egypt was guided by a misapprehension that the Egyptian Army could best be built around the "martial races" whose innate fighting qualities were their best guarantee in battle. After 1884 the British transferred all their faith to training. In confronting the Beja's tactics (described in part 1), Baker decided to have his men form one large square, as he feared that a series of smaller battalion squares might fire on each other. In the end the two flanking battalion squares of Turkish infantry and the Massawa Sudanese were overwhelmed when the larger square broke. It must be remembered that many of the men in the army were scarcely trained: especially the Turks and *bazingers*.

The gendarmerie, when attacked, fired wildly in the air or from the hip, taking little aim. The only veteran troops in the column were the Sannaheit and Massawa Battalions of Sudanese, and of these the Massawa Battalion was considered the best. As the attack developed they found themselves on the flank of the square where they could do the least good. After the battle Baker admitted that a different formation, and a reliance on his Sudanese regulars, might have brought about a different result (Wylde: 108).

The Egyptian Army was well armed, with single-shot breech loading Remington rifles and carbines, two Gatling guns (never used), two rocket tubes (likewise never used), and two Krupp field guns. In addition to this the various irregulars in the force had a variety of muzzle-loading muskets and rifles.

The main defense of Suakin rested with the Royal Navy, who had a number of small ships. The two most powerful were the corvettes *Carysfort* and *Euryalus*. Both were steam-powered masted cruisers, with broadside mountings rather than turrets. The *Carysfort*, at 2,380 tons and measuring 225' x 44' x 19', carried two 7" MLR and twelve 64-pdrs. The *Euryalus*, at 3,932 tons and measuring 280' x 45' x 23.5' had fourteen 7" MLR (on slide mounts) and two 6" MLR (on trucks) (Archibald: 41, 49).

Uniforms

The Egyptian gendarmerie and cavalry were all dressed in the regular white Egyptian uniform of the early 1880's: White jacket, trousers and leggings, red fez with black tassel, black belts and shoes, brass buttons and buckles. The fezzes were often covered by a variety of styles of cloth. Sometimes a cloth like a burnoose was wrapped over the fez, falling down onto the neck and shoulders; sometimes a neck-cloth was tucked under the fez, and sometimes a strip of rolled cloth was wrapped around the base of the fez as an *imma* (turban). The gendarmerie did have a dark blue dress uniform (Sartorius: 174), and many officers are shown in the standard Egyptian dark blue frock coat and trousers. Others seem to have worn blue tunics with black frogging on the front and gold Austrian knots on the sleeves. A few officers seem also to have worn a gray or khaki tunic with gold braid.

The cavalry wore waist and cartridge belts over the shoulder, with the cartridge box resting over the right hip. They also sometimes carried a leather pouch like a haversack. They slung their carbines across their backs and hung their sabers on the left side of their saddles.

Some of the "Turkish" gendarmerie arrived in Suakin wearing their Albanian costumes of sheepskin coat, collarless Greek shirt, embroidered waistcoats, leggings and shoes (Sartorius: 139). One observer described the Turkish infantry and cavalry as wearing blue, red and yellow (ILN 9 February 1884: 130), and Melton Prior sketched one Turkish soldier in dark trousers, shirt and vest, with the front and edges of the vest outlined in a lighter color (ILN 9 February 1884: 132).

The commander of the Turks was dressed in an embroidered Zouave style waistcoat and jacket, loose dark cloth trousers, embroidered leggings, Turkish shoes, a red silk sash twisted in several folds around his middle, a scimitar tucked into the right side and two silver mounted flintlock pistols tucked in front. Over his sash was a belt with three or four silver filigree boxes for powder, shot, etc. (Sartorius: 186). The "Turks" were, of course, ethnic Turks, descendents of Muhammad Ali's original troops. There were no regular Turkish soldiers from the Turkish army included in any of the Sudan campaigns of the 1880's. It is likely that all mounted Bashi-Bazouks dressed in the traditional Bashi-Bazouk style. The Turks in the gendarmerie were probably issued with white uniforms before the 2nd Battle of El Teb, but it is by no means clear what the "Turkish battalion" wore.

The final troops to be covered were the "Old Soldiers of the garrison," a small group of

Illustration by Greg Rose

<u>*Egyptian Troops In The Eastern Sudan*</u>
A) Egyptian Cavalry; B) "Turkish" Infantry in Dark Uniform Showing imma Wrapped Around Fez;
B) C) Egyptian Infantry; D) Same, Showing Covered Fez; E) "Turkish" Gendarmerie; and
F) "Old Soldier of the Garrison" as Found at Suakin

about 300 night-watchmen and guards of the gate. They dressed as civilians, in white *jallabiyyas* and trousers. One officer was seen in ragged trousers, a plain overcoat and a fez (Sartorius: 104, 139).

War Game Ideas

War gaming for the Eastern Sudan in 1883-4 will present a challenge as the battles were so unlike those we associate with standard colonial warfare. It was usually the Ansar who were outnumbered, rather than the Egyptians, and the Egyptians were always better armed.

Egyptian forces should be composed of a variety of units with different morale values and fighting ability. These should reflect training and experience more than ethnic martial stereotypes. Sudanese regulars should normally be given the highest fighting ability, but Sudanese irregulars (the *bazingers*) should rank near the bottom. Turkish Bashi-Bazouks could range from quite good (as at Sinkat) to unreliable (as at El Teb). Egyptian regulars should also vary. Those who form part of the existing garrisons (especially Sinkat and Kassala) should rank higher than the gendarmerie.

The Beja can be organized into war bands under their own sheikhs, but all under an overall commander. There should be some mounted Beja, mainly on camels, primarily acting as mounted infantry. Virtually none of them had rifles at this time, and any who did would be inexperienced shots.

A variety of games can be attempted. The first assault on Sinkat is filled with possibilities. Osman Digna would have to try for some early breach of the fortifications in order to bring some of those Beja observing on the sidelines into the battle. There are also a number of cattle and camel raiding skirmishes (initiated by either side) to try.

In recreating any of the battles of El Teb, one can experiment with battalion squares to see if these would fare any better. With each side composed of a proportion of steadfast troops and waverers, the outcome of each game could be far from certain.

Footnotes

1) There is some disagreement about the size of the force. Mrs. Sartorius (66) gives it as 600 Sudanese, 200 Egyptians and 50 cavalry. Wylde (11), who was in Suakin at the time, gives the figure as 700 Sudanese, 300 Egyptians and "Old Soldiers," and 30 Bashi-Bazouk cavalry. Colvile (19) gives the total figure of 700 Sudanese, while Royle (101) says the column totaled 700 men, of whom only 400 were Sudanese. Wingate (95) says there were 200 Bashi-Bazouks and 500 Sudanese, while Jackson (41) breaks down a total number of 700 men into 400 Sudanese, 225 Egyptians and 25 Bashi-Bazouk cavalry (though this totals only 650!). It would seem that the column numbered no more than 700 men, of which about 200 were Egyptians, up to 50 Bashi-Bazouk cavalry, and between 400-500 Sudanese, and an undetermined number of gunners for the single mountain gun.

(2) Both Sartorius (67) and Jackson (41), who used her as a source, claim that the square broke ranks when it reached the wells. Wylde (11), who got his story from a Sudanese survivor soon after the battle, gives the scenario used here. Wingate appears to accept it (95).

(3) Precise numbers vary, but these are based mainly on Royle (106-7), and Jackson (63). Sartorius (232) has figures which compare better with Royle (who used the official report) than with Jackson.

(4) Sartorius (232) says the force marched out in two parallel columns with the artillery and escort in between. Both Royle and Wingate used the official report as their source and is used here.

References

Archibald, E.H.H., THE METAL FIGHTING SHIP IN THE ROYAL NAVY 1860-1970, Blandford, London, 1971.
Clowes, Sir We., THE HISTORY OF THE ROYAL NAVY, Vol. VII, Boston, 1903.
Colville, H.E., HISTORY OF THE SUDAN CAMPAIGN, Part 1, HMSO, London, 1889.
Haggard, A., UNDER CRESCENT AND STAR, Blackwood, Edinburgh, 1895.
Jackson, H.C., OSMAN DIGNA, Methuen, London, 1926.
Royle, C., THE EGYPTIAN CAMPAIGNS, 1882 TO 1885, Vol. II, Hurst & Blackett, London, 1886.
Sartorius, E., THREE MONTHS IN THE SUDAN, Kegan, Paul and Trench, London, 1885.
Shaked, H., THE LIFE OF THE SUDANESE MAHDI, Transaction Books, New Brunswick N.J., 1978.
Wingate, F.R., MAHDIISM AND THE EGYPTIAN SUDAN, 2nd Edition, Frank Cass, London, 1968.
Wylde, A.B., '83 TO '87 IN THE SUDAN, Vol. 1, Negro Universities Press, New York, 1969 (reprint of 1888 edition).

Sources For Maps And Material

ILLUSTRATED LONDON NEWS, 1884 (ILN).
Grant, J., CASSELL'S HISTORY OF THE WAR IN THE SOUDAN, London, ca. 1886.
Sandes, E.W.C., THE ROYAL ENGINEERS IN EGYPT AND THE SUDAN, The Institute of the Royal Engineers, Chatham, 1937.

"A Desert Pool"

Wars in Eastern Sudan Part 3: Graham's First Expedition of 1884
by Doug Johnson

Major-General Sir Gerald Graham

On 6 February 1884, the day after Baker's defeated army sailed back to Suakin, Admiral Hewett landed a force of 150 sailors and Marines and two Gatling guns from the Red Sea division of the Mediterranean Fleet then at Suakin. The Royal Navy vessels moored in the harbor were the gun-vessel H.M.S. *Ranger* (Commander W.E. Darvall), the gunboat H.M.S. *Coquette* (Captain Alexander Plantagenet), and the corvette H.M.S. *Euryalus* (flagship). A further 120 Marines were taken off the transport H.M.S. *Orontes* which was then at Suez, homeward bound from China. Another 280 Marines were sent from Egypt with the corvette H.M.S. *Carysfort* (Captain W. Stewart) and the torpedo-depot ship H.M.S. *Hecla* (Captain A. Knyvet Wilson). All the Marines at Suakin were originally from the Portsmouth and Plymouth Divisions of the Royal Marine Light Infantry (R.M.L.I.) and were placed under the command of Col. Tuson. (Clowes: 350-1; Field: 195-7; Jackson: 68).

Col. Henry Hallam Parr

On 9 February Admiral Hewett declared Suakin under a state of siege, and the next day he took over command of Suakin and the Red Sea Littoral.

The defense of the town was undertaken by the Naval Brigade detachment and same 3,000 remnants of the Egyptian garrison. Three British officers of the new Egyptian Army— Hallam Parr, Pigott, and Andrew Haggard (Rider Haggard's brother)— were sent to take over from Baker and his staff and help organize the defense of the town. Haggard took command of 900 discontented Sudanese soldiers from Massawa and Zubair's *bazinger's*. Hallam Parr organized a small detachment of British "Horse Marines" for scouting, and there were a further 50 mounted Abyssinian irregular scouts armed with Remington rifles under the merchant Augustus B. Wylde.

The Royal Navy ships were usually stationed off Trinkitat, though sometimes they moored in Suakin harbor. (Royle: 119; Haggard: 132, 135, 139; Wylde: 115, 141).

Orders for a campaign to relieve Tokar were issued on 12 February, and on the following day troops in Egypt began to embark for Suakin. Pending their arrival, the defenses of the town of Suakin were improved. The Egyptian Army garrisoned the earthworks around El-Geif, the left and right water forts, and the redoubt at Tabiat al-Fula ("The Fort of Beans") outside the town. The Marines took over two flat-roofed brick and stone buildings within the line of entrenchments and renamed them forts

Hallam Parr's "Horse Marines"

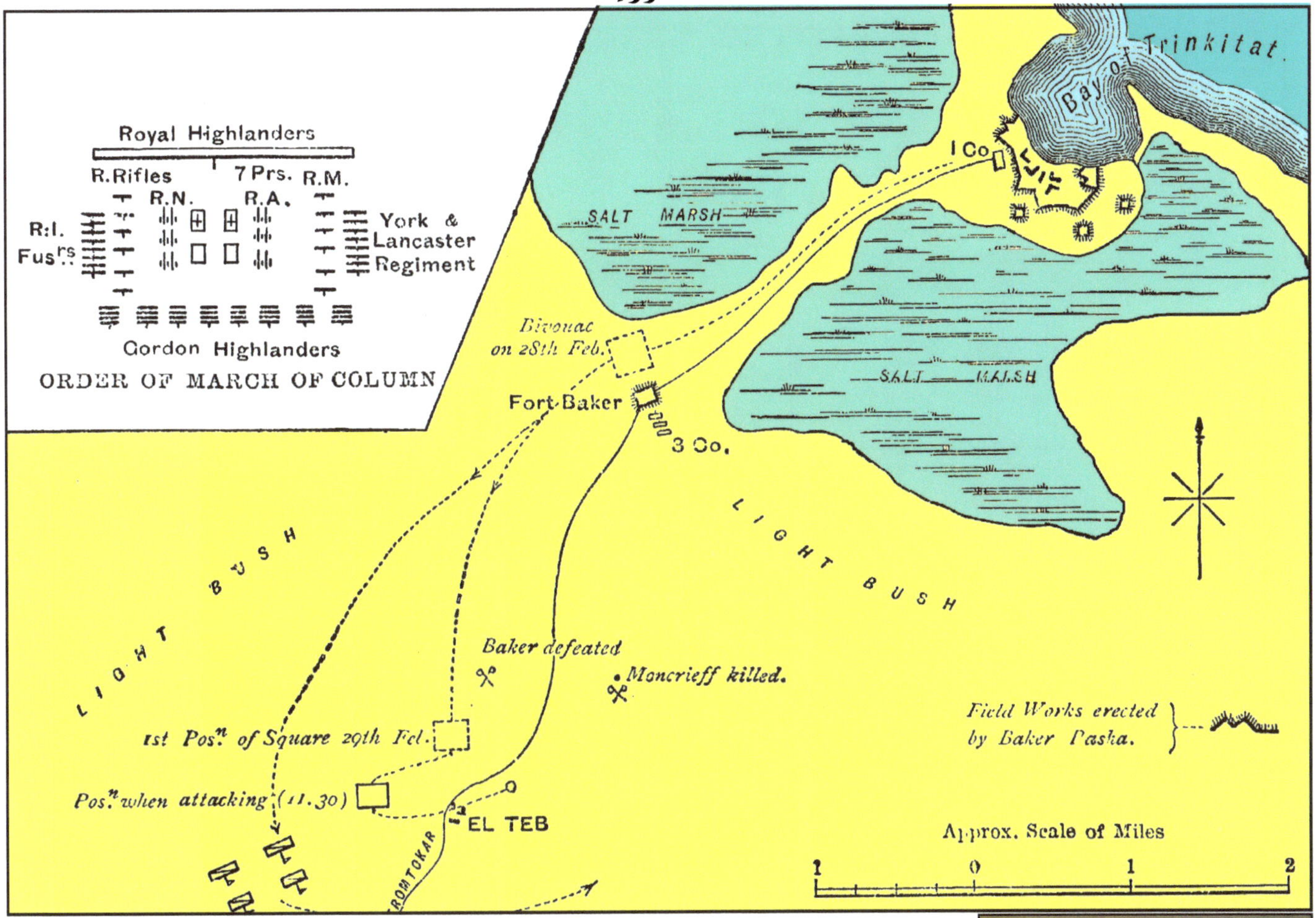

"Euryalus" and "Carysfort." Prior to the departure of Baker and his staff, the town was "in a constant state of night alarms," with the Mahdists coming outside the lines at night and firing into El-Geif. The land outside the earthworks originally consisted of gardens of melons and vegetables, but the townspeople abandoned them and the Mahdists "Had a playful way of descending upon these gardens and thoroughly raiding them at night whenever there was anything in them to raid." (Haggard: 133-5).

Col. Sir Redvers Buller

The British force raised to relieve Tokar came from the garrisons in Egypt, Aden and India. From Egypt came the 42nd Royal Highlanders (Col. Green), the 75th Gordon Highlanders (Col. Hammill), the 3rd Battalion, 60th King's Royal Rifle Corps (KRRC) (Col. Ashburnham), the 19th Hussars (Col. Webster), the Mounted Infantry (Maj. Humphreys), the 6th Battery, 1st Brigade, Scottish Division, Royal Artillery (Maj. Lloyd), and the 26th Company, Royal Engineers (Maj. Todd). The 65th York and Lancaster Regiment (Col. Byam) and some artillery (to be formed into "M" Battery, 1st Brigade at Suakin) were sent from Aden, and the 89th Royal Irish Fusiliers (Col. Robinson) and the 10th Hussars (Col. Mood) were diverted to Suakin on their way home from India. Major General Sir Gerald Graham, V.C., K.C.B. was sent from Egypt to command the force, with Col. H. Steward (later to be killed commanding the Desert Column in 1885), Col. Sir Redvers Buller, and Col. Davis as brigade commanders. Sir Valentine Baker acted as Chief of Intelligence, assisted by Major Harvey.

Graham learned of the surrender of the Tokar garrison on his arrival at Suakin, but decided to push on at least is far as El Teb in any case. Between 26-28 February

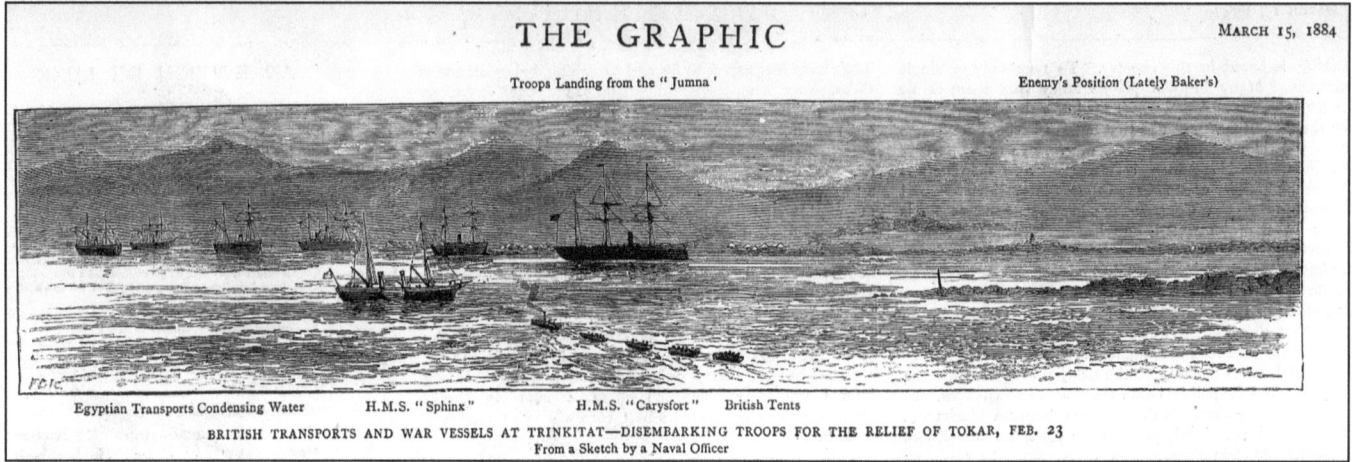

BRITISH TRANSPORTS AND WAR VESSELS AT TRINKITAT—DISEMBARKING TROOPS FOR THE RELIEF OF TOKAR, FEB. 23
From a Sketch by a Naval Officer

he concentrated a force at Trinkitat, preparatory to beginning his march. By the 28th he had a total force of 2,850 infantry, 750 mounted troops, 150 Naval Brigade, 100 Royal Artillery, and 80 Royal Engineers, supplemented by six machine guns and eight 7-pounder mountain guns (Colville; 21).

On the 28th February the entire force concentrated at Fort Baker, and an the 29th Graham marched out "With his entire available force," leaving Fort Baker under the command of Lt. Col. Ogilvy, with four companies of KRRC, armed departmental details, and one Krupp and two bronze guns manned by the Royal Marine Artillery (Royal: 139).

The cavalry were sent out ahead as scouts, with the Mounted Infantry in front. Before the infantry set off, H.M.S. *Sphinx* fired four rounds toward El Teb, but fell a mile short of the Mahdist positions, exploding closer to the British cavalry than to the Ansar. It was signaled to cease fire (Burleigh: 45). A short cloud-burst before daybreak turned the first two miles of the march into a muddy quagmire, slowing the pace and requiring frequent halts to rest the artillery and Naval Brigade, who were dragging their guns by ropes.

The infantry marched in square formation (see inset with map, page 142), with the Mounted Infantry ahead, one squadron of the 10th Hussars covering the front, and the rest of the cavalry marching in the rear. The Gordon's formed the front face and the 42nd (Black Watch) the rear, both marching in company columns of fours at company intervals. In the angles of the front face were the Naval Brigade machine-guns (2 Gatlings and 1 Gardner in the left, 1 Gatling and 2 Gardners in the right), with the Royal Engineers in support. The rear face had four 7-pdrs of the RA at each angle. The 89th marched on the right flank, with part of the 4 companies of the KRRC on line, with the rest of the KRRC in quarter columns support. The 65th were in line on the left flank, with 360 RMLI in quarter columns support. The flanks marched in open company columns with intervals at the angles for the guns, and the ammunition and hospital camels in the center (Royle: 139-141; Burleigh: 42-45; Vetch: 267, 375-376).

When Osman Digna learned that the English force had landed an the coast, he sent his nephew, Madani ibn Ali, to reinforce Abdullah ibn Hamid, the Emir of the coast (Shaked: 138). Osman had captured some 45,000 rounds of ammunition at Tokar, as well as a number of artillery pieces at previous engagements. Abdullah ibn Hamid and Madani ibn Ali fortified an abandoned sugar refinery near the old battlefield of El Teb, manning it with some 6,000 men, 4 Krupp guns, 2 bronze guns and 1 Gatling. The main Mahdist force was drawn from the Hadendowa, Gemilab, Ashraf, Arteiga and Hassinab (Colvile: 22; Royle: 136, 142-144, 156; Jackson: 71).

Graham's force made no contact with the Ansar for the first mile out of Fort

An image of the 19th Hussars meeting both Beja afoot and mounted at once. Again, as can be seen in most other examples of art depicting British defeats, the suggestion is made that enemy numbers were ultimately responsible, rather than blunders by the "home side."

Graham's square in front of the "brick house" and the old boiler late in the battle.

Another on the spot sketch by Prior of the Naval Brigade's machine guns in action at El Teb.

Prior's famous drawing of the Ansar battery at El Teb clearly showing the Krupp and bronze mountain guns, as well as the lone Gatling.

The dirty little secret of battle against "Native" soldiers by Victoria's Armies is recorded here by eyewitness correspondent, Melton Prior, showing the fate of wounded enemies after the fight in the immediate vicinity of the old boiler in the Beja lines.

Baker. For the next two miles they were subjected to some long range sniping. The Ansar entrenchments at El Teb were sighted at about 10AM, and the square inclined to its right to approach them.

At about 11:20AM the force found itself immediately in front of a battery of 2 Krupps and 1 bronze gun behind a crescent-shaped redoubt. The square then moved well to the right front, crossing the Ansar left front (Burleigh: 46; Vetch: 376).

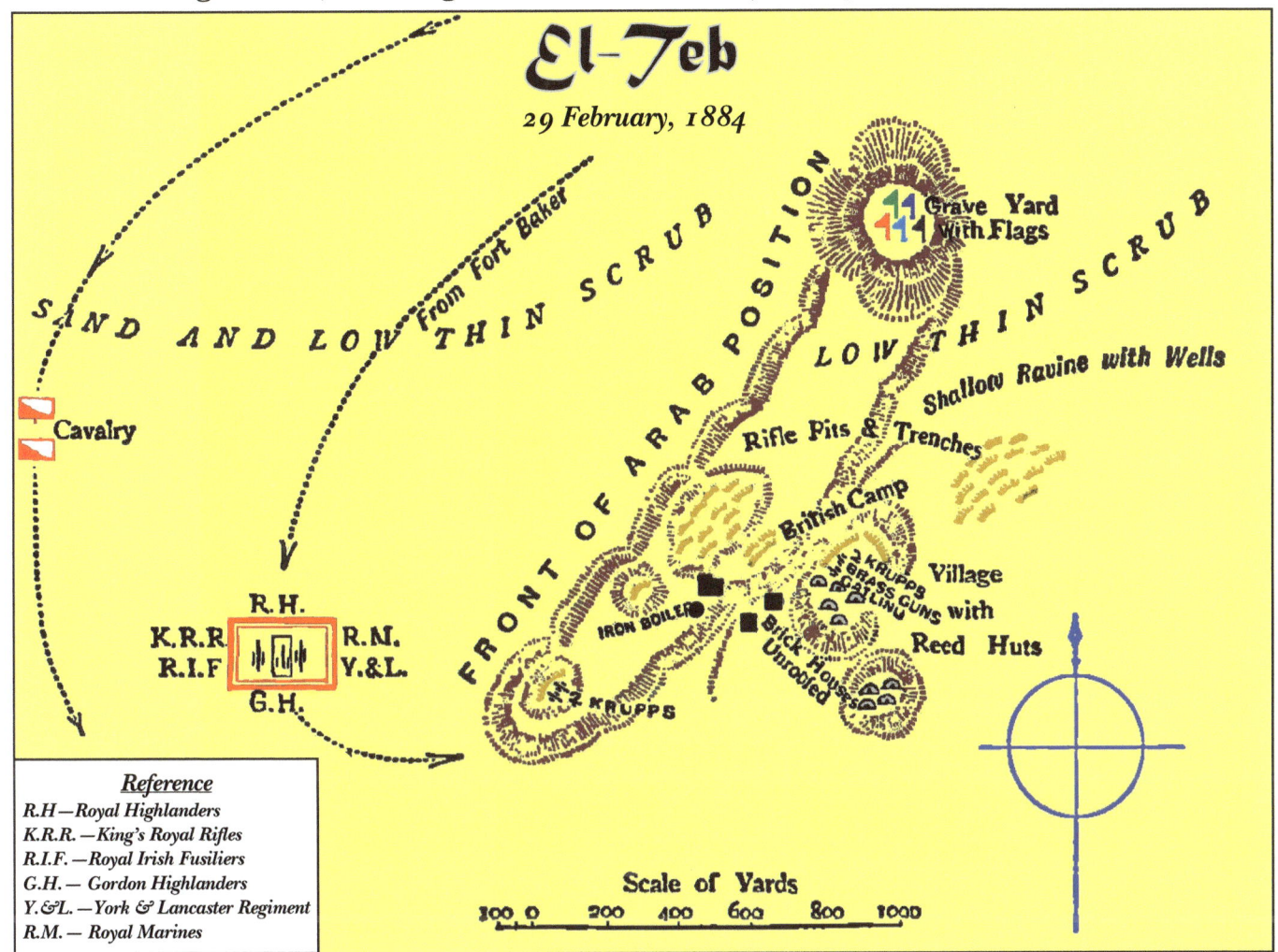

Battle Begins

The Ansar opened up with artillery and rifle fire at about 1,000 yards. The Krupps were more accurate than expected, placing shells inside the square as well as in front of it and in the rear (Villiers: 141; Haggard: 146), and in all the square lost about 20 casualties as it moved to the left. The Mounted Infantry and cavalry retired to the rear as the infantry were ordered to lie down. The Royal Artillery and Naval Brigade opened up with their guns at 900 yards, supported by rifle fire, taking the Krupp battery slightly in the rear, and silencing it by driving the gunners away.

The square now moved forward, with the left face as the front, the Yorks and Lancs, supported by the RMLI, in the fighting line, while the Gordons and Black Watch were in columns of fours on either flank, and the KRRC and Royal Irish were in the rear (Vetch: 268, 376-377; Royle: 141; Burleigh: 46-48).

The Ansar were spread out along the front, about 2,000 men in scattered cover, with large groups poised on the flanks of the square. The infantry fired as it advanced; first volley fire, and then independent fire. At about 200 yards the Ansar launched their first charge. The York and Lancs fell back for about 30-40 yards, opening up a gap in the formation into which some Ansar charged, but were dispatched by the Marines who moved up in support. The square formation now became somewhat irregular as a second charge was launched on all sides of the square and the flanks were briefly engaged in hand-to-hand fighting. The second charge being repulsed the Yorks and Lancs, and Marines rushed the redoubt in front of them and seized the guns which were there (Royle: 141, 147-148; Burleigh: 48-50).

When these early charges were repulsed the Sudanese withdrew slowly and in good order to their positions in and around the sugar refinery and in El Teb village. Stewart, mistaking the withdrawal for a retreat, ordered both the 10th and 19th Hussars, supported by the Mounted Infantry, to charge. The broken ground and thick bush prevented a knee-to-knee charge, and to their surprise the cavalry found that the Ansar held their ground.

Three charges were launched. The war artist Frederick Villiers later described the scene: "Backward and forward the cavalry charged, but still the enemy were not flurried; they stood their ground and gave battle, and some rolled under the horses' bellies, cutting and slashing with their two-handed swords, hamstringing several animals and bringing their riders to the ground" (Villiers: 145).

An even more graphic picture was provided by the correspondent Bennet Burleigh:

"The enemy showed the greatest indifference to the cavalry, waiting their approach, throwing themselves prone at the proper moment alongside a bush or knoll, dodging around like lightening to hamstring with swords or knives the troopers' horses, dispatching riders checked or thrown by such dexterous manoeuvre. The Hussars' swords were too short to reach the crouching foe, and our weapons were badly-tempered compared with the Arabs' lances, which would have been more effective in a cavalry pursuit. Even the enemy's horsemen—total estimate, 130—when attacked, rode forward to meet our regiments, the Arabs jumping off, sheltering under horses, and cutting at the troopers in passing in the same way the footmen did."

(Burleigh: 65-66).

"At last, out of sheer weariness, the enemy made off" (Villiers: 145), leaving the cavalry such the worse off, with 20 killed and 28 wounded, the total of the rest of the force for El Teb being 10 killed and 94 wounded (Anglesey: 316).

Part of the cavalry's difficulties were later attributed to the small Egyptian horses they were riding, which the British troopers found difficult to control. At the same time, Stewart seems to have badly miscalculated the state of the enemy when he ordered the charge (Anglesey: 316).

But the main reason for the failure of the charge was the tactics the Ansar used, and the Hadendowa proved too acrobatic for the cavalry (Haggard: 150). The tactics they used in meeting the charge were a foretaste of Omdurman: The troops who set and checked the charge of the 21st Lancers in 1898 were all from Osman Digna's command. After El Teb the British cavalry in Graham's force armed themselves with captured Sudanese spears (Burleigh: 71, 85), but they never attempted a charge again.

While the cavalry were engaged in their combat, the infantry, now on the left of the Ansar positions around the refinery and the wells at El Teb, advanced on their enemy's rear. The RNA manned the captured Krupps and bronze gun to silence the remaining battery of Krupps. The Ansar infantry held an to the sugar mill and rifle pits tenaciously and had to be rooted out slowly by the Highlanders. They were forced to withdraw to their third position near the wells and even shelled the Gordons in their rear before the battery of 2 Krupps and 1 bronze gun and 1 Gatling was silenced. The Gordons took the village and the last battery (including two unused rocket tubes as well as the other guns) after an hour of constant firing from the infantry's rifles and the Naval Brigade's machine-guns. In the final assault on the last position the formation of the square had become so irregular as to be almost circular (Royle: 142, 150- 151; Burleigh: 51-52).

The Ansar fought stubbornly and withdrew only gradually. Their losses were put at 2,100 killed by Graham, but 1,500 killed and an equal number wounded by Osman Digna (the latter figure being adopted by later authors, including Wingate). The dead included the Emirs Abdullah ibn Hamid, Madani ibn Ali, al-Tahir ibn al-Hajj (cousin of Shaykh al-Tahir al-Majdhub), Omar Qamar al-Din al-Majdhub, and Musa Qilay (Shaked: 138-139).

Some 400 Black Watch under Col. Green were left at the camp at El Teb, along with a troop of the 10th Hussars and 20 RNA to man the captured guns. The rest of the force marched to Tokar on 3 March, reaching it without any further fighting, and being received by about 600-700 soldiers, women and children of the old garrison who had previously surrendered to the Ansar. These were removed to Trinkitat an 4 March, and the entire force returned to Suakin on the 5th.

Sortie to Tamai

Following the battle of El Teb and the evacuation of Tokar, there were no significant defections to the government, or desertions from Osman's force. A second demonstration was then decided on, this time a sortie to Tamai.

The Black Watch (623 officers and men) secured in old *zariba* site 8.5 miles out of Suakin on the Sinkat road on 9 March. The rest of the force concentrated there on 11-12 March, leaving some 100 Marines and 5 guns at Suakin. A new battery of Royal Artillery, armed with 9-pdrs from the Royal Navy was added to the force.

On the 12th of March the force marched out in two brigade squares, with "M" Battery and the Royal Engineers marching in the interval between them. The Naval Brigade once again hauled their guns by ropes, and the Abyssinian scouts were sent out ahead with the cavalry.

On the first day out the force camped within 1.5 miles of Tamai, having been informed that the Ansar held the ravine there and the small stream that ran at the bottom of it. The two brigades formed one large square for the night, the troops sleeping in their greatcoats. They were harassed throughout the night by snipers but these were dispersed by the 9-pdrs and one Gardner gun in the morning (Royle: 162-165; Burleigh; 134-151).

The next morning half of "M" Battery was transferred to the 1st Brigade square. The two brigades marched in echelon of squares, Graham, with the 2nd Brigade,

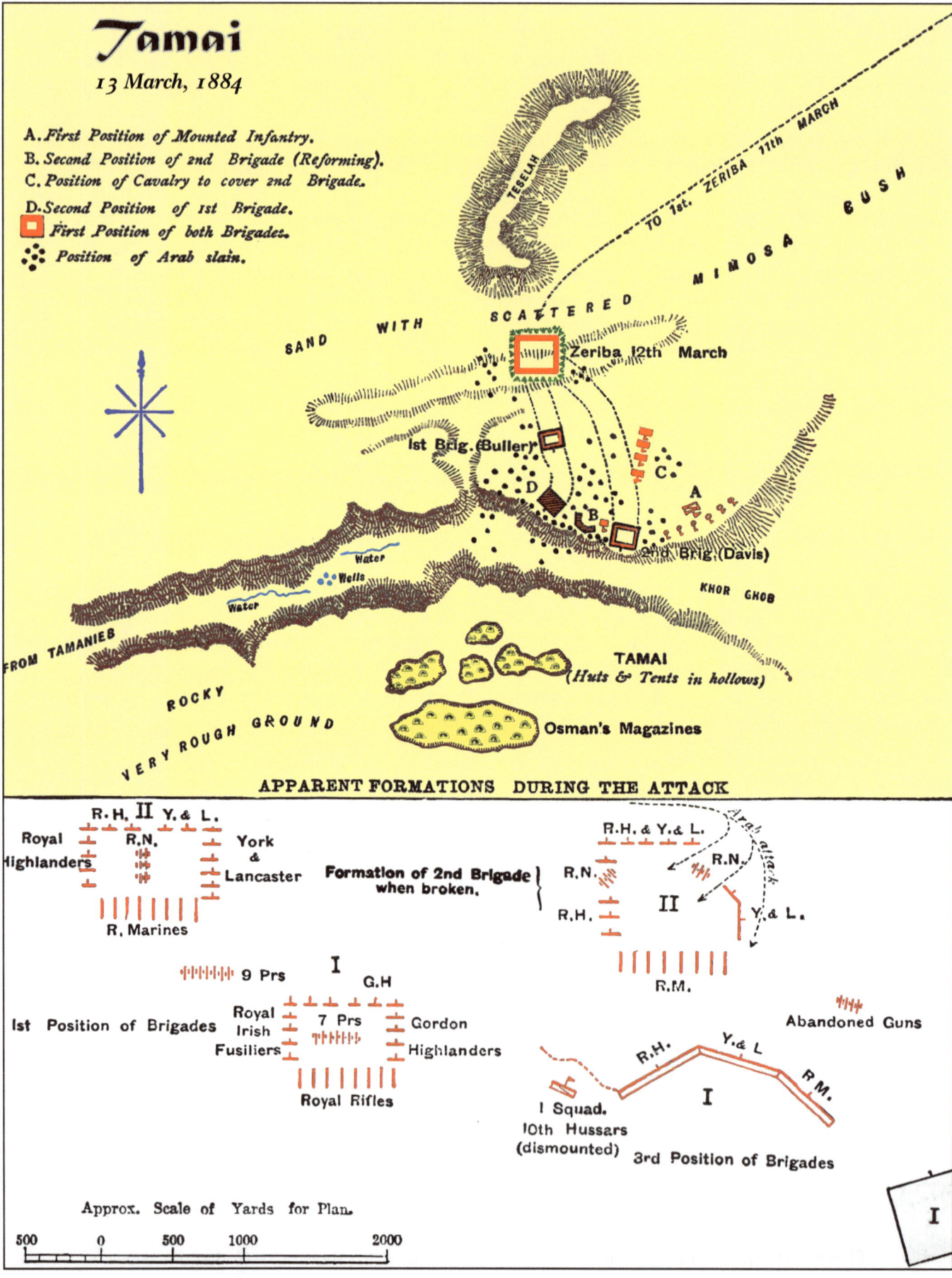

A certainly "too orderly" Press impression of the collapse of the square's corner held by the Yorks & Lancs.

leading. The main body of cavalry were echeloned to the left rear on the 2nd Brigade.

Graham had been informed that the Ansar were camped in the ravine ahead. Estimates of the total Ansar force, under Osman Digna's cousin, Mahmud Musa, vary. There may have been between 9,000-12,000 total (Royle: 179); Mahdist records put their own forces at about 6,000 (Shaked: 147). There seems to have been 5,000-6,000 in the ravine itself, with some hundreds hidden in the bushes to the right of the squares (Royle: 171).

Battle Joined

Neither the two squadrons of cavalry scouts, nor the Abyssinians, were able to see the entire force hidden in the bushes or ravine. Graham ordered the advance, 2nd Brigade leading, with the 1st Brigade under Buller 700 yards to the right rear. The Ansar in the bushes began firing at the squares, but their shots were high. When the square was some 200 yards from the ravine, it was charged in a series of rushes, which were cleared away by rifle fire. Graham ordered the Black Watch to charge up to the ravine, which they immediately did, commencing independent fire on the Ansar to their left and right when they were 30 yards from the ravine. The 65th were not ordered to charge, though some tried to follow the Black Watch. A larger gap opened up in the square than had opened at El Teb. The Gatling and Gardner guns were now outside the square.

The Ansar began a charge an the right flank, some

The struggle around one of the Gatling Guns as portrayed by the popular press.

Buller's 1st Brigade on the point of advancing to the support of Davis' 2nd Brigade.

disappearing into the ravine as they ran, before reappearing almost on the square itself. Visibility was already bad since there was no breeze to clear the rifle smoke. The Ansar rushed in on the guns, same of which had to be abandoned, and threw the 65th back. The right flank of the Black Watch was now exposed and the Highlanders recoiled under the impact of the charge which hit them. The Marines were the next to be hit, and the entire square was pushed east some 800 yards. Little groups of men fought back to back, the 9-pdrs of "M" Battery were left outside the squire but continued to fire at the charging Ansar; the 1st Brigade was also charged but, being 400-500 yards from the ravine, opened up a steady stream of fire, keeping the Ansar at bay in a radius of 80 yards from the square.

    Buller was able to advance and catch those Ansar attacking the 2nd Brigade in a cross-fire, as the 2nd Brigade square fell to his left. The 10th Hussars and mounted infantry, too, dismounted and opened fire. In about 20 minutes the attack had been repulsed and the 2nd Brigade began to reform, with the Marines on the right, the 65th in the center, the Black Watch an the left, and 160 Naval Brigade in the rear (Royle: 169-176; Haggard: 177).

    Graham's force halted for about a quarter of an hour. The 1st Brigade now moved up 200 yards on the right, firing at close range for 10 minutes until they were able to retake lost ground and abandoned guns. The Ansar had set one ammunition limber on fire and dumped one Gatling gun down the ravine.

    The 2nd brigade turned their machine-guns on the Ansar still in the ravine and drove them out. Shortly after this the 1st Brigade took a ridge 800 yards off, and the

The "victory" at Tamai that impressed others than Kipling with the appreciation of the "Fuzzy-Wuzzy" as a "First Class Fightin' Man."

village of Tamai immediately below it (Royle: 177-8; Burleigh: 159). At least 1,500 Ansar had participated in the charge on the 2nd brigade, and the British counted 1,500 dead on the field. By their own record the Mahdist force lost some 2,000 dead and an equal number wounded (Burleigh: 169, 176; Shaked: 141, 147; Jackson: 79).

The British losses were also high, with between 90-100 men killed and over 100 wounded (Royle: 179; Burleigh: 152; Prior: 196; Haggard: 174-175).

Graham recommended a further demonstration towards Berber, but this was vetoed by General Stephenson in Egypt. It was only later, when news from Khartoum became more alarming, that Wood and Stephenson advocated an advance to Berber in mid-March. Only a further demonstration to Tamanieb was sanctioned. A *zariba* was established at the base of the Handub wells an 25 March, manned by both brigades with a small force of friendlies (mainly followers of Shaykh Mirghani) added as scouts. Three hundred Marines held the line of supply. The 75th, 89th, 60th, the camel battery, the 42nd, Marines, and a few 65th with the 9-pdrs (3,000 men in all), and a small force of cavalry, occupied Tamanieb on the 27th. Osman Digna had about 3,000 men left to his following, but offered no resistance. The wells were destroyed and the village burned. The force then withdrew (Burleigh: 262; Royle 185-189; Colvile: 25).

Conclusions

The fighting during this campaign was the most stubborn either side had so far met. The British were far better organized, far more determined, and far stronger than the Ansar had come to expect from their encounters with the Egyptians.

Yet the Ansar, too, were a tougher proposition than the British had met in the field throughout their invasion of Egypt.

At both El Teb and Tamai the British were left in possession of the field, but the Mahdist forces withdrew slowly, and in good order, each time. The burning of Tamanieb was uncontested, but it was an insignificant military objective.

As the main historian of the Mahdiyya has written, "British intervention had proved practically ineffective. Uthman [Osman] Digna retained both Sinkat and Tokar and the Suakin-Berber route was controlled by the Ansar" (Holt: 86-87).

Very little of practical value was accomplished through the pyrrhic victories of El Teb and Tamai.

Formations

General Graham decided on the formation he would adopt before he arrived at Suakin; one large square with Naval Brigade machine-guns in the corners of the front face and Royal Artillery guns in the corners of the rear face; front and rear to march in company columns of fours at company intervals; flanks to march in open columns of companies (Vetch: 267).

This is the formation adopted at El Teb, where the interior was 500 x 150 yards (Royle: 139) and support troops (R.E. an the front face, Royal Marines on the left flank, and the 60th K.R.R.C. on the right flank) marched in quarter columns.

As a result of his experiences at El Teb, Graham adopted the two square formation for Tamai. On the day before the battle the two brigades formed into two squares, and marched surrounded by cavalry scouts with the main body of cavalry between them. The "M" Battery 9-pdrs and the R.E. were in a 25 pace interval in the center separating the two regiments who formed the front face of each. That night they camped in one large square.

The next morning the brigade squares marched in echelon. Each had a 200 yard front and a 100 yard flank. The 1st Brigade was to the right and rear of the 2nd, at an interval of 600-900 yards (it varied due to broken terrain). There were cavalry sections in front, with the rest of the cavalry echeloned to the left rear of the 2nd brigade.

Tactics (Cavalry)

Cavalry were used mostly in scouting. The Mounted Infantry was usually sent out ahead of the cavalry to make contact with the Mahdists and use the range of their rifles at the best advantage. They were much liked by Stewart, for "In those days, except at close range, the cavalry shooting was rotten" (Marling: 110). The nature of the ground, being broken by *Khor's* and small depressions as well as by thorn bushes, made cavalry scouting difficult. At Tamai even the Abyssinian scouts, who were used to the type of country and whose eyesight was better than the British, were unable to detect the bulk of the Mahdist force before the battle began.

Terrain also prevented the cavalry from being any use in a charge. At El Teb they made the mistake of charging the Mahdists after they had been repulsed from an attack on the square, but before they were sufficiently broken. The fact that terrain prevented a "knee-to-knee" charge only increased the cavalry's difficulties. Hadendowa tactics at evading a single rider could, and did, come into play with such effect that in all it was estimated by most British observers that the cavalry lost more than the Mahdists in each cavalry charge.

The cavalry charged three times, twice in squadron and once in squadron echelon. They had better effect in scattering a small band of Mahdist horsemen who charged them. The Mounted Infantry joined in the charges, but in the end all horsemen had to dismount to clear their way with carbine and rifle fire.

For the rest of the campaign it was decided that, aside from scouting, the best use for cavalry was to overawe the enemy in retreat and prevent them from reforming (Haggard: 151). At Tamai the 10th Hussars mounted one demonstration saber charge to make the Mahdists fall back, and then dismounted with their carbines to help the Mounted Infantry fire on them (Haggard: 174-5).

Tactics (Infantry)

The infantry tactics—square and *zariba*—were straight-forward and left little room for variations, though some were made to meet the battlefield situations.

At El Teb the men were ordered to lie down when they came under artillery and rifle fire from prepared entrenchments. The Mahdist artillery was silenced by return fire from the R.A., rifle and machine-gun fire while the square was stationary to try to entice the Mahdists to charge. When this failed, the men were ordered to stand, the square wheeled slightly so that the left face became the front face, and an advance against the first Mahdist entrenchment was made. Volley fire begin at 300 yards, and an independent fire at 100. The Mahdists charged on all sides of the square, and a gap appeared at the right corner when some of the 65th fell back and the 42nd and 75th became engaged in hand-to-hand fighting.

A few Mahdists slipped through it without causing a major breakthrough. There were three major Mahdist entrenchments to take: Earthworks mounting artillery, a brick building and iron boiler of an old sugar refinery, and fresh water wells. There were numerous rifle pits and "rabbit warrens" around and between them. As the square had to advance against these as well as receive attacks its outline became indistinct (becoming circular at times) and it had to stop and reform several times.

At Tamai Graham opted for an echelon of two squares. These provided cover for each other and were easier to manage. Unlike El Teb there were no entrenchments to take, but at one point Graham ordered the Black Watch to charge the enemy in a ravine. This they did with some of the 65th following them it a slower rate. A hole thus opened up in the square, and the opening was swiftly exploited by a Mahdist charge out of the ravine, crumbling the right front corner and pushing the square back, forcing it to abandon some of its guns. The Black Watch were able to close up and join in hand-to-hand fighting on the inside, which cleared the square of Mahdists. Covering fire from the 1st Brigade on the right flank cleared the outside of the square.

The first British Suakin campaign highlights one limitation of the square, and that is launching a charge from it. Graham was most at fault for not realizing this. The charge of the 65th at El Teb opened up a small gap, and the charge on the earthworks was probably not necessary as it could have been taken by a steady advance—its artillery had already been silenced.

Graham ordered the Black Watch to charge the sugar refinery, but this they were disinclined to do as they were advancing steadily and there was little to be gained from a charge which would break not only their own cohesion, but that of the square. Because they had not responded quickly to an order, Graham later criticized them.

At Tamai, when he ordered a charge, they did so with greater vigor than they ought otherwise have done. Graham gave no order to the rest of the square to advance, so a big hole was made. To order a charge at that point, when the enemy was known to be in a ravine, but their numbers were unknown, at a time when visibility from smoke was particularly bad, also seems peculiar.

Tamai demonstrated, as did Abu Klea later, the vulnerability of guns at the corners of a square if part of the formation advances while the rest stays put, or when an enemy charge succeeds in pushing the square back a short distance.

The *zariba*'s were stationary, and slightly more fortified squares. They were used to establish strongholds along the line of march prior to advance, and to protect the lines of supply and communication during an advance. They ranged from the low mud walls of "Fort Baker," to the thorn bush enclosure typical of the Sudan.

Tactics (Ansar)

The Ansar used the same tactics they had used first against the Egyptians. They tended to place their best men in the front, with some in reserve to hit enemy troops once they were broken up (Royle: 151).

At El Teb rifles, artillery, and one Gatling gun were used to soften up the square before the spearmen attacked on all sides. The artillery and riflemen ceased fire as the spearmen got near their target (Haggard: 146). The accuracy of the artillery fire amazed the British observers, though in fact few casualties were inflicted. The guns were manned by former Egyptian soldiers (perhaps Sudanese).

Beja rifle fire, however, was very ineffective at both El Teb and Tamai (Haggard: 146; Royle: 171). This is understandable since the rifles were distributed to warriors who were unused to them; unlike in Kordofan and the siege of Khartoum, where rifles were kept in the hands of trained soldiers in the Mahdist forces.

Uniforms of Eastern Sudan 1884
General

Troops were sent to Suakin from Egypt or diverted from India; thus they wore uniforms issued for service in those two stations. Most units serving in Egypt sees to have already been issued with a gray serge drill, while troops from India were already wearing khaki.

Melton Prior, the war artist, noted that all troops wore gray, except sailors, who wore blue (Prior in ILN, 15/3/1884: 244, 249); while Bennet Burleigh, the war correspondent, noted that the entire force was dressed in "gray, dun or blue" (186), and quoted one of Graham's dispatches in which the General stated that both officers and men usually wore khaki. Andrew Haggard noted that the 2nd Brigade at Tamai (42nd Highlanders, Royal Marines, York and Lancs Regiment) were "kharkee coated" (161). Shades of khaki varied; perhaps gray for troops from Egypt, dun for troops from India. In addition to this all troops were issued with "ample *pagri*" to go around their helmets (ILN 16/2/1884).

Melton Prior, war correspondent & eyewitness illustrator

Infantry (1st Brigade)
75th Gordon Highlanders:
Melton Prior records that the Gordons wore gray tunics, and one of his sketches has them wearing helmet spikes and no *pagris* (ILN 11/3/1884: 268). A photo in the Gordon Highlanders' scrapbook in the same museum in Aberdeen shows them in what looks to be a full dress tunic, white helmet with dark *pagri* and no spike. There is no indication that this was what they wore on drill or in battle. The Gordon's wore a white hackle in their helmet, and wore sporrans and hose tops as per the 42nd (below).

60th K.R.R.C.: Marling (80) mentions that while in Egypt after Tel-el-Kebir the 60th Rifles wore rifle green serge jackets. Milne & Terry claim that a service dress of gray brown with puttees was not introduced until as late as 1904 (33), so it is possible that the 60th did wear green jackets with red collars, black trousers, and white helmets, as indicated in a "Bird's Eye View" print of El Teb displayed at the R.E. museum at Chatham (this print gives the color of all other infantry uniforms as gray, unlike the usual practice of this series, which was to depict regiments in their home uniforms). Grant (112) describes the 60th as arriving at Suakin from Egypt in "Stained and tattered fighting kits," but gives no more description than this. Milne and Terry also state that while on service officers usually wore the same serge patrol jacket as other ranks (32).

89th Royal Irish Fusiliers: Grant (112) describes the 89th arriving at Suakin from Egypt along with the 60th rifles in "Stained and tattered fighting kits." Melton Prior depicted them in gray coats, plain helmet with *pagri*, and a blanket rolled up above the mess-tin on the back (ILN, 15/3/1884: 249). The "Bird's Eye View" print of El Teb displayed at the R.E. museum at Chatham shows the 89th in gray- khaki uniforms.

Royal Engineers: The only indication of the Royal Engineers' uniforms on display at the R.E. museum at Chatham is the "Bird's Eye View' print of El Teb, which depicts the Engineers in red tunics, black collars, blue trousers with red seas stripes, black gaiters and white helmets. This seems unlikely, however.

Royal Artillery: By this time the R.A. in Egypt were wearing blue tunics with red collar and cuffs, khaki helmet and *pagri*, khaki trousers and blue puttees.

Infantry (2nd Brigade)
42nd Royal Highlanders: The Black Watch were issued gray serge frocks for marching and walking out while in Egypt (Keltie: 449), and this probably held true for the Gordons (above). All other sources consulted also note that the Black Watch wore gray

Illustration by Greg Rose

or khaki (Haggard: 161; ILK 15/3/1884: 244, 249; "Bird's Eye View" print of El Teb, R.E. museum, Chatham). Melton Prior's sketches (188, 196) show the Black Watch with blankets rolled up an their backs, some with Glengarries strapped on the outside. Some officers are shown in trews and knee boots. The water bottle (as exhibited at Balhousie, the Black Watch Museum, Perth) was brown leather with brown straps. Helmets were probably white, with red and black hose tops. The sporran was white with two black tassels. Belts were white.

65th York & Lancs Regiment: The uniform of the York and Lancs regiment is the subject of two vivid paintings by Douglas Giles, now at the NAM. Both are available as color post cards, one was reproduced on the dust-jacket of Philip Warner's *Dervish*. Both officers and men are shown at Tamai wearing full khaki uniforms (jacket, trousers, helmet and *pagri*). The other ranks are shown wearing white, brown or khaki puttees, while the officers are wearing blue puttees. All have white belts and a dark blue blanket roll over the left shoulder. Wyllie (125) noted that the Yorks & Lancs were diverted from Aden, and when they disembarked they were ordered to take "great coats and blankets only, no kits." One sketch by Melton Prior (188) shows the Yorks & Lancs with blankets or greatcoats rolled up on back, some with cooking tins underneath, and an extra ammunition box strapped to the waist belt on the back. Troops are also shown wearing colored *pagris*. A sketch in the ILN (22/3/1884: 268), and another in Creighton-Williamson (86), show men of the regiment wearing high gaiters rather than puttees. What look like white or brown puttees in the Giles paintings may in fact be canvas gaiters.

Royal Marines: A watercolor sketch in Reynolds, Military Costume, Vol. 35, Royal Navy and Marines (ms in the Victoria and Albert Museum) (390) shows a marine in a gray khaki tunic (with 5 brass buttons) and trousers with no puttees; buff colored helmet, *pagri*, waist-belt, cartridge boxes, and rifle strap; white haversack; black boots, black bayonet scabbard with brass tip; and a blue flash with silver regimental badge on the shoulder straps.

Royal Navy: The Naval Brigade wore a variety of combinations of blue and white uniforms, and a variety of headgear. Some are shown in contemporary sketches in blue blouses, white trousers, white round caps (with black hat bands) and the haversack worn on the back, with the straps going over the shoulders and under the arms. Others are shown wearing blanket rolls. Others are in all white or all blue uniforms. When wearing a blue blouse the collar was either light blue with three white stripes, or plain dark blue (matching the blouse). When wearing a white blouse the collar again was either light blue with three white stripes or all white (to match the blouse). The neckerchief was black. The round caps had either dark blue or white tops, with the name of the ship in gold letters an the front of the black hat band. All leather belts were brown with brass buckles, the haversack was a "tanish" white, the canteen was wood with tan straps, and the cutlass was worn in a black scabbard. Leggings were either brown canvas or black leather; shoes were black. Straw hats with black hat bands were also sometimes worn.

Officers wore dark blue double-breasted jackets, with gold rank insignia on the cuff, white shirts, black neckties, dark blue or white trousers, white haversacks; all leather (boots and belts) was either brown or black.

Uniforms (Cavalry Brigade)

10th Hussars: The 10th Hussars retained their India helmets (with brass spikes and chin scales, and khaki uniforms and puttees (Liddell: 430, 444; Haggard: 171; Melton Prior ILN 15/3/1884: 241). Both officers and men wore puttees, but some officers had gold braid on their trousers (Marling: 106). The 10th were issued with 300 gray Syrian Arab horses from Baker's gendarmerie, each about 14 hands high and between 8-9 years old. They were fitted with old French cavalry pattern saddles, with an improvised carbine bucket, the carbine passing through a hole cut in the shoe cases, with the muzzle fitting into a small leather bucket. The bits were "Mamluke bits," and the head and heel ropes were improvised naval ropes (Liddell: 431- 2, 444).

19th Hussars: The uniform of the 19th Hussars in Egypt was blue tunic, drab trousers and helmet (no spike), blue puttees. They sometimes wore blue stockings rather than puttees (ILN, various illustrations, 1884-5). The regiment left Cairo with 395 horses (Biddulph 241), of which 300 were the gray Syrian type and the rest were English horses (Haggard: 151).

Mounted Infantry: The Mounted Infantry was formed in Cairo after 1882, with 30 men each from the 3rd Battalion, 60th KRRC, the 42nd, the 75th and the 35th (Royal Sussex) regiments. They used the Egyptian Syrian horses with Egyptian saddles and bridles (see description of 10th Hussars, above) (Marling: 96- 104). A painting by Douglas Giles (Marling,110) shows the Mounted Infantry in full khaki uniform, but with puttees of a darker shade, and a lighter shade (white?) helmet with a darker *pagri*. One officer is shown wearing a brass helmet spike and a regimental helmet badge.

Staff: Only two British officers on the staff (General Stewart and Col. Clery, the Chief of Staff) wore red coats, and they frequently drew enemy fire (Burleigh: 186). The British officers from the Egyptian Army attached to Graham's force wore khaki uniforms, white helmets, and red *pagri's* (to distinguish them from other officers) (Haggard: 171). A small square red flag on a short light pole was carried on horse-back behind Graham wherever he went (Burleigh: 186).

Friendlies: Only a few "friendlies" were employed in the campaigns of 1884. At this time the Ansar were not wearing the *jibba*, and both Mahdists and "friendlies" wore exactly the same costume and hairstyles, causing considerable confusion among the British around Suakin (Burleigh: 123). At Tamai, Fadlab "friendlies" were given pieces of white cloth to carry in their hands, and at Handuk the "friendlies" of Sheikh Mirghani were given red calico cloth to tie around their heads or necks (Burleigh: 139; Royle: 186).

Bibliography

Anglesey, The Marquess of, A HISTORY OF THE BRITISH CAVALRY 1816-1919, VOL. 3: 1872- 1098, London, 1982.

Biddulph, J., THE NINETEENTH AND THEIR TIMES, London, 1899.

Burleigh, B., DESERT WARFARE, London, IBB4.

Clowes, Sir W., THE HISTORY OF THE ROYAL NAVY, VOL. 3, Boston, 1903.

Colvile, H.E., HISTORY OF THE SUDAN CAMPAIGNS, VOL. 1, London, 1889.

Creighton-Williamson, D., THE YORK & LANCASTER REGIMENT, London, 1970.

Cunliffe, M., THE ROYAL IRISH FUSILIERS, 1793-1950, Oxford, 1952.

Field, C., BRITAIN'S SEA-SOLDIERS. A HISTORY OF THE ROYAL MARINES, Liverpool, 1924.

Gardyne, C.G., THE LIFE OF A REGIMENT. THE HISTORY OF THE GORDON HIGHLANDERS FROM 1816 TO 1898, Edinburgh, 1903.

Grant, J., CASSEL'S HISTORY OF THE WAR IN THE SOUDAN, VOL. 2, London, n.d. (ca. 1987).

Haggard, A., UNDER CRESCENT AND STAR, Edinburgh, 1895.

Hare, S., THE ANNALS OF THE KING'S ROYAL RIFLE CORPS, VOL. 4, London, 1929.

Headlam, J., THE HISTORY OF THE ROYAL ARTILLERY, VOL. 3, CAMPAIGNS (1860-1914), Woolwich, 1940.

Halt, P.M., THE MAHDIST STATE IN THE SUDAN, 1881-1898, 2nd ed., Oxford, 1971. THE ILLUSTRATED LONDON NEWS (ILN), 1884.

Jackson, H.C., OSMAN DISNA, London, 1926.

Another Melton Prior eyewitness rendering of Tamai. Note the Beja overrunning the guns and limbers to the left center, shell bursts at center and right, and the identification of the British units along the line.

Keltie, J.S. and Melven, W., HISTORY OF THE SCOTTISH HIGHLANDS, HIGHLAND CLANS AND HIGHLAND REGIMENTS, VOL. 5, Edinburgh, 1887.
Liddell, R.S., THE MEMOIRS OF THE TENTH ROYAL HUSSARS, London, 1891.
Marling, Sir P., RIFLEMAN AND HUSSAR, London, 1931.
Milne, S.M. and Terry, A., THE ANNALS OF THE KING'S ROYAL RIFLE CORPS, APPENDIX DEALING WITH UNIFORM, ARMAMENT AND EQUIPMENT, London, 1913.
Porter, W., THE HISTORY OF THE CORPS OF ROYAL ENGINEERS, VOL. 2, London, 1889 (Chatham, 1951).
Prior, M., CAMPAIGNS OF A WAR CORRESPONDENT, London, 1912.
Protheroe, E., THE BRITISH NAVY. ITS MAKING AND ITS MEANING, London, n.d. (ca. 1914).
Royle, C., THE EGYPTIAN CAMPAIGNS, 1882-1885, VOL. 2, London, IBB6.
Sandes, E.W.C., THE ROYAL ENGINEERS IN EGYPT AND THE SUDAN, Chatham, 1937.
Shaked, H., THE LIFE OF THE SUDANESE MAHDI, New Brunswick, 1978.
Vetch, R.H., LIFE, LETTERS AND DIARIES OF LIEUT.-GENERAL SIR GERALD GRAHAM, V.C., O.C.B., R.E., Edinburgh, 1901.
Villiers, F., PICTURES OF MANY WARS, London, 1902.
Wingate, F.R., MAHDIISM AND THE EGYPTIAN SUDAN, London, 1891 (London, 1968).
Wylde, A.B., '83 TO '87 IN THE SOUDAN, 2 VOLS., London, 1888 (New York, 1969).
Wyllie, H.C., THE YORK AND LANCASTER REGIMENT, VOL. 1, Frome, 1930.

Exhibits:
Black Watch Museum, Balhousie, Perth.
Gordon Highlanders Museum, Aberdeen.
Royal Engineers Museum, Chatham.

A contemporary illustration of the Sudan's ubiquitous thorn bush defense work, the zariba.

Ginnis: A Battle of Lasts and Firsts
by Doug Johnson

Brigadier General Francis Wallace Grenfell, here in Egyptian service.

After the fall of Khartoum, both the Nile and Desert Columns withdrew to Egypt and were disbanded late in 1885. The frontier was garrisoned against a potential Mahdist invasion by a Frontier Field Force composed of units from the British garrison in Egypt and the new Egyptian Army. Major-General Grenfell, later Sirdar of the Egyptian Army, was commander-in-chief of the Field Force with his headquarters at Assuan. The garrisons were strung along the Nile and the railroad from Assuan to Akasha, with the southern-most fort at Kosheh. Brigadier General Butler was in command of the advance posts from Wadi Halfa to Kosheh.

The Mahdist forces were under the command of Muhammad al-Khair. They were little more than provincial levies occupying the northern territories as the British forces withdrew. The invasion of Egypt, which was part of the Mahdi's strategy, was delayed by the death of the Mahdi in June, after which various provincial commanders were called back to Omdurman to swear allegiance to the Khalifa. This was followed by consolidation throughout the Sudan as a few remaining Egyptian outposts were subdued and provincial administration was organized.

Each side feared an invasion by the other, but neither had the capacity at the end of 1885 to justify their enemy's suspicion. In September, Muhammad al-Khair reported to the Khalifa that the British were encouraged by the Mahdi's death to launch an invasion of Dongola (Holt, p. 142). This was not the case, but the Khalifa increased recruitment of troops, especially from the Gezira, south of Khartoum, to be sent as reinforcements to meet this invasion. These reinforcements were first noted along the frontier in November, and Wingate later claimed that they were an advance force sent to take Wadi Halfa in preparation for Wad al-Nujumi's invasion of Egypt (Wingate, p. 270). Wad al-Nujumi arrived in Berber late in December to organize an army, but documents in the Mahdist archives reveal that his preparations were designed to thwart an expected British Invasion, not to invade Egypt. (Holt, p. 142).

The Anglo-Egyptian force on the frontier in November-December 1885 was divided as follows:
Wadi Halfa: 500 British, 350 Egyptians;
Akasha (railhead): 600 British, 350 Egyptians;
Sarkametto and Dal (two villages on opposite banks of the Nile): 200 Egyptians
Kosheh: 600 British, 300 Egyptians
Mograka: 266 Egyptians.

There were various smaller detachments of thirty to fifty men in forts overlooking the rail line at Ambigol Wells, Tanjur Road, Murrat Wells and Saras (Wingate, p. 272).

Documentation of the Mahdist force at the frontier is less clear, and it is evident that the Intelligence Department, still in its infancy, had only the vaguest idea of Mahdist strength and intentions. Some 4,000 men were reported in front of Kosheh at the end of November (Grant, p.159), and there appear to have been only 5,000 men divided under about 40 flags in late December (Grant, p.162). Wingate later claimed 6000 men were involved (Wingate, p. 279).

Muhammad al-Khair Abd Allah Khugali, a former teacher of the Mahdi and commander of Berber, was in command of the frontier troops. Abd al-flajid Nasr al-Din abd al Khalik, the commander of the Mahdists at Kirbekan, was sent as second-in-command. Among the leading Emirs in the force were:

- **Abd al-Majid KhuJali**, Muhammad al- Khair's nephew and leader of the Berber contingent at Abu Klea
- **Uthman Azraq**, who later captured Charles Neufeld, was one of al-Nujumi's
- divisional commander at Toski, as Governor of Berber opposed the Anglo-Egyptian advance of 1896, and died at Omdurman;
- **Hassan Abu Qarja** who commanded the Khartoum contingent
- **Mahmud al-Ajami Hamza**, a leading Berber Emir who had also fought at Abu Klea
- **Shaikh wad ar-Rahama**, commander of the Berber contingent
- **Wad ar-Rais** (sometimes listed as "Wad Ebrais") who commanded the riflemen and artillery
- **Bashir** who commanded the Rubtab contingent
- **Umar wad al-fakir**, a staff officer
- **Hamuda Idris** who later commanded the Mahdists at Firket.

(Cairant 1/11/55, and Hill).

It is uncertain how many rifles and cannon the Mahdists had. Four cannons (small brass mountain guns) were later captured at Kosheh and Ginnis, and one more was mounted in a fort on the west bank, so at least five guns were present.

Between November 27th, when the Mahdists were first sighted near Kosheh, and December 22nd, there were many skirmishes. The Emirs Uthman Azraq, Hamid az-Zain, and Siwari ad-Dahab were the main leaders of the Mahdist frontier raids. An early skirmish, on November 30th, involved the river boat *Lotus* (one of the Yarrow-built steamers left over from the Nile campaign), the Egyptian Cavalry and the British Mounted Infantry (Grant, p.160). Between December 2nd and 4th Hamid az-Zain led a force of cavalry, camelry, infantry and one gun in raids on the fort at Ambigol Wells and the rail line in that area. On December 12th, he raided Firka and made off with some cattle and money. The Kordofani Emir Siwari ad-Dahab raided the fort at Mograka the same night (Wingate, p. 273).

During this time the Mahdists set up camp at the village of Ginnis and moved into the village of Kosheh, completely investing the fort on its southern side. (Wingate later claimed that this concentration was ordered by Abd al-Majid abd al-Khujali against the Khalifa's orders, Wingate, p. 279). A continuous fire was poured into the fort from a high black rock directly overlooking the fort's southern wall. Some entrenchments and a gun emplacement were also set up opposite the fort on the west bank. The Mahdist artillery fire became increasingly accurate during the month-long siege, and one shell dismounted the fort's Gardner gun on December 20th.

The Anglo-Egyptian forces under the command of Lt. General Stephenson began to concentrate at Firka to meet the supposed invasion. On December 15th the Cameron Highlanders made a sortie from Kosheh against the black rock. Brigadier Butler made a stronger reconnaissance to Ginnis on December 22nd with the Mounted Infantry, Egyptian Camel Corps and the 20th Hussars. In this sortie the mounted troops were suddenly attacked and had to fall back. The Mahdist casualties were light, but the Kordofani Emir Badawi al-Azraq was killed.

On December 29th, General Stephenson ordered General Grenfell to advance

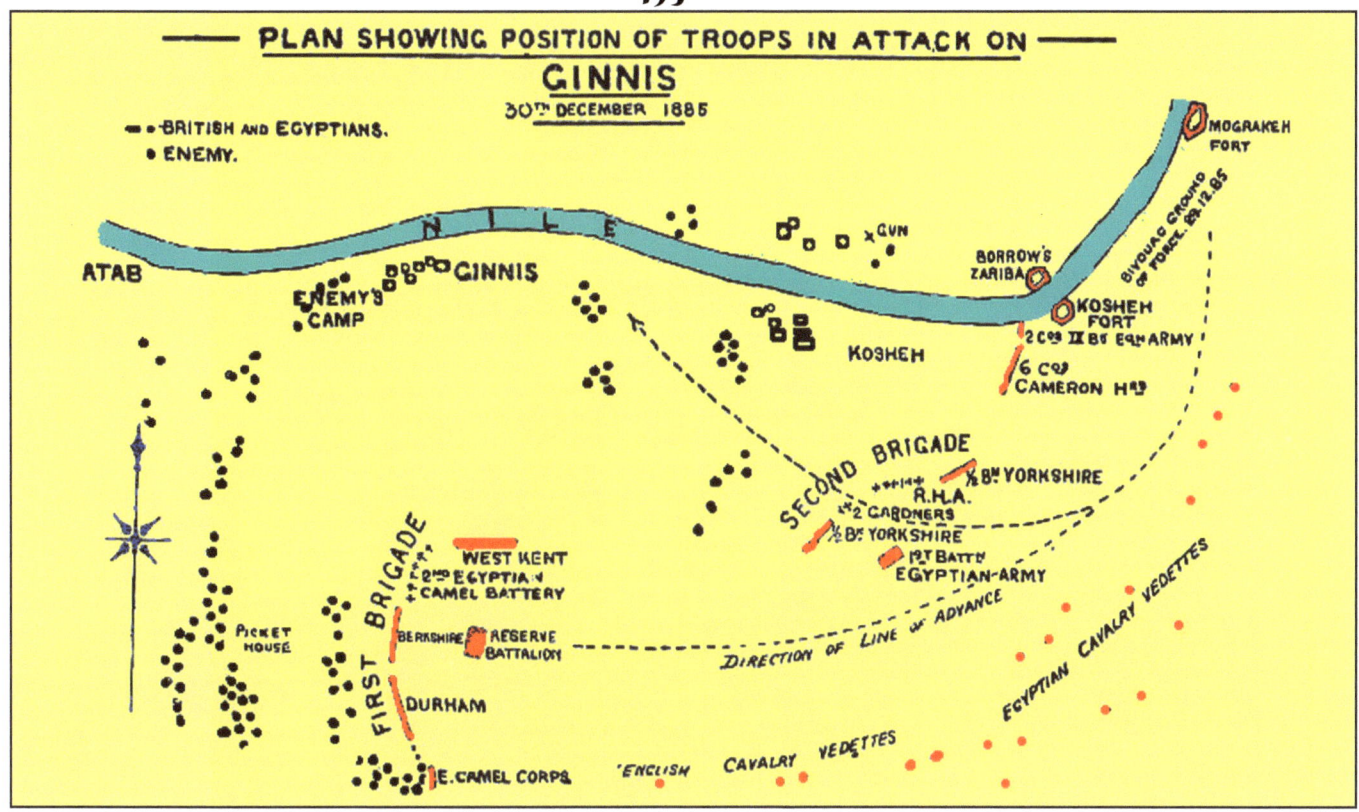

from Firka to Kosheh, bivouacking between Mograka and Kosheh forts. The Anglo-Egyptian force was divided into two brigades with a semi-independent cavalry command. General Butler commanded the 1st Brigade with the 1st Berkshires, the West Kents, the 2nd Durham Light Infantry (DLI), one camel battery (six guns) Egyptian Artillery, with a sixty-man escort from the 3rd Egyptians, and the 11th Company R. E. Colonel Huyshe, who commanded the Berkshires at Tofrek, commanded the 2nd Brigade with the Yorkshire Regiment, six companies of the Cameron Highlanders, two companies (152 men) of the IXth Sudanese, 278 men of the 1st Egyptians, the 3rd Company (39 men) of the Egyptian Camel Corps, a detachment of the British Camel Corps (the last time such a unit appeared in the Sudan), one mule battery (screw guns) of the 2nd battery, 1st Brigade, South Irish Division R.A., and two Gardner guns.

The mounted troops under Colonel Blake consisted of the 1st Company (11 men) Egyptian Camel Corps, one company Mounted Infantry (referred to in one dispatch as the Royal Highlanders Mounted Infantry), the 20th Hussars, and one squadron of about 57 men) of the Egyptian Cavalry. Two companies of the IXth Sudanese were left in Barrow's *zariba* opposite Fort Kosheh on the west bank, 200 men of the 3rd Egyptians were at Mograka Fort, one company of the Camerons in Kosheh fort and one company Camerons with one Krupp gun in the redoubt outside the fort (see pp. Wingate 215-278; Haggard, pp. 367-368; and Cairint 1/11/55).

The Battle:

At 5:00 AM on December 30th the Anglo-Egyptian force marched out of its camp. All men were issued with 80 rounds of ammunition. The British infantry wore their red coats, leaving greatcoats and blankets in the camp. The First Brigade plus the 1st Company Egyptian Camel Corps marched off first with the mounted troops following and keeping in touch. The British Camel Corps followed the mounted troops maintaining contact with them and the 2nd Brigade behind them. The *Lotus* had its steam up

The field before Ginnis from the RHA Battery. Note the "Black Rock" on the horizon and the town at the upper center with its back to the Nile.

and was manned by a rifle detachment from the West Kents and a Gardner gun manned by the IXth Sudanese.

The 1st Brigade marched three miles south-east into the desert, hidden by the hills, until they were able to take up a position on the ridges opposite Ginnis. The cavalry was spread out in vedettes on their left. The 2nd Brigade, minus six companies of the Cameron Highlanders and two companies of the Sudanese, took up a position overlooking Kosheh village, while the Egyptian Cavalry occupied vedettes in the rear. The Cameron Highlanders and the IXth Sudanese formed up in front of Kosheh fort.

The battle began at 6:10 AM after the 2nd Brigade mounted a crest 1,200 yards from Kosheh village with the Yorkshire Regiment in half battalions on either side of the Royal Artillery and the Gardner guns and the 1st Egyptians in the rear. The battery opened fire on the village, taking the Mahdists by surprise. They replied with a "sharp but ill-directed fire," which was in turn answered by the Yorkshires. After fifteen minutes of bombardment the Camerons and the IXth began their advance along the river, while the *Lotus* steamed alongside them slightly in front.

The Camerons met the order to advance with great relief after one month pent-up in the fort. They headed directly for the village while the IXth stormed the black rock. The *Lotus* trained its Gardner gun and rifles on groups of Mahdists driven from hut to hut. The IXth cleared the black rock after stiff hand-to-hand fighting and captured one brass gun. When the Camerons joined the IXth on the other side of the rock they met them with a loud cheer.

By 6:50 AM Kosheh village had been cleared. The *Lotus* reported a Mahdist force advancing from Ginnis. She was ordered to continue steaming slightly ahead of the

Camerons, bringing fire to bear an both banks. The Camerons and Sudanese continued their advance through the palm groves and cultivation towards Ginnis, and were joined by the rest of the brigade.

When the Mahdists in the camp behind Ginnis found that the 1st Brigade had taken a position in the ridges to the south-east they began an attack of their own screened by riflemen. The riflemen lined the crests and opened fire for about forty minutes, though this was described as "heavy but ill-directed" (Cairint). Some spearmen were able to advance unseen along a *khor* and attack the Egyptian Camel Corps while it was dismounted, forcing it back. But the attack was broken by fire from the DLI and the Camel Corps' own right flank troops.

"The Last Rush." Ansar spearmen come boiling up out of the khor against the Egyptian Camel Corps at the battle's climax.

The 1st Brigade now swung to the left, fighting for each crest as it continued to advance towards the camp at Ginnis. It occupied the camp as the Camerons and IXth Sudanese cleared the houses of Ginnis village. The British cavalry and Mounted Infantry had formed on the left of the 1st Brigade and pursued the Mahdists through the Atab Defile. This was weakly held, and the Mahdists were dispersed by a bayonet charge of the Mounted Infantry. The cavalry then watched the Mahdists retreat "sullenly," an adjective used when natives withdrew slowly and in good order. When the commander of the cavalry was later taken to task for not pursuing the Mahdists more vigorously, he replied, rather testily, that he hadn't an independent command and didn't feel he could take such an initiative (Cairint).

With the Mahdist camp and both villages now in Anglo-Egyptian hands it was found that a small band of Mahdists were still occupying a house in Kosheh village. They were finally dislodged by a screw gun and the 1st Egyptians. The battle was over by 10:00 AM.

The Aftermath of Battle

The Anglo-Egyptian casualties during the battle were light. They were reported as two British killed and 25 wounded, 8 Egyptians killed and 13 wounded (Cairint). Later sources placed the dead at 20 Egyptians and 12 British (Haggard, p. 384).

It is hard to say what the Mahdist casualties were, as the official dispatches give no figures either of the force or its losses. Wingate gives casualty figures as 500 killed and 300 wounded (Wingate, p. 279). Andrew Haggard, who commanded the 1st Egyptians in the battle, later claimed that an official estimate of 600 casualties was too high (Haggard, p. 384). It should be noted that Haggard's figures are usually at variance with the official figures. The loss of Emirs seems to have been high, including as it did Abd al-Kajid, abd al-Khalik and Umar wad al-fakir among the high command, the commanders of the Rubatab, Berber and Khartoum contingents, and Hamid at-Zain. Abd al-Majid al-Khujali was wounded. The official dispatch erroneously claimed Uthman Azraq and Mahmud al-Ajumi Hamza among the slain (Cairint).

The Mahdist forces were rallied by Uthman Azraq at old Dongola, which served as the northern most Mahdist outpost during most of the rest of 1886. Muhammad al-Khair reported to the Khalifa that his forces were taken completely by surprise. He was later blamed for the defeat and was removed from his command of Berber and Dongola in 1886.

The Mahdists continued to fear an invasion from the north until the Anglo-Egyptian forces, now satisfied that they faced no immediate threat from the south, abandoned Kosheh and withdrew to Wadi Halfa, where they remained until the beginning of the Re-conquest.

Conclusions About The Battle

Most of the front-line fighting was done by the British Army, but it cannot be denied that all branches of the Egyptian Army acquitted themselves well. Both the Camel Corps and the 1st Egyptians were involved in difficult hand-to-hand fighting, and all four guns captured during the battle were captured by the Egyptian Army. The honors of the day went to the recently formed IXth Sudanese, the first, and at that time the only, Sudanese battalion in the Egyptian Army. Sergeant Major Ali Abdullah of the IXth, formerly a gunner on one of Gordon's steamers, was mentioned in dispatches and recommended for promotion for his skill in handling the Gardner gun on the *Lotus* (Cairint). In the battle, the battalion captured two guns. A bond was formed between it and the Cameron Highlanders during the month they shared the siege in Kosheh, and the Camerons presented the IXth with a set of colors, suitably inscribed with "Kosheh" and "Ginnis" as their first honors. The success of the IXth on the frontier led to the raising of a second Sudanese battalion, the XIIIth under Smith-Dorrien.

Even with the honors the Egyptian Army won, so great was the rivalry between the British officers of the Egyptian Army and those of the regular army that one officer attached to the Egyptian Army rushed into the Mahdist camp at Ginnis, bundling Mahdist banners under his arms, shouting "Don't let the English get the flags!" (Haggard, p. 376)

Ginnis marked the end of the active involvement of the British Army on the Nile frontier. The *ad hoc* Camel Corps and Mounted Infantry disappeared from all future engagements and the regulars returned to garrisons further down the river. It was also the last time that large units of British and Egyptian troops were brigaded together. The defence of the Frontier devolved on the Egyptian Army and over the next few years certain units such as the Sudanese Battalions and the Egyptian Camel Corps gained a reputation for fighting that was carried through the Re-conquest. It was the Egyptian Army that later defeated Wad al-Nujumi's army at Toski (only one British unit, the 20th Hussars was present), and it was the Egyptian Army that carried out the early stages of the Re-conquest. It was only with the Atbara and Omdurman campaigns that large numbers of the British Army were used, and then they were brigaded separately.

The armed steamer Lotus, another Yarrow built vessel providing yeoman service in support both in combat and supply roles.

It is hard to make an assessment of the Mahdist performance, because intelligence reports about them at this time are so incomplete. Aside from the want of accurate numbers, there is no complete list of the different contingents. There seems to have been a separate command of riflemen, but it is unlikely that they were a regular unit of the *Jihadiyya* (former Sudanese soldiers in the Mahdist army), as the *Jihadiyya* at this time was still under the command of Hamdan Abu Anja, and he was using them in 1885 to put down various revolts in Kordofan and the Nuba Mountains.

There are varying opinions about the accuracy of the Mahdist riflemen at Kosheh and Ginnis. One Cameron Highlander Sergeant claimed that the Mahdists did not use their Remingtons well and fired high, even at close range (Lawton, pp. 31 and 68). Andrew Haggard stated that some of the snipers were very good shots (Haggard, p. 367). The official reports speak of heavy or sharp, "but ill-directed fire," yet the Sirdar attributed the low casualties of the Anglo-Egyptian force to the complete surprise it achieved in its attack, not to the inaccurate rifle fire (Cairint). In the fighting around Kosheh Fort prior to the battle, Wingate commented that "very harassing" Mahdist rifle fire forced the defenders to build additional earthworks, and it was the excellence of these that kept casualties low. Yet Smith-Dorrien, who visited the black rock above the fort after the battle claimed that every movement in the fort could be seen, and the low casualties were due to "the extraordinary bad shooting of the Arabs" (Smith-Dorrien, p. 59).

During the month preceding the battle, the Mahdists showed a high degree of ingenuity and skill in their many raids around Kosheh and along the railroad. In particular their enemies noted their use of riflemen as skirmishers, and the well-placed gun emplacements along the river and overlooking the railroad (Grant, p. 160). They were unable to counter the Anglo-Egyptian ability to bring in reinforcements quickly by train or steamer , and in the end they were totally surprised by the appearance of a large army where they were aware of only a small garrison.

The brevity of reports does not give us a very clear idea of the abilities of the different Mahdist commanders. Muhammad al-Khair was in over-all command of the Frontier, but he does not seem to have been directly involved at Ginnis. The force there seems to have been commanded by Abd al-Majid al-Khujali, who proved to be somewhat careless. Hamid at-Zain was a very good hit-and-run frontier fighter, and Wad-ar-Rais placed his guns and riflemen well during the siege of Kosheh.

What has to be emphasized is that the Mahdist army at Ginnis was not the vanguard of an invading army, but the first line of defence. While Wad al-Nujumi raised an army for the defence of the frontier, Muhammad al-Kahir and Abd al-najid al-Khujali were to contain the enemy. Their tactics were mainly defensive, aimed at forcing the withdrawal of the Kosheh garrison without risking a major assault.

What is surprising is that although the Mahdists were expecting a large invading force, they were totally unprepared for the one that attacked them, but Ginnis was not a major defeat. It allowed the Anglo-Egyptians to withdraw to Wadi Halfa without harassment, but it left the Mahdists in possession of a longer stretch of the Nile than they previously held.

Of Firsts and Lasts

The Battle of Ginnis was a small affair notable for three points: it ended the phase of the Sudan campaign that began with Graham's battle of El Teb in 1884, it was the first battle of consequence in which the new Egyptian Army took part, and it was the last battle in which the British Army wore red coats.

Orders Of Battle For The Sudan Campaigns And Actions, 1883-1885
Researched And Compiled By Andrew Preziosi
As Part of The Preziosi Orders of Battle Collection

Hicks.00
Order of Battle, Soudan Field Force (Hicks Pasha Expedition), Kasghil, Nov. 5, 1883

Nominal Commander in Chief: *Sulieman Pasha Nyasi*
Chief of Staff: (Actual Field Commander)
　Major General William Hicks Pasha,
　(ex-1st Baluch Battalion) Bombay Staff Corps
Second in Command: *Ala al-Din Pasha,*
　Governor General of the Sudan
Quartermaster General: (Chief of Staff to Hicks Pasha)
　Major (Kaimakam [Brevet Colonel]) Arthur Farquhar,
　Grenadier Guards
Deputy Assistant Adjutant General (Intelligence/Civilian Interpreter): (Honorific) *Major Edward B. Evans*
Principal Medical Officer:
　Surgeon General Georges D. Douloglu Bey
Correspondents/Extra Staff Officers: *Edmund O'Donovan, Frank Viztelly*

Infantry Division: (approx. 7,600) *Hussein Pasha Mazhar*
2nd Brigade: (i.e, 2nd Egyptian Infantry Regiment) *Hussein Pasha/Abd-el-Kadr*
<u>1st Battalion</u>
　Miralai Rajab Bey
<u>2nd Battalion</u>
<u>3rd Battalion</u>
<u>Sudanese *Bazinger* Battalion</u>
　Miralai Salim Bey (attached)

3rd Brigade: (i.e, 3rd Egyptian Infantry Regiment) *Ala-al-Din*
<u>1st Battalion</u>
<u>2nd Battalion</u>
<u>3rd Battalion</u>
<u>Sudanese *Bazinger* Battalion</u> (attached)

4th Brigade: (i.e, 4th Egyptian Infantry Regiment) *Abbas Bey*
<u>1st Battalion</u>
<u>2nd Battalion</u>
<u>3rd Battalion</u>
<u>Sudanese *Bazinger* Battalion</u> (attached)

The Cavalry Brigade: *Major Baron Gotz von Seckendorff* (German)
　Major Warner, ex-Baker's SAH

HICKS PASHA, LATE COLONEL IN THE INDIAN ARMY
Commander-in-Chief of the Soudan Field Force

Bashi-Bazouk Cavalry Regiment (2 sqdns-400)
 Captain Arthur Herlth & Captain A. Matygna (Austro-Hungarian Officers)
Egyptian Regular Cavalry Regiment (untrained) (500)
 Captain Massey, ex-Middlesex (currently British Militia Officer, also ADC to Hicks Pasha)
Cairo Cuirassier Regiment (100 Circassian Cuirassiers)
 Lieutenant Morris Brody (also spelled Brady, ex-RSM, RHA)

Artillery: (approx 300)
4 Krupp Field Guns
10 Brass Mountain Guns
6 Nordenfelts

Camp Commandant: *Surgeon Major Rosenberg*
Camp Followers (2,000)
Camels (5,500)
Horses (500)

Khartoum.01
Order of Battle, Egyptian-Sudanese Division, Khartoum, January, 1885

Egyptian-Sudanese Division: (4,800) *Major General Charles George Gordon Pasha*, RE 
1st Egyptian Brigade: (actually the 1st Egyptian Inf. Regt—800 men
 Behki Bey el-Petrachi
1st Battalion/1st Infantry Regiment
 Behkit Bey (1st through 4th Coys)
3rd Battalion/1st Infantry Regiment
 Mohamed Ibrahim (9th- 12th Coys)

5th Egyptian Brigade: (5th Inf Regt-200 men) Hassan Bey
1st Company/5th Infantry Regiment
 Osman Hicmet
5th Company/5th Infantry Regiment
 Hassan Bey

Egyptian Gendarmerie:
Two Companies (200
 The Sudanese (*Bazinger*) Battalion
Sudanese Irregulars (400)
(1st) Bashi-Bazouk Irregular Infantry Regiment:
 Muhammad Ali Pasha Husayn
1200 Shaiqi Irregulars
(2nd) Bashi-Bazouk Irregular Infantry Regiment
 Faraj Allah Pasha Raghib
600 Ja'li(in?) Irregulars
600 Bari Irregulars

Armed Slave Battalion:
200 Nilotic Slaves

European Civilian Volunteers (unorganized):
300 Greeks
300 Austrians
200 Italians

Artillery Battalion:
Nine (9) pieces—100 Egyptian gunners

Khartoum.02
Order of Battle, Egyptian-Sudanese Division, Khartoum, January 25, 1885

Commander in Chief: (Governor General of the Sudan)
Major General Charles George Gordon Pasha, RE

Egyptian-Sudanese Division:
Lieutenant General Farag Pasha Ezzeini

1st "Sudanese" Brigade: *Behki Bey Betraki*
1st Egyptian Infantry Regiment (800 regulars)
Bashi-Bazouk and Shaggieh (3 *ordu's*))
1st Battalion/1st Egyptian Infantry Regiment (1st through 4th Coys)
    Major Ali Effendi Sakr
Bashi-Bazouk (9 *ordu's*)
    Surrur Bey Bahgat
2nd Battalion/1st Egyptian Infantry Regiment (5th-8th Coys)
    Major Mohammed Effendi Osman
Bashi-Bazouks (2 *ordu's*)
    Major Ahmed Eff. Hemaya
3rd Battalion/1st Egyptian Infantry Regiment (9th- 12th Coys)
    Major Mohammed Effendi Desuki

5th Egyptian Brigade: *Hassan Bey el Bahel Bahmassawi* (5th Egyptian Infantry Regt)
1st Battalion/5th Infantry Regiment (White Nile line) (320 men)
    Yussef Effendi Effat
Shaggiehs & Volunteer Bashi-Bazouks (10 *ordu's*)
    Osman Bey Hishmet
2nd Battalion/5th Infantry Regiment
    Farag Ali Bey & Ibrahim Bey Saleh

Reserve:
Bashi-Bazouk Cavalry (both mounted and dismounted)

Notes:
#1: The troops listed above run in a line from the Blue Nile to the White.
#2: The Volunteer forces are in reserve!

Khartoum 03
Mahdist Order of Battle, Siege and Assault of Khartoum, January, 1885

Commander in Chief: *Mohammed Ahmed* (The Mahdi)
Principle Subordinates: *Fiki Mustafa* (?), *Khalifa Wad en Nejumi* (replaced Emir Abu Girgeh)

Wing: (10,000 men and 9 cannon) *Khalifa Abd el Alai*
Sheikh Abou Hanga (1000 men and 4 cannon)
Sheikh El-Helou (1000 men and 5 cannon)
Sheikh Ali Cherif (1000 men)
Emir Fudhl (1000 men)
Sheikh Abd el Kader (*Wad om Miriam*) (1000 men)
Emir Mustafa Ibn el Amin (5000 men)

Wing: (4000 men and 4 cannon) *Sheikh El Obeid/ Sheikh Wad*

Wing: (20,000 men and 7 cannon) *Khalifa Wad en Nejumi*
Emir Wad Gubara (8,000 and 5 cannon)
Emir Abdullah Wad en Nur (8,000 men and 2 cannon)
Sheikh Abu Girgeh (1,000 men)
Sheikh Wad el Basir (1,000 men)
Sheikh Fudhl (1,000 men)
Sheikh Abd el Kader (1,000 men)

Suakin.00
Order of Battle, Egyptian Forces, 2nd Battle of El Teb, Feb. 4th, 1884

Commanding Officer: *Lieutenant General Sir Valentine Baker Pasha,*
   Egyptian Gendarmerie (ex-10th Hussars)
Aide-de-Camp: *Captain (Brevet Major) A.B. Harvey,*
      Black Watch
Second in Command:
   Major General (Lt. Colonel) Euston Henry Sartorius Pasha, VC, E. Lancs
Aides-de-Camp: *Major Izzat Effendi, Captain Goodall*
Egyptian Chief of Staff: *Colonel Abd El Rassak*
British Chief of Staff: *Lt. Colonel Fitzroy-Hay*
Paymaster: *Lt. Colonel James Anderson Morrice Bey*, RMLI (K)
Senior Medical Officer: *Dr. Leslie* (K)
Attached: (along for the ride)
   Lt. Colonel Frederick Gustavus Burnaby, The Blues
1st Gendarme Division:
   Major General (Lt. Colonel) Euston Henry Sartorius Pasha, VC, E. Lancs
Chief of Staff: *Lt. Colonel (A.M?) Harrington Bey*, ex-Rifle Brigade
1st Brigade:
<u>Alexandria Gendarme Battalion</u> (560)

Baker Pasha

Cairo Gendarme Battalion (500)
Turkish Infantry Battalion (429)
>   *Captain (Brevet Major) Holroyd*

2nd Brigade:
Massawa Sudanese Battalion (560)
Senhit [Sennaheit] Sudanese Battalion (400)
Zobair's *Bazinger* Regiment (2 bns) (678)

Divisional Troops:
Cavalry: *Yusuf Bey*
Egyptian Cavalry (Seven Squadrons)
Bashi Bazouk Cavalry (Three squadrons [troops], 150)
>   *Captain (Brevet Major) G.D. Giles*, Indian Cavalry

Artillery: *Captain (Brevet Major) R.H. Forrestier-Walker*, hp (ex-RA?) (K)
4 Krupp Field guns
2 Gatling guns
2 Rocket tubes
Gunners (128)

Provost Guard:
European Police (40) *Major Maletta*

Garrison of Suakin: *Colonel Alexander Bey*
Cairo Gendarme Battalion (108)
Alexandria Gendarme Battalion (68)
Massawa Sudanese Battalion (72)
1st Battalion/Zubair's Bazingers (107)
2nd Battalion/Zubair's Bazingers (639)
The Turkish Battalion (35)
Pensioners (320)
Bandsmen (50)
Turkish and Arab Horse (33/54)
Gunners (186)

Naval Support: Red Sea Squadron:
>   *Rear Admiral Sir William Nathan Wright Hewitt*, VC, KCB, KCSI, RN
>   *HMS Carysfort*
>   *HMS Coquette*
>   *HMS Euryalus*
>   *HMS Ranger*
>   *HMS Sphinx*
>   *HMS Woodlark*

Egyptian Gunboats:
>   *Deb-el-Bar*
>   *Gefferiah*
>   *Tor*

Trinkitat Camp Guard:
200 Egyptians
300 Sha'iqiya Arabs

Admiral Hewitt

Fort Baker:
Massawa Battalion (detachment)
2 Krupp's guns

Suakin.01
Order of Battle, British Suakin Expeditionary Force, Battles of El Teb and Tamai, February 29th and March 12th, 1884

Commander in Chief:
Major General Sir Gerald Graham, VC, CB, RE
Assistant Military Secretary:
Captain Kenneth Schalch Baynes, Cameron Highlanders
Aides-de-Camp:
> *Lieutenant Frederick William Romilly*, Scots Guards
> *Lieutenant W.A. Scott*, Cameron Highlanders
> *Lieutenant C.G. Lindesay*, RN, HMS *Euryalus*

Assistant Adjutant General:
Major (Brevet Lt. Colonel) Cornelius Francis Clery, ex-DCLI
Deputy Assistant Adjutant Generals:
Major (Brevet Lt. Colonel) R.W.T. Gordon, A&SH
Captain Andrew Gilbert Wauchope, CMG, Royal Highlanders
Provost Marshal: *Captain G.C.P. William-Freedman*, Sussex
Military Police: (HQ Flag bearer) *Sergeant Major Burke*
Signals: *Lieutenant F.M Beaumont*, 3rd KRRC, *Sergeant Sherwood*
Deputy Assistant Adjutant General (Intelligence) and Chief of Royal Engineers:
> *Major (Brevet Lt. Colonel) John Charles Ardagh*, CB, RE

Deputy Assistant Adjutant Generals (Intelligence):
> *Lt. Colonel Frederick Augustus Burnaby*, The Blues
> *Major Elliott Wood*, RE
> *Captain Arthur Octavius Green*, RE
> *Captain (Brevet Major) Frederick George "Keggy" Slade*, RA
> *Lt. Colonel Henry Edward Colville*, Grenadier Guards

Principal Medical Officer(s): (order of seniority)
> *Deputy Surgeon General Edmund Greswold McDowell*
> *Surgeon J. Prendergast*
> *Surgeon Major William Alister Catherwood* (Base)
> *Surgeon Major J.J. Greene* (Base)
> *Surgeon Major W. Venour* (Troop Ship HMS *Jumna*)

Principal Veterinary Officers:
Charles Clayton & Henry Thomson

Commissariat and Transport:
> *Assistant Commissary General Robert Arthur Nugent*, CB
> *Deputy Assistant Commissary General Marcus Edward Read Rainsford*
> *Deputy Assistant Commissary General George Vaughan Hamilton*

Transport Officers:
> *Major J.F. Forster*, DCLI
> *Lieutenant C.C. Turner*, Shropshire LI
> *Lieutenant R.L. Bower*, 3rd KRRC
> *Conductor Henry Hickie*

Ordnance Store Department:
Assistant Commissary General of Ordnance Herbert James Mills, OSD
Deputy Assistant Commissary General of Ordnance E. Houghton, OSD
Army Paymaster: *Major Robert Bent Farwell*, APD
Army Chaplains:
Reverend G. Smith (Co E)
Reverend John McTaggart (Presbyterian)
Reverend Father Robert Brindle (RC)
Reverend J. Webster (Wesleyan)
Staff Supernumeraries: Naval Commander in Chief, Red Sea Station:
Rear Admiral Sir William Nathan Wright Hewitt, VC, KCB, KCSI, RN
Naval Staff: *Captain Arthur Knyvett Wilson, RN, VC* (HMS *Hecla*)
Commander Pine Coffin, RN

Commander in Chief, Egyptian Constabulary:
Lieutenant General Sir Valentine Baker Pasha, Egyptian Gendarmerie (ex-10th Hussars)
1st Brigade: *Brigadier General Sir Redvers Buller*, VC, KCMG, CB, ADC
Aide-de-Camp: *Lieutenant John Townshend St. Aubyn*, Grenadier Guards
Brigade Major: *Captain William Freeman Kelly*, Sussex Regiment (W)
Intelligence Officer: (along for the ride)
Major (Brevet Lt. Colonel) John Charles Ardagh, CB, RE

Principal Medical Officer: (Infantry) *Surgeon Major William Deane Wilson*
3rd Kings Royal Rifle Corps (19/546)
Lt. Colonel (Brevet Colonel) Sir Cromer Ashburnham, KCB, ADC/
Lt Colonel William Lewis Kinloch Ogilvy
1st Gordon Highlander Regiment (23/689)
Lt. Colonel Denzil Hammill, CB
2nd Royal Irish Fusilier Regiment (17/326)
Lt. Colonel Barnes Slyfield Robinson/Captain John Gordon
26th Company, RE (5/57)
Major Killingworth Richard Todd (Field Engineer)/*Captain James Ford Dorward*

2nd Brigade: *Major General John Davis*
Aide-de-Camp: *Lieutenant C.C. Douglas*, Scottish Rifles
Brigade Major: *Captain Thomas Burnett Hitchcock*, Shropshire LI
42nd Royal Highland Regiment (Black Watch) (19/604)
Lt. Colonel William Green
1st York and Lancaster Regiment (14/421)
Lt. Colonel William Byam
Royal Marine Light Infantry Battalion (14/464)
Lt. Colonel (Brevet Colonel) Henry Brasnell Tuson, CB, ADC, RMAf

Army Medical Department
Deputy Surgeon General Edmund Greswold McDowell
The Abyssinian Scouts

The Cavalry Brigade:
Brigadier General Sir Herbert Stewart, CB, ADC
Aide-de-Camp: *Lieutenant Francis William Rhodes*, 1st Royal Dragoons
Brigade Major: *Major (Brevet Lt. Colonel) A.M. "Billy" (William?) Taylor*, 19th Hussars
Principal Medical Officer: *Surgeon Major B.B. Connolly*
<u>10th Hussar Regiment</u> (16/235)
    Major (Brevet Lt. Colonel) Edward Alexander Wood
<u>19th Hussar Regiment</u> (19/343)
    Lt. Colonel Arthur George Webster/
    Lt. Colonel Percy Henry Stanley Barrow, CMG
<u>Imperial Mounted Infantry</u> (6/118)
    Lieutenant (Local Captain) H. Humphreys,
      Welsh Regiment

General Sir Herbert Stewart

Naval Brigade: (attached to 1st Bde)
    Commander Ernest Neville Rolfe, RN
<u>6 Gatling guns</u> (150)

Artillery: *Major Francis Thomas Lloyd*, RA
<u>6th Battery/1st Brigade/Scottish Division</u> (8-7 pdrs/camel) (7/100)
    Major F.T. Lloyd, RA/Captain Josceline Heneage Wodehouse, RA (Egyptian Army)
<u>Battery "M"/1st Brigade, RA</u> (4-9 pdr mule battery) (3/66)
    Major Edward Hunt Holley, RA

Base Commandant: *Lt. Colonel R.W.T. Gordon*, A&SH
<u>RMLI</u> (100) (w/5 guns in position)
Invalid (Sick) Details (Camp guards)

Note: Unlike most OB's where the second officer listed usually took command upon the death or wounding of his CO, most of the "spare" (or second) officers are listed here because they performed an important function/duty/service at one point during the campaign.

Suakin.02
British Expeditionary Force, Suakin (Suakin Field Force), March 1885

Commander in Chief:
    Local Lt. General (Major General) Sir Gerald Graham, VC, KCB, RE
Military Secretary: *Major Edwin Henry Hayter Collen*, BSC
Assistant Military Secretary: (appointed but not present)
    Major (Brevet Lt. Colonel) Geoffrey Barton, R. Fusiliers
Aides-de-Camp:
    Lieutenant the Hon. J.M. Stopford, Grenadier Guards
    Lieutenant W.C. Anderson, RA
    Lieutenant C.G. Lindesay, RN (Naval ADC)
Army Staff:
Chief of Staff: *Major General Sir George Richard Greaves*, KCMG, CB
Aide-de-Camp: *Major Alexander Nelson Rochefort*, RA
Staff: *Captain (Brevet Major) Kenneth Schalch Baynes*, Cameron Highs

Assistant Adjutant and Quartermaster Generals:
>*Colonel D.S. Warren*, Regimental District (subsequently transferred to base)
>*Colonel G.F. Gildes (Gildea?)*, ADC, hp (succeeded Warren, then invalided out, ill)
>*Colonel J.M. Leith*, CB, Cameron Highlanders (succeeded Gildes)

Deputy Assistant Adjutant and Quartermaster Generals:
>*Major R.H.L. Anstruther*, hp
>*Major William R. Cooke-Collis*, RIF

Deputy Assistant Adjutant and Quartermaster Generals, Intelligence Department:
>*Major George Edward Grover*, RE
>*Captain George Sydenham Clarke*, RE
>(SSO, ex-acting Military Secretary, vice Barton)
>*Captain W.H. Sawyer*, KOR Lancs.
>*Captain P.H.N. Lake*, E. Lancs
>*Captain George Hand More-Molyneaux*, BSC

Deputy Assistant Adjutant and Quartermaster Generals: (Special Service Officers)
>*Captain (Brevet Lt. Colonel) R.H. Murray*, Seaforths (attached, Co's)
>*Captain (Brevet Major) C.W.H. Douglas*, Gordons (attached, AAG Dept.)
>*Captain (Brevet Major) William Christopher James*, Scots Greys (attached, AAG Dept., then Camel Corps OC)
>*Lieutenant James Moncrieff Grierson*, RA (attached QMG Dept.)

Provost Marshal: (Assistant Adjutant and Quartermaster General)
>*Major (Brevet Lt. Colonel) R.W.T. Gordon*, A&SH
>*Major J.M Morris*, RMLI (DPM)

Signaling Department: *Major Edward Thomas Browell*, RA
District Paymaster: *Staff Paymaster R.G. Craig*, APD
Chaplains:
>*The Reverend W.H. Bullock* (Co E)
>*Reverend Father Reginald F. (B?) Collins* (RCC)

Commissariat and Transport:
>*Lt. Colonel John Leslie Robertson* (Assistant Commissary General)
>*Lt. Colonel Stephen Beckett*, BSC (Assistant Commissary General, Transport, ISC)
>*Lt. Colonel Charles Elliott Walton (Watson?)* (Assistant Commissary General, Transport)
>*Major E.G. Skinner*, OSD (Assistant Commissary General of Ordnance)
>*Captain (Brevet Major) G.H.E. Elliott* (Deputy Assistant Commissary General, Transport, ISC)
>*Major James Alleyne Clarke* (Assistant Commissary General)
>*Captain Edward Willis Duncan Ward* (Deputy Assistant Commissary General)
>*Captain Emilius Albert de Cosson*, Reserve of Officers (ditto)

Medical Staff:
>*Deputy Surgeon General Oliver Barnett*, CIE (PMO)
>*Deputy Surgeon General George Langford Hinde*
>*Brigade Surgeon J. Warren*
>*Brigade Surgeon W. Tanner*
>*Surgeon Major J.A. Shaw*
>*Surgeon Major J. Fleming*
>*Surgeon Major G.J.H. Evatt*

Veterinary Staff: *Inspecting Veterinary Surgeon W.B. Walters*

1st (Guards) Brigade: *Major General Arthur James Lyon-Fremantle*

Aide-de-Camp: (subsequently Brigade Major)
 Captain the Hon. Frederick William Stopford, Grenadier Guards
Brigade Major: *Captain the Hon. North de Coigny Dalrymple-Hamilton,* Scots Guards
<u>2nd Grenadier Guards Regiment </u>(840)
 Lt. Colonel (Brevet Colonel) Reginald Thomas Thynne
<u>2nd Coldstream Guards Regiment </u>(834)
 Lt. Colonel (Brevet Colonel) Arthur Lambton
<u>1st Scots Guards Regiment </u>(840)
 Lt. Colonel (Brevet Colonel) the Hon. Walter Randolph Trefusis
<u>New South Wales Battalion </u>(attached)
 Lt. Colonel John Soame Richardson (OC, NSW Contingent)
 Lt. Colonel Wells

2nd Brigade: *Major General Sir John C. MacNeill,* VC, KCB, KCMG
Aide-de-Camp: *Lieutenant the Honorable Allan Dudley Charteris,* Coldstream Guards
Brigade Major: *Major (Brevet Lt. Colonel) William Freeman Kelly,* Sussex
<u>1st Berkshire Regiment </u>(650)
 Lt. Colonel Alfred George Huyshe
<u>1st Shropshire Light Infantry Regiment </u>(800)
 Lt. Colonel Robert Holt Truell
<u>2nd East Surrey Regiment </u>(600)
 Lt. Colonel (Brevet Colonel) William Henry Ralston
<u>Royal Marine Light Infantry Battalion </u>(500)
 Lt. Colonel Nowell Fitzupton Way

3rd Brigade: (The Indian Contingent)
 Local Brigadier General (Colonel) John Hudson, CB, BSC
Assistant Adjutant and Quartermaster Generals:
 Major Robert Macgregor Stewart, RA
Deputy Assistant Adjutant and Quartermaster Generals:
 Captain (Brevet Major) Norman Robert Stewart, BSC
 Major A.J. Pearson, RA
Brigade Major: *Major John Cooke,* BSC, VC
Provost Marshal: *Captain H.R.L. Holmes,* BSC
Chief Commissariat Officer: *Lt. Colonel Edmund Scopoli Walcott,* BSC
Chief Transport Officer: *Major George Robert James Shakespeare,* BSC
Medical Staff: *Brigade Surgeon James Howard Thornton,* MD
  Brigade Surgeon Morice
<u>15th Ludhiana Sikh Infantry Regiment </u>(725)
 Lt. Colonel (Brevet Colonel) George Robertson Hennessey, BSC
<u>17th Bengal Infantry Regiment </u>(843)
 Major J.M.W. Von-Beverhoudt, BSC (K)
<u>28th Bombay Infantry Regiment </u>(245)
 Lt. Colonel (Brevet Colonel) Francis Corbett (H?) Singleton

Column Troops:
Cavalry Brigade: *Colonel Henry Peter Ewart,* CB, hp
Brigade Major: *Captain Charles Fitzgerald Thomson,* 7th Hussars
<u>The Camel Corps</u>
 Captain (Brevet Major) William Christopher James, Scots Greys

Mounted Infantry Regiment (196)
    Lt. Colonel Henry Fane Grant, 4th Hussars
9th Bengal Cavalry Regiment (581)
    Lt. Colonel (Brevet Colonel) Arthur Powell Palmer
HM 5th Lancer Regiment (2 sqdns) (248)
    Major Alfred Bissell Harvey/Captain L.H. Jones
HM 20th Hussar Regiment (2 sqdns) (261)
    Lt. Colonel Cecil Mangles/Major Francis John Graves
Mounted Infantry/Police (13)
Artillery: *Lt. Colonel Stuart Nicholson,* RA (C, RA)
Adjutant: *Captain R.A. Bannatine,* RA
5/1 Scottish Division, RA (Mountain Battery) (6 – 2.5" guns)
    Major J.J. Congdon, RA
6/1 Ammunition Column, RA (mules and camels, later manned Gardner guns on the Armored train)
    Captain E.R.M. Cooke, RA
"G" Troop, "B" Brigade, RHA (6 – 9 pdrs)
    Major John Forbes Meiklejohn
New South Wales (Australian) Field Battery (6x 9-pndrs)
    Lt. Colonel Warner Wright Spalding
    Major Henry P. Airey/Lieutenant Robert Nathan, NSWA
Naval Brigade: *Commander William Cecil Henry Domville,* RN, HMS *Condor*
Naval Gardner Gun Battery

Engineers: (Staff) *Colonel J. Bevan Edwards,* CB, RE, hp (C, RE)
Brigade Major: *Captain (Brevet Major) H. Whistler-Smith,* RE
18th (RR) Company, RE-*Lt. Colonel Elliott Wood*
11th Company, RE (attached to Mounted Infantry)
    Captain (Brevet Colonel) Edward Pemberton Leach, VC
17th Company, RE (105)
    Lieutenant F.C. Heath
24th Company, RE (124)
    Lieutenant A.G. Thompson
"A" Company, Queen's Own Madras Sappers and Miners
    Captain Charles Boyd Wilkieson, RE, (W)
Balloon Corps Detachment
    Major James Lethbridge B. Templer, 7th KRRC
2nd and 3rd Section, Telegraph Battalion
    Major H.F. Turner, RE

Base (and LOC): *Local Major General (Brigadier General) Charles Brisbane Ewart,* RE
Aide-de-Camp: *Lieutenant C.R. McGrigor,* KRRC
Deputy Adjutant and Quartermaster General: (Base and LOC Commandant)
    Colonel William Arbuthnot, hp
Assistant Adjutant and Quartermaster General: (Base and LOC)
    Major (Brevet Lt. Colonel) H.G. Macgregor

Deputy Assistant Adjutant and Quartermaster General: *(Base and LOC)*
Major Alfred Allen Garstin, Middlesex
Staff Officers: (Base and LOC)
Lt. Colonel F.A. Le Mesurier, RE
Major J.H. Barnard, CMG, Munsters (SSO)
Captain R.C. De'E. Spottiswoode, 10th Hussars (SSO)
Captain (Brevet Major) Henry Hare, Munsters (SSO)

Royal Navy Contingent: (Red Sea Squadron/Division of the Mediterranean Fleet/Squadron)
Commodore Robert Henry More-Molyneux, CB
Harbor Master:
Lieutenant Thomas MacGill
Principal Transport Officers:
Captain John Fellowes
Commander William L. Morrison (APTO)
Current Squadron:
HMS Sphinx (Flag)—
Commodore R.H. More-Molyneux/
Lieutenant Archibald T. Carter
HMS Carysfort—Captain Walter Stewart (invalided out)
  Acting Commander Edwin N. Price
HMS Dolphin—Captain Sidney M. Eardley-Wilmot
HMS Condor—Commander William Cecil Henry Domville
HMS Coquette—Lieutenant Fritz H.E. Crowe
HMS Starling-Lieutenant James B. Young
HMS Cygnet-Lieutenant Alexander M. Carter

Commodore R.M. Molyneux

Sudan.00
Order of Battle, British Staff, The Gordon Relief Expedition, 1884

Commander in Chief: *General Sir Garnet Wolseley*, GCB, GCMG, etc...
Military Secretary: *Lt. Colonel Leopold Victor Swaine*, CB, RB
  (invalided out after Fall of Khartoum [NB])
Aides-de-Camp:
Captain Lord Charles William de la Poer Beresford, RN
    (Naval Brigade)
Colonel Zohrab Bey
Major Frederick Meyer Wardrop, 3rd Dragoon Guards
Major Arthur Gethin Creagh, RA
Lieutenant John Adye, RA
Lieutenant Erskine Spencer E. Childers, RE
Personal Surgeon: *Surgeon Major William Simson Pratt*

Army Staff:
Chief of Staff: *Major General Sir Redvers Buller*, VC, KCB, KRRC, etc...
Aide-de-Camp: *Lord Edward Fitzgerald*
Chief of Intelligence: (DAAG[I]) *Colonel Sir Charles Wilson*, KCMG, RE
Quartermaster General: *Major General Sir A. J. Stewart*

Captain Beresford

Deputy Quartermaster General and Deputy Assistant Adjutant General: (Field)
Colonel Henry Brackenbury, CB, RA
Assistant Quartermaster General: (Director of Transport)
Lt. Colonel George Armand Furse, Black Watch
Assistant Adjutant General: **(Boat Service)**
Colonel William Francis Butler, CB
Assistant Adjutant Generals:
Colonel George Benjamin Wolseley, CB, Y&L
Colonel Charles Edmund Webber, RE (Telegraphs)
Lt. Colonel Coleridge Grove, E. Yorks (Boat Service, later Military Secretary)
Lt. Colonel James Alleyne, RA (ditto)
Deputy Assistant Adjutant Generals: (Intelligence)
Lt. Colonel Henry Edward Colville, Grenadier Guards
Major Frederick George "Keggy" Slade, RA
Major Alfred E. Turner, RA
Captain Herbert Horatio Kitchener, RE (*Bimbashi*, EA)
Captain William Willoughby Cole Verner, RB
Deputy Assistant Adjutant Generals:
Captain (Brevet Major) John Hartley Sandwith, RMLI
Captain Robert George Kekewich, E. Kents
Chief of Artillery: *Major Woodburn Hunter*, RA (OC, 1st/1st Scottish Division)
Chief of Engineers: *Major W.H. Mulloy*, RE
Commissariat and Transport Department:
Deputy Commissary General Emilius Hughes, CMG
Commissariat: *Assistant Commissary General James Tierney Skinner*, CB, DSO, ASC
Transport: *Assistant Commissary General Robert Arthur Nugent*, CB
Ordnance Store Department:
Deputy Commissary of Ordnance M.J.T. Ingram
Assistant Commissary of Ordnance Thales Pease
Provost Marshal: (HQ Commandant)
Lieutenant (Staff Captain) R.H. Maxwell, Black Watch
Signaling: *Lieutenant (Staff Captain) F.M. Beaumont*, KRRC
...and other, lesser luminaries (medical, veterinary, pay, post, etc.)

Col. Henry Brackenbury

Staff Supernumeraries: (Designated Field Force and Column Commanders)
Major General: *Major General William Earle*, CB, CSI
Aide-de-Camp: *Lieutenant John Townshend St. Aubyn*, Grenadier Guards
Brigade Major: *Major Mordaunt Charles Boyle*, KRRC
Brigadier General: *Brigadier General Sir Herbert Stewart*, KCB
Aide-de-Camp: *Captain Francis William Rhodes*, Royal Dragoons
Brigade Major: *Captain David Stanley William, The Earl of Airlie*, 10th Hussars
Line of Communications Staff: (primarily and overwhelmingly Egyptian Army officers)

The Sirdar: (C-in-C, Egyptian Army)
Lieutenant General Sir Evelyn Wood, VC, GCMG, KCB, 17th Lancers
Aide-de-Camp:
Lieutenant (Brevet Major) Francis Reginald Wingate, RA

Brigadier General:
 Local Brigadier General (Lt. Colonel and Colonel) Francis Wallace Grenfell, KRRC (EA)

Aide-de-Camp: *Captain (Brevet Major) David Phelps Chapman, S. Lancs* (EA)

Colonel on the Staff: *Colonel Richard Edes Harrison,* CB, RE

Assistant Adjutant Generals:
 Major (Brevet Lt. Colonel) John Charles Ardagh, CB, RE (Base Commandant)
 Major (Brevet Lt. Colonel) Thomas Fraser, CMG, RE (Colonel, EA)
 Major (Brevet Lt. Colonel) John Frederick Maurice, RA
 Colonel K.G. Henderson (h.p., commanding Assuan)

Deputy Assistant Adjutant Generals:
 Major E.T.H. Hutton, KRRC
 Major E.A.W.S. Groves, RW Kents
 Lt. Colonel Frank Thomas Lloyd, RA (h.p., commanding Assuan)

Special Service Officers:
 Colonel the Hon. Everard Primrose, Grenadier Guards
 Colonel Frederick Augustus Burnaby, RHG (The Blues)
 Colonel R. Blundell-Hollingshead-Blundell
 Lt. Colonel R.W.T. Gordon, A&SH
 Lt. Colonel Henry Hallam Parr, CMG, Somersets (Colonel, EA)
 Lt. Colonel Francis Duncan, RA (ditto)

Not Listed:

Commanding Officer, Egypt (and Staff):
 Lt. General Sir Frederick Charles Arthur Stephenson, CB, KCB, Scots Guards

General Sir Evelyn Wood

Sudan.01
Dispositions and Concentrations of Anglo-Egyptian Troops, Nov. 18, 1884

Commander in Chief: *General Sir Garnet Wolseley,* GCB, GCMG, etc...

Dongola:
HQ (45)
Mounted Infantry Camel Regiment (440)
1st Royal Sussex Regiment (820)
Details (50)

Between Dongola and Dal:
Guards Camel Regiment (320)
1st South Staffordshire Regiment (600)
Royal Engineer Company (50)

Between Dal and Gemai:
2nd Duke of Cornwall's Light Infantry Regiment (670)
2nd Essex Regiment (620)
42nd Highland Infantry (Black Watch) (225)
Canadian Voyageurs and West African Kroomen (370)

Naval Brigade (70)

South of Halfa:
Egyptian Troops:
Five Infantry Battalions (20/99/2381)
Five Troops of Cavalry (1/14/345)
Camel Battery (1/4/115)
Camel Troop (2/5/154)

Between Halfa and Dongola:
19th Hussar Regiment (300)

At Halfa, Serras and Gemai:
1st Black Watch (450)
Royal Artillery (85)
Royal Engineers (300)
Heavy Camel Regiment (225)
Light Camel Regiment (135)
Royal Marine Light Infantry (100)
Commissariat and Transport Corps (150)
Bearer Company and Mobile Field Hospital (170)
Departmental Troops (60)
Sick (220)

Between Halfa and Assuan:
1st Gordon Highlanders (720)
Heavy Camel Regiment (230)
Light Camel Regiment (250)
Transport Company (70)
19th Hussars (50)
Royal Engineers (50)

Assuan:
1st Royal West Kents (750)
1st Royal Irish (750)
1st Gordon Highlanders (50)
2nd Essex (120)
Sundry Troops (50)
1st Cameron Highlanders, plus Details (500)
1 Egyptian Battalion (2/24/451)
1 Troop, Egyptian Cavalry (5.65)
1 Egyptian Artillery Battery (5/93)
Sick (120)

Assuit:
Details (75)

Sudan.02
Order of Battle, The Desert Column, January-February 1885
(Note: For campaign purposes, this Order of Battle is post-Jakdul Wells centric)

Commanding Officer: *Brigadier General Sir Herbert Stewart*, KCB
Aide-de-Camp: *Captain Francis William Rhodes*, 1st Royal Dragoons
Column Brigade Major: *Captain David Stanley William, The Earl of Airlie*, 10th Hussars
Staff: Deputy Assistant Quartermaster General and Adjutant General: (Field)
　Major Frederick Meyer Wardrop, 3rd Dragoon Guards
Deputy Adjutant General, Intelligence: (2nd in Com)
　Colonel Sir Charles William Wilson, KCMG, RE
Deputy Assistant Adjutant Generals: (Intelligence)
　Captain William Willoughby Cole Verner, RB
　Major J.B.B. Dickson, 1st Royal Dragoons (attached, boats)
　Captain Richard Frederick Thomas Gascoigne, Yorkshire Dragoons
　　(Yeomanry Militia) ex-RHG (attached, ADC to Burnaby)
　Lieutenant (Brevet Major) Edward James Montagu Stuart-Wortley ("Wortles"),
　　KRRC (Egyptian Army) (attached)
Principal Medical Officer: *Surgeon Major F. Fergusson*
Baggage Master: *Captain Lord Cochrane*
　(either *Major Douglas Mackinnon Baillie-Hamilton, The Earl of Dundonald*,
　2nd Life Guards **or** *William Francis Dundonald Cochrane*)
The Camel Corps: *Colonel Frederick Augustus Burnaby*, RHG
　　(The Blues— (Special Service Officer))
<u>Guards Camel Regiment</u> (19/365)
　Lt. Colonel the Hon. Evelyn Edward Thomas Boscawen, Coldstream Guards
<u>Heavy Camel Regiment</u> (24/376)
　Lt. Colonel the Hon. Reginald Arthur James ("Reggy") Talbot, 1st Life Guards
<u>Light Camel Regiment</u> (21/387) (not present at Abu Klea)
　Lt. Colonel Stanley de Astvel Calvert Clark, hp
<u>Mounted Infantry Camel Regiment</u> (24/359)
　Major the Hon. George Hugh Gough, 14th Hussars
Column Troops:
Cavalry:
<u>19th Hussar Regiment</u> (2 sqdns) (8/127)
　Lt. Colonel Percy Henry Stanley Barrow, CB, CMG

Artillery:
<u>1st Battery/1st Southern Brigade, RA</u> (Camel drawn Half Troop) (4/39) (3- 2.5 muzzle loading screw guns)
　Captain Gilbert Frederick Allan Norton, RA

Naval Brigade: *Captain Lord Charles William de la Poer Beresford*, RN
Sailors, gunners and artisans (5/53) (1- 5 barreled Gardner gun)

Miscellaneous Troops:
<u>1st Royal Sussex Regiment</u> (8/250)
　Major Marsden Samuel James Sunderland
　(*Colonel John Ormsby Vandeleur* commanded Base Garrison at Jakdul Wells)

Royal Engineers:
<u>Detachment, 26th Company, Royal Engineers</u> (2/25)
   Captain James Ford Dorward

Medical and Transport Column:
   Assistant Commissary General Robert Arthur Nugent, CB
Bearer Company (2/40)-*Surgeon A. Harding*
Movable Field Hospital (2/20)-*Surgeon William Hamilton Brigg*
Transport-*Assistant Commissary General Marcus Edward Read Rainsford*

Reinforcements: *Major General Sir Redvers Buller*, VC, KCB, KRRC, etc...
<u>1st Royal Irish Fusilier Regiment</u>
   Lt. Colonel Hugh Shaw, VC

Sudan .03
Order of Battle, The River Column, Korti, January 4, 1885

Commanding Officer: *Major General William Earle*, CB, CSI
Aide-de-Camp: *Lieutenant John Townshend St. Aubyn*, Grenadier Guards
Brigade Major: *Major Mordaunt Charles Boyle*, KRRC
Principal Staff Officer: (2nd in Command)
   Brigadier General (Colonel) Henry Brackenbury, CB, RA
Assistant Adjutant Generals:
   Colonel William Francis Butler, CB
   Lt. Colonel James Alleyne, RA
Staff Officer:
   Lieutenant D.V. Pirie, 1st Life Guards
Deputy Assistant Adjutant Generals: (Intelligence)
   Lt. Colonel Henry Edward Colville, Grenadier Guards
   Major Frederick George "Keggy" Slade, RA
   Captain (Brevet Major) John Hartley Sandwith, RMLI

Staff Captains:
   Lieutenant (Staff Captain) Charles Reginald Orde, RB
   Lieutenant (Staff Captain) W.F. Peel, 2nd Life Guards
   Lieutenant (Staff Captain) H.G. Morris, DCLI
   Lieutenant (Staff Captain) J. Macrae, Black Watch
   Lieutenant (Staff Captain) Barry Nugent, Viscount Lord Avonmore, Hampshires
Signaling Officer: *Lieutenant (Staff Captain) F.M. Beaumont*, KRRC
Supply and Transport: *Deputy Assistant Commissary General John Alexander Boyd*
Principal Medical Officer: *Surgeon Major Charles Hamilton Harvey*
Infantry Brigade: *Brigadier General (Colonel) Henry Brackenbury*, CB, RA
<u>1st South Staffordshire Regiment</u> (600)
   Lt. Colonel Phillip Homan Eyre
<u>1st Black Watch Highlander Regiment</u> (675)
   Lt. Colonel William Green, CB
*2nd Duke of Cornwall's Light Infantry Regiment** (650)
   Lt. Colonel George Clayton Swiney
<u>1st Gordon Highlander Regiment</u> (720)
   Lt. Colonel Denzil Hamill, CB

Rear Echelon Troops:*
2nd Essex Regiment (740)
Lt. Colonel Charles Elphinstone Rennie
1st Royal West Kent Regiment (750)
Lt. Colonel David John Dickson Safford/Lt. Colonel John Lannoy Tweedie
1st Royal Irish Regiment (750)
Lt. Colonel William Richard Erskine Dawson
1st Cameron Highlanders (500)
Lt. Colonel Henry Hungerford St. Leger

Column Troops:
Cavalry:
19th Hussar Regiment (350)
Major John Compton Hanford Flood
Egyptian Camel Corps (Two companies, 161)
Captain (Brevet Major) Reginald Adams Marriott, RMA
Artillery:
Camel Battery, Egyptian Artillery (6 x 7-pndrs) (120)
Miscellaneous Troops: (mostly LOC and Support)
Engineers:
8th (RR) Company, RE
11th (Transport) Company, RE
Captain Blackburn, RE
26th Company, RE
Naval Brigade (70)
Canadian Voyageurs and West African Kroomen (370)
Lt. Colonel Frederick Charles Denison, Canadian Militia
The Mudir's Troops:
The Vakeel Ahmad Effendi Sulayman
Black *Bazinger* Regiment (310)

Note: Officers commanding the five regiments marked with an asterisk (*) are based either on regimental records during the entire campaign and the Brevet promotion list, it is possible for one or two to be mistaken.

Sudan .04
Order of Battle, The River Column,
Battle of Kirbekan, February 10, 1885

Commanding Officer:
(See previous Order of Battle for full Staff details)
Major General William Earle, CB, CSI (K)
Aide-de-Camp: *Lieutenant John Townshend St. Aubyn,*
Grenadier Guards
Brigade Major: *Major Mordaunt Charles Boyle,* KRRC
Field Force:
1st South Staffordshire Regiment (23/533)
Lt. Colonel Phillip Homan Eyre (K)/Lt. Colonel Henry Beal
1st Black Watch Highlander Regiment (20/417) (7 Coys.)

General Earle

Lt. Colonel William Green, CB/Junior Lt. Colonel Robert Charles Coveney (K)
19th Hussar Regiment (5/78)
    Major John Compton Hanford Flood
Camel Battery, Egyptian Artillery (2 7-pndrs) (2/22) (1 section)
1st Company, Egyptian Camel Corps (6/42)
    Captain (Brevet Major) Reginald Adams Marriott, RMA

Troop Dispositions:
Covering Troops:
Zariba:
    Major (Brevet Lt. Colonel) Charles John Eden, Black Watch
Staff Officer: *Captain (Brevet Major) John Hartley Sandwith, RMLI*
Black Watch (1 Coy.) (w/ boats and baggage and HQ [staff])
Blocking Force: (Hillock)
    Lt. Colonel James Alleyne, RA
2 Companies, South Staffs and Egyptian Artillery section
Covering Force: (Left Flank)
1st Company, Egyptian Camel Corps
    Captain (Brevet Major) Reginald Adams Marriott, RMA
Main Column: *Major General William Earle, CB, CSI*
    Brigadier General (Colonel) Henry Brackenbury, CB, RA
    Colonel William Francis Butler, CB (Cavalry)
19th Hussars (in front)
1st South Staffs (6)
    Lt. Colonel Eyre (1/2 BN columns at intervals of 2 companies)
1st Black Watch (6)
    Lt. Colonel Green (same formation)
Field Hospital
Reserve Ammunition Camels

Versus

Dervish Forces: (Monasir and Robatat tribesmen)
Emir Hamid al Kalik
Emir Musa Wad Ali Hijal
Emir Ali Wad Hussain

850 Spearmen
150 Riflemen

Sudan.05
Order of Battle, The River Column, Return to Meroe, February 24, 1885

Commanding Officer: *Brigadier General (Colonel) Henry Brackenbury, CB, RA*
1st South Staffordshire Regiment (566)
1st Black Watch Highlander Regiment (582)
2nd Duke of Cornwall's Light Infantry Regiment (575)
1st Gordon Highlander Regiment (511)
19th Hussar Regiment (96)
Camel Battery, Egyptian Artillery (6 7-pndrs) (90)
The Egyptian Camel Corps (1 Coy.) (97)

26th Company, RE (22)
Egyptian Cavalry (Detachment) (7)
Naval Brigade (12)
Canadian Voyageurs and West African Kroomen (66)

Sudan .06
Dispositions and Concentrations of Anglo-Egyptian Troops, June 26, 1885

Commander in Chief: *General Sir Garnet Wolseley*, GCB, GCMG, etc...
Dongola:
1st Royal West Kents
19th Hussars (1 sqdn)
1/1 Southern Division, RA (1 section- 2 guns)

Hafir:
1st South Staffordshires (2)
19th Hussars (1)
1/1 S/Div, RA (2)

Fatma:
1st South Staffs (2)

Kabuda: (600)
Baker's Egyptian Gendarmerie
9th Sudanese Battalion

Kaibar:
Whaler Crews
Egyptian Troops (500)

Kaibar-Abri:
19th Hussars (1)
1/1 S/Div, RA (2)

Abri & Dal:
2 small Egyptian garrisons

Akasha:
Egyptian Troops (500)
1st Royal Sussex (300)

Wady Halfa-Akasha RR:
Egyptian Troops (400)

Wady Halfa:
Mounted Infantry Camel Regiment
2nd Duke of Cornwall's Light Infantry Regiment (4)
2 Egyptian Camel batteries

*General
Sir Garnet Wolesley,
"Our only General."*

Egyptian Camel Corps

Wady Halfa-Assuan:
½, Light Camel Regiment

Assuan:
HQ
1st Yorkshire Regiment
1st Royal Sussex Regiment (4)
26th Company, RE

North of Assuan:
1st Black Watch
2nd Essex
1st Gordons
1st Royal Irish
Guards Camel Regiment
½, Light Camel Regiment
½, 2nd DCLI
Heavy Camel Regiment

Sudan.07
Dispositions and Concentrations of Anglo-Egyptian Troops, December 10, 1885

Commander in Chief:
Lt. General Sir Frederick Charles Arthur Stephenson, CB, KCB, Scots Guards

General Sir Frederick Stephenson

North of Assuan: (8,300 British Troops)
19th Hussar Regiment
Three Batteries, Royal Artillery
26th (?) Company, RE
1st Black Watch (Royal Highlanders)
1st Royal Sussex Regiment
1st Royal Dublin Fusilier Regiment
1st East Kent Regiment (heading to the front)
1st King's Royal Rifle Corps
1st Oxfordshire Light Infantry Regiment
1st Essex Infantry Regiment (heading to the front)

Suakin:
1st King's Shropshire Light Infantry Regiment (KSLI) One Battery, RA

The Frontier Field Force: (5,400 British Troops)
Local Brigadier General (Lt. Colonel and Colonel) Francis Wallace Grenfell, KRRC (EA)

Assuan: (2,000)

1st South Staffordshire Infantry Regiment (LOC troops)
2nd Duke of Cornwall's Light Infantry Regiment
20th Hussar Regiment (half)
One Battery, RA
Detachment, Royal Engineers

Korosko: (500)
1st Yorkshire Infantry Regiment (Princess of Wales Own)

Wady Halfa: (1,100, mainly detachments)
1st Yorkshire Infantry Regiment (Princess of Wales Own)
1st Berkshire Infantry Regiment (Princess Charlotte of Wales Own)
1st Royal West Kent Infantry Regiment
20th Hussar Regiment (half)
Detachment, Royal Engineers

Akasheh: (900, mainly detachments)
1st Berkshire Infantry Regiment (Princess Charlotte of Wales Own)
1st Royal West Kent Infantry Regiment

Kosheh and Environs:
1st Queen's Own Cameron Highlanders (600)
IXth Sudanese Battalion
Detachment, 20th Hussar Regiment

Fort Moggrakeh:
3rd Egyptian Battalion
Egyptian Troops: (8,000) Distributed as above, but in reverse order of strength (ie, most troops forward)
1st Egyptian Battalion
Egyptian Artillery
Egyptian Cavalry
Egyptian Camel Corps

OB Sources List
Compiled and Researched by Andrew Preziosi

Alford & Dennistoun, *The Egyptian Sudan*
Alford & Sword, *The Egyptian Sudan…Its Loss and Recovery*
Anglesey, Marquis of, *History of the British Cavalry, Vol. 3*
Brackenbury MG H., *The River Column*
Burleigh, Bennet, *Sirdar and Khalifa; Or: The Re-conquest of the Soudan, 1898* (Official Dispatches)
Burleigh, Bennet, *Desert Warfare-The Eastern Soudan Campaign*
Dennis L. Bishop, Researcher (Wichita State University Library)
Lt. Dave Bullock, "Weep for Hicks, Parts 1 & 2"; *Savage & Soldier*
Churchill, Winston, *Dispatches*
Churchill, Winston, *The River War*
Colville, Lt. Col. H.E., (Official) *History of the Sudan Campaign, 1884-85*
Colville, Lt. Col.; *History of the Sudan Campaign, Vol. 1*
Colborne, J.; *With Hicks Pasha in the Sudan* Ed., *Frontier and Overseas Expeditions*

from India, Vol. 6
Gleichen, Lord Edward, *The Anglo-Egyptian Sudan: A Compendium Prepared by Officers of the Sudan Government*
Gozzi, Daffroso, *Note Alla Buona Sugli Avvenimenti di Egitto e Sudan dal 1882 al 1885*
Hunter, Archie, *Kitchener's Sword Arm*
Haggard, Andrew *Under Crescent and Star*
Keown-Boyd, Henry, *A Good Dusting*
Knight, Edward Frederick, *Letters from the Sudan*
The London Gazette (various notices)
The London Gazette & *London Times*: *Official Dispatches and Accounts*
Official Dispatches, *London Gazette*, Tuesday, January 30, 1900
Official Dispatches, *London Times* and *London Gazette* Various Reports, London Times (February 1891)
Maurice, Col. J.F., *The Campaign of 1882 in Egypt*
Preston, Adrian (Editor), *In Relief of Gordon: General Wolseley's Khartoum Campaign Journal*
Royle, C.; *The Egyptian Campaigns, 1882-85*
Smith, Peter C., *Victoria's Victories*
The Times of London, December 10th, 1885 through January 2nd, 1886 (including Official Dispatch)
The Times of London, November 8th through December 28th, 1888 (including Official Dispatch)
The Times of London, Cable Reports, May 11th through July 9th, 1889
Vetch, Robert Hamilton, *Life, Letters and Diaries of Lieut. General Sir Gerald Graham*, London, MCMI (Official Dispatches)
Whitehouse, H., *Battle in Africa*
Major F.R. Wingate, *Mahdism and the Egyptian Sudan*
Major F.R. Wingate, *The Siege and Fall of Khartoum*
Ziegler, *Omdurman*
Zulfo, I.; *Karari*

British Soldier graves outside Metemmeh today, a century-and-a-quarter later, and still they look almost fresh. The twin graves in the foreground may possibly be those of officers as it was customary to mark theirs with stone.

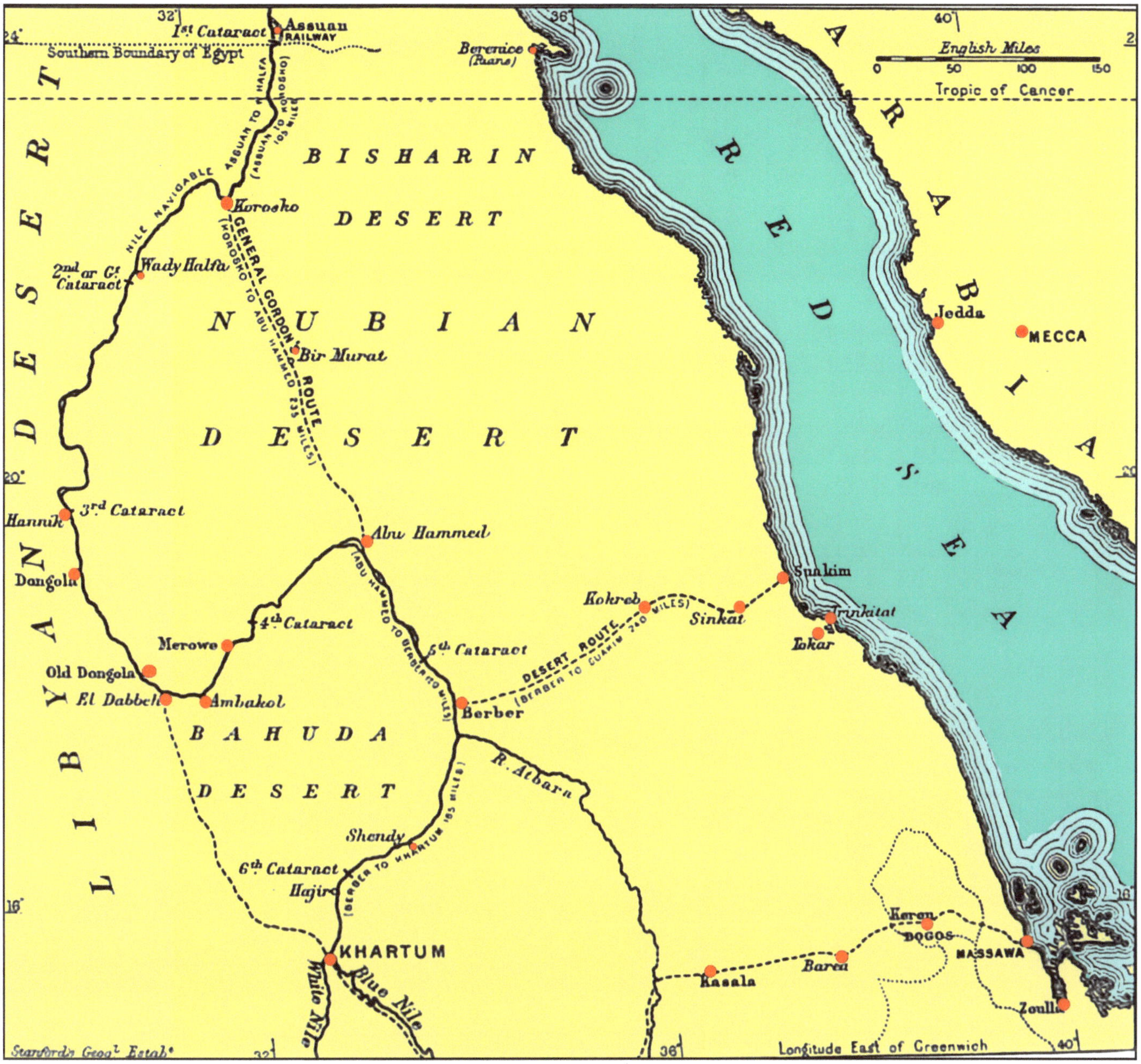

Gordon's route from Assuan to Khartoum

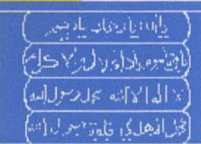

The Mahdist Wars Flag Collection
Designed By Eric Cox

The latest project by Eric Cox, designer of the 19th Century Chinese Flags Collection for the Tai-P'ing and Boxer Rebellions, TVAG is proud to announce the best researched and most authentic collection of flags for the Sudan Wars of 1883-1899.

As part of the editorial efforts to produce the *Mahdist Wars Source* Book, and with the help of renowned *Mahdiyya* expert and former Archivist for the South Sudan Government, Douglas Johnson, plus other contributors in the UK, we have been able to learn more details of more Mahdist Flag than previously available. The first five Sets are now available, with others to follow as more information is collected.

Working from photographs taken in Museums from Omdurman to Blair Atholl, and with his constant attention to detail, Eric has created each flag virtually pixel-by-pixel, copying not only the colors and texts, but even matching the different lettering styles of the individual flag makers. All texts are in their proper Arabic and come with translations whenever they vary from the Muslim Creed appearing on the vast majority of examples.

As ever, all flag Sets are available in your choice of 54mm, 28mm, 20mm, 15mm, and 6mm scales, and all for the same price. Sets may be bought singly, or the entire Collection may be bought at a discount. The Sets currently available are as follows:

MWF-01—The New Egyptian Army (1883-1899), some 58 flags including Battalion colors for all 18 Fellahin and Sudanese units raised, plus those of the Khedive, the National Flag, and six sets of individual Company flags in their proper colors. There are also two versions of the presentation colors for the IXth Sudanese, one for the early period, and one for the late (Omdurman) period. **Price: $10.00**

MWF-02—Mahdist Ranking Commanders, a Set of 10 Flags, each the personal color of key figures in the *Mahdiyya*, including the Mahdi himself, all four of his Khalifas, and several important Emirs (Zaki, Mahmud, Nejumi, *et al*). **Price: $10.00**

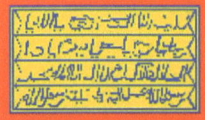

MWF-03—General Mahdist Flags Set 1, 75 flags representing 15 different designs and provided in groups of 5 alike—one large Emir's Flag and 4 smaller identical versions which can be carried by each of four *Rubs* under his command. **Price: $15.00**

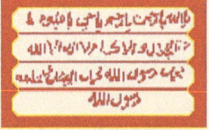

MWF-04—**General Mahdist Flags Set 2** (same mix as Set 1) **Price: $15.00**

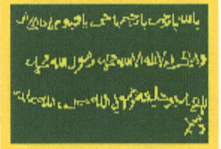

MWF-05—**General Mahdist Flags Set 3** (same mix as Set 1) **Price: $15.00**

Full Collection Deal: Buy all five Sets in any scale (some *278* flags) for $50.00, postpaid in the U.S. ($6.00 more to Canada and Overseas).

www.thevirtualarmchairgeneral.com   TVAG@worldnet.att.net

www.ingramcontent.com/pod-product-compliance
Lightning Source LLC
Chambersburg PA
CBHW041512220426
43661CB00048B/1544